Figures in a Famine Landscape

Figures in a Famine Landscape

Ciarán Ó Murchadha

Bloomsbury Academic
An imprint of Bloomsbury Publishing Plc

B L O O M S B U R Y
LONDON • OXFORD • NEW YORK • NEW DELHI • SYDNEY

Bloomsbury Academic
An imprint of Bloomsbury Publishing Plc

50 Bedford Square	1385 Broadway
London	New York
WC1B 3DP	NY 10018
UK	USA

www.bloomsbury.com

BLOOMSBURY and the Diana logo are trademarks of Bloomsbury Publishing Plc

First published 2016
Reprinted 2016

© Ciarán Ó Murchadha, 2016

Ciarán Ó Murchadha has asserted his right under the Copyright, Designs and Patents Act, 1988, to be identified as Author of this work.

All rights reserved. No part of this publication may be reproduced or transmitted in any form or by any means, electronic or mechanical, including photocopying, recording, or any information storage or retrieval system, without prior permission in writing from the publishers.

No responsibility for loss caused to any individual or organization acting on or refraining from action as a result of the material in this publication can be accepted by Bloomsbury or the author.

British Library Cataloguing-in-Publication Data
A catalogue record for this book is available from the British Library.

ISBN: HB: 978-1-4725-1453-0
PB: 978-1-4725-1155-3
ePDF: 978-1-4725-0863-8
ePub: 978-1-4725-0666-5

Library of Congress Cataloging-in-Publication Data
Names: Ó Murchadha, Ciarán. | Ó Murchadha, Ciarán. Sable wings over the land.
Title: Figures in a famine landscape / Ciarán Ó Murchadha.
Description: London ; New York : Bloomsbury Academic, an imprint of Bloomsbury Publishing Plc, 2016. | "The origins of this book go back to an earlier study of 1998, Sable Wings over the Land"–Preface.
Identifiers: LCCN 2016000481 (print) | LCCN 2016009235 (ebook) | ISBN9781472514530 (hardback) | ISBN 9781472511553 (paperback) | ISBN9781472508638 (PDF) | ISBN 9781472506665 (ePub) | ISBN 9781472508638(epdf) | ISBN 9781472506665 (epub)
Subjects: LCSH: Ireland–History–Famine, 1845-1852. | Famines–Socialaspects–Ireland–Clare–History–19th century. |Poor–Ireland–Clare–History–19th century. | Clare (Ireland)–Biography.| Ennis (Ireland)–Biography. | Clare (Ireland)–History–19th century. |Ennis (Ireland)–History–19th century. | BISAC: HISTORY / Europe /Ireland. | HISTORY / Modern / 19th Century. | HISTORY / Social History.
Classification: LCC DA950.7 .O534 2016 (print) | LCC DA950.7 (ebook) | DDC 941.5081–dc23

Cover design: Catherine Wood
Cover image: Detail from Little Ark painting by unknown artist, Chapel of Our Lady Star of the Sea, Moneen, Kilbaha. Reproduced by kind permission of the Diocese of Killaloe.

Typeset by Integra Software Services Pvt. Ltd.
Printed and bound in Great Britain

*Don mhuintir a mhair i Tara agus
Marymount insna sean-laethanta*

CONTENTS

List of Illustrations viii
Preface ix
Maps xii

Introduction 1
1   Hurricane from the South-West: John Busteed Knox 9
2   Intrepid Fire-Eater: Captain Edmond Wynne 29
3   The Poor Man's Magistrate: John Singleton of Quinville 47
4   The Medical Gentleman: Dr Patrick Maxwell Cullinan 65
5   The Reverend Sinecurist: Henry Murphy 83
6   The Exterminator General: Marcus Keane of Beech Park 99
7   Father Michael Meehan and the Little Ark 117
8   The Cabin-Tumbling Warrior: Crofton Moore Vandeleur 137
9   The Most Charitable Officer: Captain A.E. Kennedy 155
10 The Famine Landscape 173

Notes 186
Bibliography 214
Index 220

LIST OF ILLUSTRATIONS

Cover Illustration
Painting of Little Ark at Church of Our Lady Star of the Sea, Moneen, Kilbaha.

John B. Knox's residence.	12
The Ennistymon courthouse.	36
Interior of Ennistymon courthouse.	40
John Singleton in old age.	54
Harmony House, Dr Cullinan's residence.	70
Residence of Dr Michael Healy.	73
Green Park, home of Reverend Murphy.	89
Marcus Keane in later life.	105
Bridget O'Donnell and her children.	124
Father Michael Meehan.	129
Crofton Moore Vandeleur in later years.	144
Captain Kennedy and his daughter Elizabeth.	167
Captain Arthur Kennedy, early in his colonial service.	171

PREFACE

The origins of this book go back to an earlier study of 1998, *Sable Wings over the Land*, and to the cull of accumulated paper that followed its publication. Sifting through an immensity of photocopies at that time – printouts from microfilm, filled notepads and decks of scribbled index cards – I was struck by how much of this material I had not used, and by the possibilities it seemed to present for the construction of a set of individual character analyses, and a new way perhaps of approaching Famine history, complementary to that of traditional narratives of the kind I had just completed. I remember wondering at one point indeed if I had written the right book.

Each of the candidates I now began idly to consider for inclusion in a new study had featured briefly in *Sable Wings* – some also in general Famine histories, in passing references by historians with little awareness of them beyond the anecdotal uses to which they had been put and the quotes they supplied. Only two had ever been subjected to scholarly analysis, the majority being almost unknown in Famine historiography. As I sketched out a possible work along these lines, it became clear that one of its benefits would be to lend each of these locally dominant figures a wider significance in the overall Famine story, and that in addition it would dovetail pleasingly with the working historian's appetite for micro-history and *mentalité*. And as I worked on the idea, the concept of geographical mobility through landscape suggested itself with increasing strength in relation to each figure: when I came across the painting which adorns the front cover of the book, the title became inevitable.

Although I published one study (Marcus Keane) separately in 2000 as a kind of pilot for the others, when I went to work for the National University of Ireland, Galway, the following year, the *Figures* project vanished beneath the mountain of work involved in returning to my early modernist roots, and with teaching, research supervision and other duties, not to mention a tiring daily commute to Galway. During the seven years I worked for the NUI Galway. History Department, however, the idea never quite faded away, and it was fanned into life when under the encouragement of Michael Greenwood, then of Hambledon Press, I wrote my own Famine history. In the writing of this book, which occupied the years immediately following my departure from NUI Galway in 2008, I came across some of the figures again, against a larger national canvas that added another dimension to my understanding of them.

PREFACE

It was some time after the publication of the Famine history, under the title *The Great Famine: Ireland's Agony 1845–1852* that I returned to *Figures* and found myself again in the company of individuals whom I had come to know very well. When I began finally to write, one last change of perception imposed itself: this related directly to my own ageing and the fact that over the years since I first learned of these figures, I had gone from being younger than the youngest of them as they were in Famine times to being of comparable age to the oldest. As I wrote, the comparative youth of all of them, as indeed of so many of those who had acted or suffered in the Famine, was never far from my consciousness. In addition, my own perspective had changed over the years as a result of life experienced and knowledge earned; and because of all these things I was obliged to rewrite my earlier drafts in their entirety. I would continue to rework the book's architecture in fact to the very end, the last changes being prompted by the strange assailing resonances of that time, as related in the last chapter. *Figures in a Famine Landscape* is the result of all these labours.

In the years it has taken this study to come to fruition, I have availed of the resources of the following institutions, which I acknowledge with gratitude: the National Library of Ireland, Dublin; Royal Irish Academy, Dublin; National Archives of Ireland, Dublin; Representative Church Body Library, Dublin; James Hardiman Library, National University of Ireland, Galway; National Library of Australia, Canberra; State Library of Western Australia, Perth; British Library, London; Public Record Office of Northern Ireland, Belfast; Archives of the Diocese of Killaloe, Ennis; Clare County Archives, Ennis; and Clare County Library, Ennis. Of my former colleagues from NUI Galway and current friends there, eager respondents all to calls on their expertise, I thank in particular Niall Ó Cíosáin, Caitriona Clear, John Cunningham, Gerry Moran, Padraig Lenihan, Enrico Dallago and Laurence Marley. Other Famine historians have provided insight and encouragement, and I am especially grateful to Jim Donnelly and Cormac Ó Gráda in this regard. In this category I also include Perry Curtis, who continues to write with distinction on nineteenth-century Ireland and who has been far too kind a critic of my own efforts.

On the ground in Clare I have benefited greatly from the generously shared knowledge of Paddy Nolan of Kilkee and the expertise of John O'Brien in regard to the interpretation and presentation of visual images; Peter Beirne and Brian Doyle at the Manse, Ennis, have been patient with my many demands on their time and their catalogues, as has Rene Franklin at the Clare County Archives. To Paddy Naughton, whom we lost in summer 2015 I owe much, not least memories of marvellous tour through his home town of Kilrush some years ago. My family continue to be a great rock of support for my work; Niall and Deirdre have been particularly situated to lend specific assistance, Cathal once again a bastion against computer chaos and my niece Ciara a discerning observer.

The following, in no particular order, have been of assistance in ways they will individually know (or indeed may not!): Matt Lynch, Brian Ó Dálaigh, Kieran Sheedy, Maureen Comber, Eric Shaw, Harry Hughes, Martin Breen, Carmel Honan, Mark Dunphy, Eddie Lough, Luke McInerney, Aidan Courtney, Lucille Ellis, Paddy Waldron, Paul O'Brien, Declan Barron, Fr John Jones, Fr Pat O'Neill, Fr Patrick Culligan, Fr Joe McMahon, Rev. Bob Hanna, Martin Lynch, Canon Reuben Butler, Máire Ní Ghruagáin, Anne McNamara, Jane Halloran Ryan, Marian O'Leary, Cynthia O'Dell, Michael Greenwood, Joe Byrne, Amy Harris, Kathryn Comber, Arthur Ford, Michael O'Loughlin, Joe Queally, Michael and Marie Corley, Mary Hester, Clare Curtin, Pat O'Brien and Paschal Brooks. I owe special debts to Katrina Vincent (Australia), Deirdre Collery (Sligo), Pat Lynch (Clogher) and Liam Ashe (Edenvale) for support or assistance at critical junctures. Thanks also to the people at Scéal Eile (Ennis) and the Kilbaha Gallery (Kilbaha). I am happy also to record my great gratitude to Teresa Beirne for the warmth of her interest and enthusiasm as the project neared completion. Throughout, the team at Bloomsbury, Frances Arnold, Emma Goode and Emily Drewe, have been efficient, kind and patient.

Killashee, Naas, County Kildare
March 2016

Map of Clare from Lewis's Atlas Comprising the Counties of Ireland *(London, 1837). Lewis's maps were much used by travellers in the Famine landscape.*

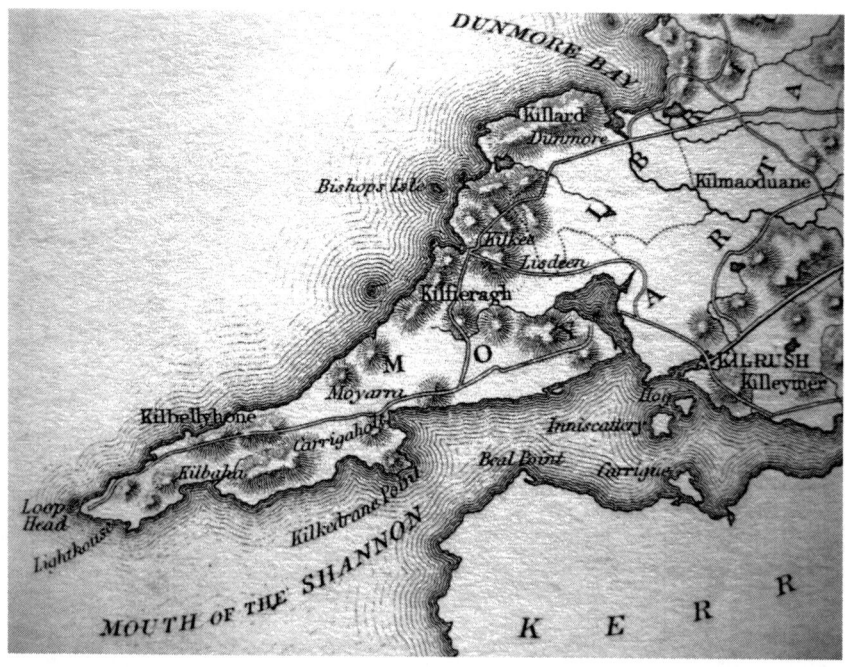

West Clare and the Loop Head peninsula, detail from Lewis's Atlas.

Introduction:
Figures in a Famine Landscape

The Chapel of Ease at Moneen is a plain structure that stands solitary on the coastal plain at the end of the peninsula that ends in Loop Head in West Clare. Inside the chapel, in front of the altar, repose the remains of its builder, Michael Meehan, for nearly three decades pastor of the united parishes of Moyarta and Kilballyowen.[1] In an annexe to the chapel, entered through an arched doorway to the left of Meehan's unmarked resting place, the battered shape of his Little Ark sits on sturdy wooden trestles. Nearby on the walls framed photographs record Ark-related commemorative events from recent and more distant times. Conspicuous amidst this pictorial record by reason of age and fragility are two images: one a contemporary painting of a scene representing the Ark in the days of its deployment by Father Meehan, and the other a detailed drawing which it resembles substantially.[2]

For the moment it is these images that command our attention, and we shall leave the Ark story to its place in Chapter 7. Technically, neither the drawing nor the painting is an accomplished work, although they are all the more affecting for the want of artistry. Both depict a crowd of worshippers gathered reverentially around the Ark, which has been placed at the centre of the crossroads hamlet of Kilbaha, while inside Father Meehan says his Mass.

In the painting, which is considerably more evocative than the drawing, the priest is the only figure to be realized fully, if still indistinctly; and apart from some female figures at the front, the crowd is no more than an agglomerated mass in which facial features and body shapes are suggested rather than delineated. Yet the grouping radiates a strong sense of devotion, enhanced by the figures of two latecoming worshippers hurrying along the sloping cove road towards the scene. High on the hill overlooking the hamlet, the residence of the land agent Marcus Keane looks threateningly down on the little assemblage, whose human frailty is conveyed so well by the unknown and unschooled artist.

For the historian of the Great Famine, the painting is expressive of many aspects of the calamity and its aftermath that are more easily appreciated from visual than written evidence. Foremost among these is the collective manner in which many victims experienced the Famine: from the earliest community meetings to the hunger marches, from public works musters to trailing soup kitchen lines and from workhouse *melées* to localized post-Famine episodes, of which the Little Ark is one. In its depiction of these forlorn survivors, the painting is poignant indeed in what it conveys of the evanescent nature of crowd scenes in each of the Famine's phases, a function in so many instances of the progressive physical deterioration of participants and their eventual demise. From the painting, in addition, we seem to obtain an almost palpable sense of the fears and anxieties of the afflicted poor and the absolute trust which their helplessness saw them reside in authority and which was so often and so cruelly disappointed.

Another aspect again of the Great Famine which the Ark painting illuminates relates to the frequency with which so much human suffering took place in landscapes of natural loveliness. The west coast of Clare is certainly beautiful, and the visitor who has just stepped into the Moneen chapel from the vista outside becomes conscious of its replication in the painting, as gaze moves from the crowd scene to the road winding picturesquely upwards towards the agent's house and the surrounding hill fields where cattle graze tranquilly. The mind registers each successive detail as the eye widens its focus across to the seashore and the pier alongside which two pilots manoeuvre their trim craft, while out to sea the Kilrush steamer merrily exhales smoke into a cottony sky as it passes, heedless of the drama being enacted at the painting's centre.

One further reflection inspired by the painting relates to the extent to which during the Famine, the landscape itself became an increasingly dominant reality in people's lives, for the simple reason that movement through it became more frequent, sometimes more frantic, and for so many fraught with physical difficulty. If this was especially the experience of the sickly and the starving, as aware in their debilitated state of distances that had to be traversed in search of food or work as they were of agonizing topographical undulations lying between, it has application also to many other groups. It applies to the mass scramble of hundreds of thousands towards the country's ports of emigrant exit; to the movement of countless evicted families along the roads and into the bogs after clearances, and to the last tortured wanderings at the Famine's end of starving people, individuals and straggling groups, moving in silent pain through the countryside.

But we can extend our envisioning of the Famine in terms of movement through landscape well beyond the suffering and the despairing, to those who exercised authority against them – the minions of the relief bureaucracy or the police, for example, and to the landlords and their agents, under-agents and drivers – all those whose well-clad and well-shod robustness stood out against the physical decrepitude of the hunger-worn and the fever-stricken. We can apply it even to the wide-ranging rampages of wrecker gangs in their destruction of human dwellings and lives; to the journeying of God-crazed evangelical missionaries and their Catholic opponents at the end of the Famine, as indeed to the path beaten to the districts of the south and west by journalists and philanthropists who travelled long distances in order to bear witness to the annihilation of innumerable rural communities.

The paradigm has particular relevance to the individual personality studies that are the subject of this book; the Ark painting indeed might be seen as a detail from the larger canvas which these figures inhabit, one encompassing the entire county of Clare, one of the most afflicted and longest-suffering places in Ireland during the Famine. Extending the metaphor further, we might see our various subjects as foreground figures whose vanished existences we can actualize in some detail, unlike the victims whom the documentation at very best leaves half-realized, in a manner analogous to the crowd in the painting.

A number of factors have determined the selection of our subjects in this book: the richness of the evidence, the strength of the narrative thread that can be drawn from it and its potential to furnish new insight with regard to different areas of the Great Famine. A winnowing process has run side by side with the writing, in which a number of initially promising subjects were discarded because they did not meet one or more of these criteria or because they were so similar to others already selected that they added very little.

Given that the trail of surviving evidence that has had to be followed throughout is an erratic one, the selections and individual depictions necessarily exhibit a certain untidiness; as regards the former there are two major, if unavoidable, gaps. As indicated above, the first of these relates to the absence of first-hand evidence from Famine victims, few of whom were in a position to record their personal dissolution. Discovery of a surviving document from even one who did so remains an intriguing possibility, although no trace of any such document has come to light that might suit our purposes here.

The other great lacuna relates to the absence of a female perspective, to a great extent a function of the repressed social position of women in the mid-nineteenth century. One would dearly have wished for memoir or diary material as bountiful as that left behind by Asenath Nicholson or Elizabeth Smith, who travelled other Famine landscapes; as regards ours, however, the manuscript material that came under consideration was found to deal so exiguously with Famine issues and was so insufficiently supported by other documentation that, regrettably, it had to be laid aside.

Chapters in the book follow no particular template, except insofar as each broadly addresses the background of individual subjects, how each behaved during the Famine years, why they did so and how they explained their behaviour, to the extent that we possess the data with which to answer these questions. Where we encounter particularly reprehensible behaviours, including those which at the time escaped censure as well as those which many contemporaries regarded as murderous and today might fall under a rubric of mass murder, examining the dynamic of these actions represents only half the analytical task; to complete it we try to understand individual motivations and mental processes.

It will be noticed that the paths of certain protagonists in the book intersect and that a minor character in one chapter is often reprised later on as a major one or vice versa. All of our subjects knew each other personally, or knew of each other, in varying degrees of knowledge, acquaintanceship, friendship or enmity. In this sense the chapters are parallel narratives; each subject travelling his own path and sometimes encountering one of the others, and the individual trajectories furnishing the motive thrust of each chapter and collectively the book as a whole. Readers will probably obtain most benefit from the book if it is read sequentially since it broadly follows the chronology of the Famine. At the same time each chapter can be read independently and in any order without losing significant narrative value.

We begin with John Busteed Knox, owner and editor of the *Clare Journal*. A Protestant in religion and a Tory in politics, with a chauvinistic attachment to empire, Knox was very much an outsider among the nationally minded Catholics who constituted the vast bulk of his advertisers and his readers. But even among Protestants Knox was an outsider, since as a newspaperman he belonged neither to the landed gentry, the professional classes, nor fully to the urban business community. In addition, even within his own community his voice was often that of a maverick and a critic. In any society Knox would have been unusual: in mid-nineteenth-century Clare he was unique.

What we know of Captain Edmond Wynne's background suggests that for much of his life he too had been an outsider, although in a different sense to Knox. Wynne came of landed gentry stock but was significantly distanced from his social origins, and we suspect isolation also in the two obscure decades he spent in rural Tipperary with his first wife's family. The social and psychological alienation we may infer on his part helps explain many of his highly individual actions during his brief, turbulent career as Board of Works Inspector in Famine Clare and the level of controversy he was to generate while there.

By contrast with Edmond Wynne, John Singleton was very much at ease in his world, living as he did in material comfort at his Quinville estate, at the centre of a circle defined by family, friends and neighbours. In many respects Singleton is a recognizable model of the Western European landed gentleman: possessed of a refined taste in art and literature, he combined poetic sensibility with a consciousness of civic responsibility and the devotion of a family man. Singleton's deep social conservatism is captured in the family motto, 'Mutare Sperno', or 'I Detest Change'.[3]

Well-known to Singleton and cordially disliked by him was the physician, Dr Patrick Maxwell Cullinan, as also probably his colleague, the surgeon, Dr Michael Healy. As the Famine began Healy and Cullinan had just become established in their professional careers and were on terms of professional cordiality, if not personal amity. But very soon a change was to take place in their relations, which deteriorated proportionately with the onset and escalation in their immediate vicinity of starvation and fever conditions, in the palliation of which both men were active and, to the best of our knowledge, professionally competent.

Documentation relating to Reverend Henry Murphy, the incumbent of Dr Cullinan's parish of Dromcliffe, uncovers a confined little world with echoes of Anthony Trollope's Barchester novels, most evident in the microscopic detail revealed of the everyday life of a Protestant cleric, with its domestic concerns, Church politics, evangelical issues and the search for a better living, as all the while the shadow of greater personages hover in the wings. However, none of Trollope's characters resemble the humourless Reverend Murphy, and his existence unfolds in a chronically impoverished Irish town very unlike sleepy Barchester, one about to endure a cataclysm that no Barchester chronicle could have encompassed.

Among Reverend Murphy's acquaintances was the wealthy land agent Marcus Keane of Beech Park, an unusual social connection that is explained by a shared interest in evangelical ideology. In 1845, Marcus was a young man of parts and promise, for some years already developing the land agency inherited from his father. There was every reason to suppose that the heir would continue the reputation for humanity which his father's kindness had gained for the Keane family, and as expressed in the family motto, 'Felix de Mulcta Mitis', or 'Fortunate in Being Kind-hearted'.[4] From the outset, however, there were some signs of a very different tendency on Marcus's part, but so imperceptible were they that none could have predicted what he would have become by the Famine's end.

On a number of issues, Father Michael Meehan, the combative west Clare priest, was to become Marcus Keane's greatest antagonist. Athletic, articulate and forceful, Meehan was endowed with literary leanings of a kind that make for an interesting comparison with John Singleton, although the two men do not seem to have been personally acquainted. Throughout the Famine, Father Meehan would prove empathic with his people's sufferings, which he sought to alleviate insofar as it was within his power. The Famine years would discover in him also an extraordinary ability to attract national and international publicity to the distress endured by the inhabitants of his remote corner of Ireland.

Father Meehan would come into conflict not just with Marcus Keane, but also with Crofton Moore Vandeleur, the great landed magnate of west Clare, with whom he had been on friendly terms in earlier years. Vandeleur's vast domains centred on the town of Kilrush, where he had added to the embellishments made by his father in the previous generation. A cold figure who disliked publicity, Vandeleur would not have featured as a significant historical protagonist but for the large-scale consolidation of his property which he engaged in towards the end of the Famine.

Captain Arthur Edward Kennedy, the last of our figures, arrived in Kilrush at the height of the Famine in 1847. Kennedy was a career army officer who resigned his commission in order to take up the post of Temporary Union Inspector under the new Poor Law, the policing of which was his new professional remit. Welcomed to Kilrush by Crofton Vandeleur, Kennedy may have thought that this temporary posting would prove less onerous than the career for which he had exchanged it; if so he was to be mistaken, since he was soon to be faced with the greatest physical and moral challenges he had so far encountered in his life.

The larger landscape of the maritime county of Clare through which our figures moved lies midway along Ireland's Atlantic coast. Locked in by physical features that make it almost an island – the indentations of Galway Bay and the Shannon Estuary to the north and south respectively, and the River Shannon to the east – in the nineteenth century the region's ages-old cultural distinctiveness still sheltered within their insulating embrace. Bisected by the north–south flow of the Fergus which hurries through Ennis before disgorging its estuarine waters into those of the lordly Shannon some miles below the town, the county is low-lying, the topography varied. Among the geographical anomalies familiar to nineteenth-century travellers as to their latter-day equivalents were the surreal rocky plateau of the Burren and the dramatic Cliffs of Moher in the north, the squat mass of Mount Callan above Ennis and the low mountain ranges of the county's eastern borders.

Clare comprises just over 12,300 square miles in extent, the land ranging in fertility from the rich alluvial plains about Newmarket-on-Fergus to the marginal upland that takes up much of the county's centre. The county population, something over 300,000 persons as the Famine began, was about three times its present-day level. Overwhelmingly agricultural in 1845, the land of Clare was owned by no more than 200 resident landlords and a few absentee English magnates who rarely if ever visited their Clare estates.

Their past record left little reason to suppose landlords would come to the aid of the poor when starvation began, and as late as May 1846 Colonel T.L. Goldie, a British officer involved in the relief programme, reported that landed gentlemen in his district were neither subscribing to relief committee funds nor engaging with them.[5] 'Between the better classes and the peasantry of this county', wrote the colonel, who was fated to die under fire in the Crimea, 'there is an antagonism greater than in any other part of Ireland that I have been in'. The wealthier landowners were 'generally absentees, and their places supplied by agents who are generally also magistrates'. These gentlemen, according to Goldie, 'seldom reside on their properties, but mostly in the towns whence they make sorties at the risk of their lives to collect rents and to eject tenants'.

In such circumstances, a relief programme based on gentry-managed committees, as was inaugurated in the early part of the Famine, could not be effectual. But matters were to become infinitely worse from the end of 1847 as grotesquely misconceived new government measures came into operation that placed landlords' financial interests in direct conflict with the relief needs of the poor. For their part, the poor remained essentially passive through all their travails, and although we should not fall into the temptation of idealizing them as endlessly patient, or of attributing to them impossible levels of stoic virtue as some contemporaries did, they were entirely blameless in the calamities that descended on them during the Famine. As Dr Cullinan was to comment in 1851, responding in a rare moment of sympathetic irony to an obtuse remark by a Poor Law Guardian suggesting poor people were to blame for their own plight, 'he did not think that those persons voluntarily reduced themselves to such a state'.[6]

In 1845, as now, Ennis was the county's urban economic hub and administrative capital, home to its governing courts and Grand Jury, although communities on the northern fringe leaned towards Galway City, those on the southern one towards grimy little Limerick. Neither the communities of Killaloe thirty miles to the east nor Kilrush approximately the same distance to the west of Ennis were much known to each other, nor indeed were those of Ennis known to either of the other two. Long-distance travel in the county was the preserve of administrators and police, landlords and tourists – the better-off classes generally with access to saddle horses or wheeled vehicles. And although people walked astonishing distances on foot, the poorest classes spent their lives almost entirely within the confines of their own communities.

A network of county roads linked more distant centres of population with the county capital, and although the road system was less developed in the south-western coastal districts, the deficiency was to some extent supplied by steamships plying along the Shannon. In north Clare, Ennistymon and Miltown were close enough to the coast to constitute summer resorts for various classes, while the more genteel watering place of Kilkee, eight miles from Kilrush, struck an incongruous note of Victorian Englishness in a desperately impoverished, Irish-speaking hinterland.

The county landscape was a green place, its verdure altering in shade and density with the seasons, retreating briefly with the autumnal leaf-fall. There were few winters where grass or hedges disappeared beneath snow, which made the iron-hard harshness of the first Famine winters a dreadful additional shock to the hardships endured by the vulnerable. From March to October each year, seasonal changes of colour and shade were overlain by more subtle ones relating to potato cultivation: planting of early and late crops first deepened the brown, red or black tones of last year's re-dug potato plots and the new ground coming under the spade; this in turn became carpeted with the light green of young stalks that darkened gradually over the months until by late June, both crops grew together in the same green sea, before harvesting of the early potatoes began the months-long reversal of the process.

Away from the jagged seaboard, which was subject to the occasional raging fury of the Atlantic, the landscape was gentle on the eye and dotted with the remains of ancient and more recent human settlement, devotion and burial. Those of our figures who travelled it in Famine times would have idly registered, as we do, the grey stone of medieval church ruins, cemeteries and blank-windowed tower-houses that interspersed cropfields and pastures, and which nature tirelessly worked to reclaim to herself by the action of wind and seasonal rains, starring them with white-grey lichens to the consistency of the living rock. And everywhere by day were to be seen the diminutive and indistinct figures of human beings, in potato fields, cabins, villages, towns and along roads, those multitudes who form the background figures in our Famine landscape.

1

Hurricane from the South-West: John Busteed Knox

The centre of John Busteed Knox's world was a modest three-storey residence situated halfway down Jail Street in Ennis and a set of offices attached to it. It was here that Knox composed and printed the *Clare Journal*, of which he was editor and proprietor, and here also he carried on the general printing business that accounted for a great portion of his income. A stone archway at the side of the house afforded access to the *Journal* offices down a short alley, and through this rather elegant structure, reporters and correspondents, or messengers and letter carriers on their behalf, made their way each working day with articles and notices for publication. Shopkeepers, merchants and members of the public, clutching manuscript and advertising material, also passed this way daily, as did paper and ink suppliers, a range of tradesmen, clerks and clerics, and from time to time gentlemen in search of information or with information to impart. Welcoming all this human traffic, the lifeblood of his trade, by the time the Famine began Knox was already the human repository of a vast quantity of data relating to town and county: no one knew more about Ennis or Clare than did John Busteed Knox.

Occasionally Knox would venture forth from his Jail Street lair to attend public meetings, to tend to duties on certain public bodies to which he gave diligent if opinionated service, to go to church or merely to perambulate the narrow, untidy streets of the town he loved so well. Much less frequently he would travel further afield, to other Munster towns such as Tralee and Clonmel, or to Limerick some twenty-five miles to the south. Paradoxically, Knox was the least travelled of all our figures in the landscape of the county he knew so well, preferring, it would appear, that such knowledge should come to him.[1] During the later years of the Famine, the absence of first-hand information on his part, and reliance on sources that were convenient but compromised, would be a factor in the fatal clouding of Knox's editorial judgement.

Much of Knox's private life is closed to us for want of evidence, and a great deal of what we know is derived from the *Clare Journal*, the archival treasure house that was his family's great gift to posterity. For the Famine years its files are laden with the reportage and correspondence, and the advertisements and editorial comment with which he filled it, issue after issue, week after week and year after year. Painstaking scrutiny of the *Journal*'s files opens a window to a vanished world which we perceive to a great degree – often very vividly – through Knox's eyes. His own personality emerges from the *Journal* too strongly, to the extent that we learn to gauge his different moods: sympathetic, enraged or depressed as they were by turns, and much less often, bitter, dark and narrow-minded.

Printing and journalism were in John B. Knox's blood. His mother's family, the Busteeds, were well known in the Munster newspaper trade; his maternal grandfather had founded the *Clare Journal* in 1778 and his father, T.S. Knox, was its proprietor for a generation.[2] For twenty years after his father's early death, the *Journal* was operated by Knox's mother, who relinquished editorial control to John B., as he was universally known, early in the 1830s; he would become proprietor only with her death in September 1846.[3] Under Mrs Knox, the *Journal* had been arch-Tory and anti-Catholic, suspicious of priestcraft and its many wiles, and antagonistic on public issues from the 1798 Rising to the Union of 1801 and in more recent times Catholic Emancipation. Under John B., these tendencies were moderated, his views as fair-minded as could be expected from someone of his background, although atavistic ancestral passions did occasionally flare into unexpected life. In general, however, notwithstanding a fiercely independent nature, Knox's *Journal* reflected a provincial Irish Protestant mindset, that of respectable townsfolk and professional and landed gentlemen.

But the *Journal* could not have subsisted on such a narrow readership (Clare Protestants amounted to less than 2 per cent of the population), and the majority by far of its readers were Catholics strongly opposed to its political stance, yet who valued it for its advertising; much of its news coverage and features; the lightness of its prejudices and, since the *Journal* was the only newspaper published in Clare, the absence of an alternative that might reflect theirs.[4] As editor, on many subjects Knox was mild and tolerant, and irritatingly paternalist though he might be at times, his devotion to the public interest, to Clare, to Ennis and especially to its poor was unquestioned.

Social improvement was one of Knox's recurring themes, his greatest preoccupation the elevation of the lower classes of county and town from what he saw as the degraded condition to which ignorance and poverty – as well as, he sometimes indiscreetly implied, their religion – had condemned them. Grasping at all possible vehicles for reform, he used the *Journal* to promote educational initiatives, public and private; mechanics' institutes; industrial employment; agricultural progress; and land reclamation and drainage. He promoted Irish manufactures at the expense of British ones, an economic nationalism that sat ill with his Tory politics. A great believer in Temperance, he supported Father Mathew's movement fully, striving the while to hide his distaste for its underpinning of Catholic ritual.

Knox employed a small staff of reporters on the *Journal* and accepted news items also from unpaid correspondents in outlying districts; on rare occasions 'special' reporters were dispatched to such places for specific assignments. From internal evidence we know something of three *Journal* reporters during the mid-1840s: Hugh O'Keeffe, Stephen Joseph Meany and James Knox Walker. O'Keeffe was a talented journalist, a rumbustious personality who on one memorable occasion poked fun at John Singleton, the ponderous landlord of Quinville Abbey in the presence of his editor, and to his evident enjoyment.[5] Meany was the son of a Ballyea smallholder, a mere teenager when Knox, impressed by his precocious poetic gifts and his public speaking abilities, took him on as reporter. Alas for Knox, who mentored Meany to the extent of publishing an anthology of his poems, on the eve of the Great Famine his protégé deserted him for the *Freeman's Journal*, the moderate Dublin daily.[6] Worse again, Meany became an ardent Young Irelander and would later serve a prison sentence for complicity in the 1848 Rising.[7] The third reporter, James Knox Walker, who may have been Meany's replacement, was a northern Protestant of extreme confessional views. As with Meany, Knox would quarrel with Knox Walker in time, although for very different reasons.

All three young reporters would have known the Jail Street house very well and would have been on terms of familiarity with its occupants; with Knox's brand new, twenty-something wife, Mary, whom he married in October 1845 just as news of the first great potato failure began to spread; with Knox's adult daughter Eliza, child of an earlier marriage (Knox had been twice married and widowed), who was about the same age as her stepmother; doubtless the household servants also.[8] Perhaps the journalists were aware also of Knox's three-year-old daughter, the child of an illicit liaison that occurred between his marriages, but who would not have been mentioned in the household, and lived elsewhere. At any rate, as the Famine begins, Knox's life was entering a new phase, in which domestic fulfilment helped recharge the remarkable energies this 53-year-old man would display during the years immediately following.[9]

The major concern of all who frequented the Jail Street premises, reporters and Knox family alike, was of course the production of the *Journal*, an eight-page broadsheet that appeared each Monday and Thursday and sold at four pence per copy. Much of the *Journal* was taken up with world and imperial news lifted from an array of other newspapers (occasionally Knox allows us believe he consulted the 'Paris' or 'Hamburg' newspapers by apologizing for their arrival too late for inclusion. Perhaps he did).[10] Scattered among the pages of the *Journal* were items of national, county and local interest, side by side with advertisements and notices, literary material and the anchoring editorial, all of great interest to readers and to those who had the paper read to them, in urban reading room and cabin fireside.

John B. Knox's residence and Clare Journal *premises*. Author photograph.

Potato blight is first mentioned in the *Journal* late in August 1845 in an article lifted from an English newspaper regarding the destruction of potatoes in Suffolk by an unknown disease.[11] Sandwiched on an inside page between reports of an archery competition in Meath and recent news from India, the article's significance was overlooked, and a few days later Knox was dwelling lyrically on prospects for the tillage harvest, now luxuriating under late summer sunshine. The potato, that 'son of the sod', as he termed it affectionately, was 'in point of quality and quantity without complaint from the tillers', an unusual if not unprecedented situation.[12]

But as blight spread across the countryside in succeeding weeks, blasting to withered putrescence every potato field in its path, Knox's lyricism was replaced by a worried calm as he followed its deadly progress. In mid-October his tone became grave, as the digging out of the main crop brought the realization that the only food of the poor was rotting even as his editorial was being written and that a crisis was unfolding whose enormity the authorities did not appear to appreciate. Admitting that for weeks he had downplayed the situation 'while hope remained or prospects were doubtful', he now told his readers bluntly that the 'canker' was 'not partial, but general', and that only the most drastic measures, taken immediately, would avert 'an early and prolonged famine'.

'Let no time be lost,' he urged, 'let central and district committees be formed in all directions. Let the influential gentry and clergymen of both persuasions make reports that must bear the stamp of truth and appear as genuine records of existing circumstances'. More radically, he demanded that 'every precaution be taken that the Brewery and the Distillery do not consume the food of which mortals are deprived'. Domestic animals should be fed only 'upon the substance allotted them by nature, the herbage of the fields'. All too aware of the divided society in which he lived, he pleaded that 'party and politics ... strife and contention be banished from among us'.[13]

In his anxiety to communicate his own urgency to the authorities and public at large, in the weeks that followed Knox filled his columns with editorial pleas for decisive action, updates on the latest news regarding the potatoes and remedies for blight drawn from gardening publications and also from his readers. He was especially impressed with the ideas of the scientifically minded Newmarket-on-Fergus physician, Dr S. Patterson Evans, who correctly identified the blight as a fungus, something the government's Scientific Commission failed to do. Knox's respect for 'official' science, however, eventually had him warn readers against Evans's recommendations, which were 'diametrically the opposite' of the Commission's.[14]

Exasperated by the apathy and complacency he encountered all about him, Knox was now on the offensive, both in print and speech. He was scathing of landlord assertions that the potato failure had been hugely exaggerated, and before the Ennis Poor Law Guardians and Town Commissioners (he was a member of both bodies), and at meetings convened to address the crisis, he struggled against the self-interested and ineffectual proposals that emerged from such thinking. In early November at a Guardians' meeting, he sought and failed to have a memorial to government bolstered with amendments proposing a ban on whiskey distilling and the export of food, and the immediate commencement of public works. The weak resolution that was adopted in the event, he described as 'absurd', and the meeting that passed it as 'worth less than a diseased potato'.[15]

Knox had better luck with the Ennis Town Commissioners, who adopted a resolution drafted by him, including all the measures omitted from the Guardians' memorial. The price he had to pay was a temporary alliance with the Repealers on that body and the risk of taint by association with a cause that was anathema to him.[16] This slight victory, however, was more than outweighed by a hopelessly vague resolution passed at a County Meeting about the same time, a pernicious development since such meetings were weighty affairs, attended by magistrates and members of Parliament, their deliberations taken seriously by government. On this occasion, the most influential voices were those of Crofton Moore Vandeleur, the landed magnate of Kilrush who moved the resolution, and John Singleton who seconded it. The proceedings of this meeting, Knox told his readers witheringly, 'amount to nothing'.[17] Unexpectedly for Knox, his greatest source of disappointment was government, the Peel-led Tory administration whose leader he had held in high esteem, and in whose 'wisdom, foresight and activity' he had earlier resided utmost confidence.[18] Eroded by official procrastination in regard to relief measures, in mid-November Knox's faith in the Tories was shattered by the brusque treatment accorded a delegation from the distinguished Mansion House Committee by the Lord Lieutenant, Lord Heytesbury. Enraged, Knox turned on both leaders of the 'sleeping administration', Heytesbury and Sir Robert Peel:

> Nero fiddled while Rome was burning – so with Sir Robert Peel, Her Majesty's Prime Minister, and Lord Heytesbury, Her Majesty's Lord Lieutenant of Ireland. The one calls the Cabinet Ministers together, who meet and talk and adjourn – the other receives a deputation composed of the first men in the country, in a way that no deputation was ever received before. He tells them that he has heard everything they had to communicate respecting the probability of a famine, that he is quite alive to the subject, that he has appointed scientific men to make experiments how rotten potatoes may be made sound, and how long pigs can live on blackberries ... There now, Gentlemen, good morning.

Widening his attack to local Tories, he spoke of the despair now seizing on the people, and the indifference to it of the county establishment, 'who would not indeed wish to disturb my Lord Heytesbury over his wine and walnuts by telling him the honest truth', that is, that the people had no food and were desperate for relief. 'The heart sickens at such trifling', he declared, 'such disregard for the lives of the people'.

If we are taken aback at the depth of Knox's anger towards his political role models and the Clare Tories whom he antagonised at his peril, we are less surprised, probably less even than he was, that his jeremiad elicited not the slightest reaction from any quarter. Disheartened, he lapsed into silence, rage expended. Only occasionally does he bestir himself afterwards from time to time when further data or correspondence came to hand; on one occasion he admitted that he was only doing so lest 'our silence ... be construed into an acknowledgement that the potato crop in this county has not been as greatly reduced by the present distemper as was first reported'.[19] But Knox had lost heart, and his last editorial of 1845 is gloomy, as he reflects on the impossibility of impressing on authority at any level the necessity of meeting to discuss the hugely important crisis-related topic of Corn Law Repeal or 'almost any other subject'.[20]

January, however, brought two developments that revived Knox's enthusiasm and the cautious hope that his appeals had not been in vain. This first was a flurry of petitioning from all over Clare to government, demanding that employment-generating infrastructural works be started at once: drainage schemes, navigation improvements and railway construction. Petitioning, to be sure, was a passive activity, with little measurable effect, but it did at least give some indication to government that among a responsible public over a wide area great concern existed with regard to the immediate future of poor people.[21]

The second development was imminently practical and of immediate effect. This was when, rather than wait for government relief employment legislation, magistrates in west Clare instead activated an old and little-used Public Works Act.[22] Knox was an early and enthusiastic supporter of this initiative, and his recommendation that it be emulated by magistrates elsewhere soon bore fruit; within weeks special presentment sessions of magistrates and cess-payers were being held everywhere and works approved, all in the presence of large crowds of work-desperate labourers.[23] So successful did all this prove that after formal closure of the county Spring Assizes in March, the Grand Jury reassembled in special session and unanimously declared against operating the government programme which had just been sanctioned by Parliament, on the grounds that it was not necessary.[24] To Knox, therefore, must go much of the credit for ensuring that his county had a head start of several precious months over others in terms of public works employment.

Knox was highly critical of the new government legislation, yet he supported the establishment of district relief committees which formed part of it, and when the Ennis Relief Committee was formed, he threw himself into its activities. In this he differed from other Ennis Protestants, who remained aloof because the Committee was dominated by Catholic Repealers, whose leader, Cornelius Hickey, an administratively capable town merchant, was chairman.[25] It was typical of Knox that he was able to put aside his abhorrence of Repeal and Repealers and place his trust in Hickey's good faith and abilities. Committee duties did, however, add significantly to the burdens of public responsibility Knox was already carrying, on the Board of Guardians, the Town Commissioners and the County Fever Hospital; and given that he was at the same time ever more taken up with his newspaper, the first half of 1846 was clearly a time of overwork and strain for him.

From the end of May, however, his newspaper burden seems to ease somewhat, if we are to judge by a significant lessening in crisis-related coverage in the *Clare Journal*, fewer and shorter reports and letters concerning distress, relief committees, works administration and funding issues. Even the *Journal*'s tone seems less anxious, less harried, and reading through successive issues, we find ourselves paying attention again, as contemporary readers may have done also, to items of imperial and foreign news, to the Friday Petty Sessions reports, and the occasional town entertainment.[26] Was the *Journal* establishment, and Knox himself then, lapsing unthinkingly into the sort of complacency of which he had been so critical in others? Had he begun to believe that the crisis was at an end? Was the crisis, in fact, over? Certainly the lengthening days and improving weather enhanced hopes for the growing potatoes whose green mantle again covered the fields, as it did for the rapidly expanding public works employment it was believed would be sufficient to tide the poor over until they were ready for lifting.

At the end of June this summer optimism began to fall apart, with news of the fall of Sir Robert Peel's administration. Jolted by the prospect of a return to power of the Whig-Liberals and what this might portend for the poor, Knox was driven to a hasty re-evaluation of Peel's performance in office, allowing that 'latterly' at least, the outgoing prime minister had 'devoted laudable attention to the state of this country', and all things considered was still the 'fittest head of a Government for the times'.[27] But of course Knox's opinions and hopes were irrelevant to events, his helplessness underlined by reports that came hard on the heels of this seismic political change, of the return, with extreme aggressiveness, of potato blight, first noticed by the *Clare Journal* in a republished *Mayo Telegraph* report on 29 June, the very day Peel's government fell.[28]

Knox's reaction to this second visitation and the near-total destruction of the potatoes that followed within weeks is something that can be appreciated only over an extended period. A fortnight after the first devastating news, he was acknowledging the blight to be 'earlier manifested and more likely to be deeper and we think more prevalent than last year', a detached editorial observation that is followed by a vague injunction to government to make 'effectual efforts' and an anodyne discussion of replacement foods.[29] Three further weeks were to pass before his next editorial comment, the delay undoubtedly reflecting his own turmoil in processing the full implications of what had happened. The editorial itself is a confused one, amounting to no more than a jumble of disconnected phrases and contradictory half-statements relating to the destruction of the potatoes: 'not a single individual of the agricultural population' had escaped crop damage; the potato had failed in 'almost every part of the globe'; it was lost to Ireland and 'to the world as an article of diet'; potatoes should not be sown again, since it would be 'highly unwise and injurious to occupy the soil' with them.[30]

This and succeeding editorials present Knox in a light that is new to us, one where he is utterly at a loss: there are many aimless, helpless remarks about the spreading devastation, including one description of a journey south of Ennis, on the outward leg of which he saw just one potato field that had not been blighted and which, on his return two days later, had also been ruined. In another editorial, which reveals some attempts at self-control, he recognizes the necessity of facing up to the reality brought about by the new failure rather than hiding from them as some prints were doing; in another again, he speaks of the 'frightful' prospects facing the poor.[31]

By September, Knox's mood was little changed; Famine was not just 'making rapid strides towards the people', it was 'already at their doors'. Because Ireland's charity mechanisms had been exhausted in the previous season, 'almost the whole burden of providing food' would now fall upon government, and the 'the resources of the whole empire must be taxed' to that end.[32] 'Can the Government do so?' he asked, his own lifeless answer, 'they must do it', revealing how little he believed they would. Editorializing some weeks later on the refusal of Lord John Russell, the Whig-Liberal prime minister, to purchase relief grain abroad as Peel had done, his response was still essentially passive: on the one hand Russell's attitude was 'little short of mockery', but on the other, it must be that the cabinet did not appreciate the depth of distress in Ireland; when they received 'more definite information' they 'would see the propriety – indeed the necessity – of pursuing a more liberal policy'.[33]

It was only when government saw neither the propriety nor the necessity of changing its policies that at last Knox's combative nature reasserted itself. On 5 October, nearly three months into the second potato failure, he told his readers that 'our country' presented an 'extraordinary anomaly': the people were in great distress for want of food, yet there was 'plenty and to spare of food in the country', which was 'every day being sent out of the country', the people 'looking to receive food five thousand miles away to afford them support'.[34] A few days later, he declared that the poor had no food at all and that faced with starvation 'they must perish or plunder': they had no other choice.[35] As critical of the Whig-Liberals' public works measures as he had been of the Tory programmes, he concluded that they would dangerously encumber landed property while leaving other forms of wealth untouched; they would be utterly wasteful of resources and would not give sufficient employment or wages to the poor. As the programme came into operation he criticized delays in commencements and the way he observed them working out in his locality.[36] 'How very different from the bungling measures of relief now in operation', he editorialized on 15 October, conveniently forgetting his earlier attacks on the former Tory prime minister, 'was the plan adopted by Sir Robert Peel's Cabinet last year'.[37]

On 2 November, in a particularly blistering denunciation, Knox was savage regarding the Whig-Liberals. Russell's declaration that he would not pursue relief policies that involved interference with the markets, he described as insane; cabinet members and their officials were 'these Foreigners', men who were indifferent to the plight of the exclusion of the aged and sickly from the country's crowded workhouses; Stanley and Routh, the two senior relief bureaucrats, were 'pert officials with their hands in their pockets jingling their quarters' salary or sipping their wine and puffing their perfumed cigars, [while] disregard[ing] the misery that surrounds them'. By their 'insane and heartless conduct', Russell's government would succeed in healing the breach between Old and Young Ireland and do more 'to swell the ranks of Repealers than all the monster meetings that O'Connell could congregate for a hundred years'.[38]

By now Knox's convulsive rage, as expressed in passionate language of this kind, was well known among newspapermen, and in distant London even the haughty *Times* took heed. The *Times* had previously extracted material from the *Clare Journal* and on this occasion reprinted Knox's 2 November editorial in full, along with a short editorial comment. But the *Times* was not much interested in connecting Knox's anger with government behaviour or in the mass starvation currently engulfing Ireland, and its interest in Knox himself was confined to curiosity that such radical rhetoric was emanating from such a sober, respectable, fellow-Tory source. Ultimately it dismissed the issue by describing Knox, lightly, as 'this hurricane from the south west'.[39]

'National' newspapers, which had been inclined to misinterpret Knox's attacks on government as evidence of a patriotic awakening, at this point knew better, since they had been frequently and painfully disabused of such a notion by the editor himself. The *Limerick and Clare Examiner*, a new arrival on the scene, which early on had lauded the *Clare Journal* as one of the 'very few' conservative prints to be 'conducted with more moderation or more decency of tone and temper', had been so brutally rebuffed afterwards that by October, its reaction to one *Journal* put-down was a hurt reference to Knox's 'weathercock sentimentality'.[40] Knox's reply to this remark was made with an almost crazed destructive impulse: the creed of the *Examiner* was 'hatred to the Saxon', a '*hating and hateful* doctrine' [italics in original], a 'blind sectarianism', its concern for the poor a meretricious sham. 'And so we perceive', Knox wrote, 'the *Limerick Examiner* secretly chuckles with delight over the misery of the people, so long as he thinks it a stronger reason for Repeal'.[41]

Knox's other rival in the mid-west, the *Limerick Reporter*, which had followed the *Examiner–Journal* interchanges, was more artful; slightly before this it had praised the *Journal* as 'our well-meaning but erratic cotemporary', whose 'patriotic effusions' it had often admired when it had 'spoken out the truth honestly and fearlessly in a national tone, scarcely surpassed by any Repeal paper'.[42] For the *Reporter*, however, these 'fitful outbursts of nationality soon became obscured by the clouds of prejudice' as the *Journal* was 'made the dupe of the designing', its editor 'led astray by corrupting influences' against which he was not proof. 'We wish', the *Reporter* silkily declared, in a manner designed to infuriate Knox 'that he would "lay aside every weight and the sin which doth so easily beset him," and throw himself wholly and unreservedly into the sacred cause of his country'.[43]

In the last few months of 1846 Knox became possessed by a kind of incandescent fury, of which his flaying of nationally minded newspapers was a characteristic reflection. From deep within his Jail Street redoubt, his assaults on all the mechanisms of relief escalated outwards, his targets now extending beyond government and officials, and focusing increasingly on the shortcomings of landlords and merchants. Landlords had attracted his ire when the potatoes had first failed, and as he turned on them anew, it was in more sustained and specific criticism of their failure to provide employment or to import grain on their own initiative. Merchants were criticized for profiteering, most bitingly in one sally in October against 'the grasping avarice of unprincipled merchants who care little and feel less, for the miserable destitution of the people'. Since Knox was now ranging in on resident landlords as well as absentees and on specific types of merchant, the risk of alienating people he knew and to whom he was in some degree economically bound grew accordingly. Landlords and merchants with whom he was friendly would inevitably see themselves as being under personal attack, especially the merchants who included friends and acquaintances with whom he did business every day. It may be significant in this connection that Knox's criticisms of merchants were the least frequent and the shortest lived of any launched by him.[44] Names were never mentioned at any point.

Nevertheless, at one point Knox seems to have been flailing indiscriminately all around him; and while doing his utmost to promote an awareness of the sufferings of poor labourers and cabin occupiers, he could on occasion accuse them of lazy and sullen idleness.[45] He became as likely to criticize Catholic priests as to praise them and in one instance signalled his regard for the parish priest of Ennistymon, Father John Sheehan, while simultaneously insulting him with insinuations of jobbery in his opposition to the construction of a relief road near his house. Knowing Knox, who had facilitated him repeatedly by publishing his eloquent letters regarding the state of the poor, Sheehan did not take offence and merely reiterated his own respect for the choleric editor.[46]

Knox was to maintain the pace and intensity of his criticism over the first half of 1847, especially during February and March in parallel with the explosion to omnipresence of mass death by starvation and fever. Excoriating all those whose sins of omission and commission had led to this state of affairs, his writing becomes infused with what can only be called consternation, arising out of what he was witnessing on a daily basis or processing in his mind from those who brought incident after appalling incident in endless succession through the Jail Street archway to his office.

Whole communities were perishing silently, Knox told his readers in one editorial in January, without any notice being taken of their disappearance; public works labourers in many places were dropping dead of exhaustion where they stood. Upon government would rest the blood of the people if they persisted in allowing a general famine to continue and all the scenes of riot, anarchy and bloodshed that would eventually accompany it.[47] So many were perishing, he wrote in February, that the coroners were unable to hold inquests on one in fifty of the dead. Upon those still surviving, the want of sufficient food was 'traceable upon the countenances of the people as visibly as the glare of a July sun!' It was all 'a record for the eternal disgrace of the rulers of these countries'. The land lay uncultivated, the occupiers having no seed.[48] By the end of February, Knox's rage had reached such a level as to have him issue a reproach to the sovereign he revered, in a remarkable passage that manages to combine obsequiousness with anger: 'We ask does her Majesty ever read a newspaper? Does she ever cast her eye over the *London Times*, where the dying groans of the Irish are ridiculed, and the wail of the starving infant is laughed to scorn?'[49]

In these months Knox attacked every aspect of relief policy and every new proposal in regard to it. He opposed the planned emergency system of relief by soup kitchen; he called repeatedly for action to prevent fluctuations in the price of grain; in April and May he railed at committee members who failed to turn up for duty, leaving all the work to two or three individuals, and he pounded away at the callous, brutally abrupt closing of the public works.[50] One of the most extraordinary of all his editorials came in early June, after the death from typhus of his friend, Thomas Mahon, the Chairman of the Ennis Relief Committee. 'Lord John Russell', it begins, 'at your door we lay the death[s] of all the good men who have fallen victim in this hour of peril'. It was 'the good, the kind hearted and humane', those 'whose generous feelings' were horrified at the 'distresses' of the people, it was these individuals whose sufferings Russell had 'tenfold augmented', and who 'were every other day taken from amongst them':[51]

> But you, Lord John Russell, have neglected the charge committed to you, and you disregarded the warnings, you despised the cautions which were borne to you on almost every breeze, and the result has been, that thousands are sacrificed by your neglect. To make the rich richer, you sacrificed the poor Irish, as if we were a second class in the scale of society. We will not curse you in our hour of trial and of suffering, but we will hold you up to the scorn and indignation of the world at large, and demand justice against your cruelty, and the outrages you have wantonly inflicted upon our country. The blood of the slain will we require at your hands.

When this was written Knox had to have been close to exhaustion: from April we know he had accepted extra responsibilities at the Fever Hospital, the County Infirmary and Fergus Drainage boards, and his other responsibilities cannot have been decreasing either.[52] How he managed to give full value to each is difficult to know, but *Clare Journal* reports show regular attendance and active participation in each. A clue to his state of mind may be found in one section of his Russell denunciation of June, where he ascribes a state of physical and psychological prostration to certain relief committee personnel, those 'whose minds have been worn out by their efforts to provide food for a famishing people, whose sleepless nights have prevented any restoration of strength to their over-worked bodies, [and] whose powers have been prostrated by their anxiety to preserve the people'.[53] Without consciously realizing it, Knox was surely speaking of himself.

Looking backwards from the vantage point of midsummer 1847 to the aftermath of the first potato failure in October 1845, we can take full measure of the extraordinary figure who was John Busteed Knox: a conscientious contributor to Famine relief operations, and a staunch Repeal-hating Tory newspaper editor who over an extended period subjected the relief programmes pursued by two successive British governments – the first of them led by a man he had deeply admired – to intense, articulate and devastating criticism. He had also criticized what he saw as the besetting sins of individuals and bodies in his own vicinity who he felt were in some sense negligent or blameworthy with regard to the plight of the Famine-stricken poor. His criticisms in both cases went very much against his personal and commercial interests.

But if we change from a backward to a forward perspective, we are arrested by an utterly unexpected development: instead of the continuation and strengthening of his powerful critical rhetoric we soon find ourselves in the midst of a steady process of disengagement on Knox's part from his earlier views, and a lowering to inaudibility of the fearless, independent voice that had so long had been his trademark. By 1849 his stance had reversed itself entirely, the *Clare Journal* becoming the chief apologist for the most horrendously culpable behaviour of government, of officials and landlords. By the end of the Famine the *Journal* was virtually indistinguishable from the most reactionary prints in Ireland.[54] What had happened?

The key to an understanding of Knox's retreat lies in his own nervy, volatile personality and the nature of his editorial column, so often the only forum where ideas and opinions that he struggled and failed to have considered elsewhere could be expressed clearly and directly. Written often in a highly wrought state, his verbal onslaughts tended to be reckless, intemperate and dogmatic. Essentially things of impulse, of the moment, they were launched without conscious thought as to their full implications either for their targets or Knox's own interests. The possibility of a change on Knox's part and its potential swiftness are therefore comprehensible in terms of his personality; a detailed examination of its chronology explains how and why it happened.

We become aware that Knox's views have undergone radical change only over an extended period during 1848, an uncomfortable realization that we find we have been resisting. And as we rework the evidence we have half-ignored or passed over because it hasn't fitted in, we find that anomalies go back as far as the last months of 1846, when it seemed that his indignation could not have been higher. The first significant instance here seems to be Knox's low-key response to the controversies caused by Captain Edmond Wynne, even though the *Journal* did report on the episode in some detail.[55] The next occurrence comes during the soup kitchen phase of Famine relief which, as we have seen, Knox assailed at the legislative stages.[56] Once the kitchens were in operation, however, Knox's foremost concern becomes the supposed prevalence of fraud, or 'imposition', the suffering imposed by the system relegated to secondary importance.[57]

> Outdoor relief [i.e. by soup kitchen rations] is sought for by almost every individual in the district. Man, woman, and child are crowding into the committee rooms the moment it is opened. The man who had work on Monday, instead of seeking work on Tuesday, forthwith goes to the committee for a 'share of what is going'. The old woman living with two or three sons who are all in constant work, comes for a little rice of meal, and if offered a ticket to the kitchen rejects it. The very children are seeking a ticket for the rice.

If this passage reveals a new harshness on Knox's part – disregarding momentary instances of irritation already mentioned – human sympathy still remains uppermost, and a few weeks later he could still refer to the soup kitchens as 'a mean, niggardly system of relief'.[58]

Another pivotal moment comes in late April 1847 when the Ennis Relief Committee bought a quantity of grain for soup kitchen purposes at rates that were exceptionally favourable to the broker, John MacBeth, in what the *Limerick and Clare Examiner* called a 'glaring job' amounting to 'robbing the famine-stricken'.[59] Knox's silence on the issue can only be understood in terms of his personal friendship with MacBeth, much as his failure to take a position on the Wynne dispute relates to a burgeoning relationship with the landlord, Thomas Mahon, whose death would so affect him. MacBeth and Mahon were each representatives of social groups of whom Knox had once been extremely critical, but among whom he was now increasingly to be found bedding down.[60]

Mahon's very death marks a further step in Knox's reversal of attitude, not least because he succeeded him as chairman of the Ennis Relief Committee, a post he would occupy until its dissolution in September.[61] By accepting the post Knox effectively disarmed his own critical apparatus and henceforth became an instrument of official policy. Slowly at first, but with increasing momentum he begins to justify the various official policies and bureaucratic stratagems that lay at the heart of the people's suffering, gradually sliding into the self-serving thinking that pervaded the entire relief structure. This is strikingly illustrated in his final report as chairman in September, which represents an absolute *volte face* on his part, a contradiction of every criticism he had previously made of the mechanisms of relief, and in which he effaces a year of his own admirable editorial work in one shameful prevaricating sentence. Knox also bestows praise on a Major Smith, a particularly odious relief inspector with whom the Committee had been locked in perpetual conflict, and most wondrously of all, he tenders 'grateful thanks' to the recently loathed Whig-Liberals for 'their unceasing endeavours to alleviate the distress of our people'.[62]

But all of this is incidental to the major reason for Knox's about face: the upsurge of social disturbance precipitated by food shortage. It is surely significant that the first signs of Knox's turnaround are traceable to late 1846, when communities had begun to act collectively in order to prevent the removal of grain and potatoes from their districts to markets elsewhere. From this point forward we notice a cooling of Knox's admiration for the dignified and peaceable manner in which he had imagined poor people were enduring their suffering. When protest was attended by organized shooting of the horses of market-bound farmers, and attacks against the person, as it was in some districts, he became increasingly preoccupied with the 'system' of intimidation and thuggery which he believed lay behind it.[63]

Knox had predicted violence of his kind and, as we saw earlier, had seen it as an inevitable and justifiable response of otherwise helpless people. But at that point the issue had been a theoretical one; when it occurred in practice, it unnerved him, probably because it stirred deep-seated insecurities arising out of his own childhood memories of 1798 and adult experience of the Terry Alt rising of 1828–1831. Such fears cannot have been lessened by the fact that participants in the new disturbances were referred to by all, the authorities included, as Terry Alts or Whiteboys, and that they acted according to ages-old Whiteboy rituals of engagement.

Those who lived in disturbed districts tended not to be as afflicted by worry about 'outrage' as some of those who lived outside them, as did Knox, whose anxieties were irrational to the point where even after the fading away of survival crime and social protest, concern for the poor is superseded by worry about what he calls their 'moral degradation', as evidenced in threatening notices, physical attacks and armed robberies. Welcoming the dispatch of a Special Judicial Commission to Clare at the end of 1847 to deal with Famine-related crime, Knox had been revolted at the summary hangings and transportation sentences that followed, but he was positive about the Commission's salutary effect. 'Desperate evils require desperate remedies', he wrote at that time, 'and we hope that some more severe measures than have yet been adopted may not be found necessary before peace and order are restored to this county'.[64]

It says much of Knox's law and order neuroses, and his fear of the unchaining of the lower orders that he did not feel at all threatened by the posturing of the would-be revolutionaries of the Irish Confederation, ridiculing the pretensions of the Clare Confederates indeed, in a cheerful, kindly manner.[65] The abortive Rising of July 1848 did send him into editorial tirades against those involved, lasting through the aftermath hunt for escaping Confederate leaders, but it is noteworthy that when his former protégé, Stephen Joseph Meany, who had been among the insurgents, was arrested at Gort in August, Knox merely recorded the fact.[66] It is interesting also that despite his condemnation of William Smith O'Brien's actions in the Rising, Knox never lost his regard for the hapless insurgent leader, whose brother was Sir Lucius O'Brien, the Dromoland grandee.[67]

At the very time Knox was filling up editorial and news columns with denunciation of miscreant Confederates, the process of mass eviction, soon to soar to gigantic proportions, was gathering pace across the landscapes of Famine Clare. But in contrast to many other newspapers which were soon publishing details of these horrendous events, the *Clare Journal*, which had a virtual ringside seat at some of the worst clearances to take place anywhere, was conspicuous by its failure either to report or editorialize on them to any extent. In other Tory prints this failure might have been expected, but in the case of John B. Knox's *Journal* it was a singular and significant omission.

Knox had always had a blind spot in regard to evictions. During the estate consolidations of the immediate pre-Famine era he had generally accepted the landlord's version of events, and where charges of 'extermination' were levelled against proprietors he admired, he invariably weighed in on their side, usually with indignation.[68] Scrupulous in publishing letters highlighting particular evictions, but never following up with investigative reportage, most often he disposed of allegations in a disbelieving editorial comment. Typical of this Knoxian tendency is a remark appended to a letter from Father Michael Meehan regarding evictions by Crofton Vandeleur early in 1846 (we will be revisiting these later on), which is at once mild and dismissive: 'When we bear in mind the many misstatements published from time to time regarding the turning out of tenants, we receive such statements with great caution.'[69]

Knox's disposition regarding evictions became ever more entrenched during the Famine clearances, reaching proportions of knowledge avoidance that were egregious, to say the least, and in which his admiration for Vandeleur and Marcus Keane, the two worst exterminators, remained undimmed. Equally obliging with his column space towards evictors as their opponents, he was punctilious in publishing self-exculpatory letters by Keane and by Vandeleur's partisans (Vandeleur did not defend himself in newspapers).

In March 1848 he reprinted details from another newspaper regarding one atrocious Keane clearance, at Garraunnatooha in west Clare, involving the brutal expulsion of 185 persons from their homes, including the well-known instance of Bridget O'Donnell and her family, commenting that he was 'noticing' the account only because the contributor's name had been included. Having implicitly given credence, therefore, to what was by any standards an atrocity, he disposes of it in one sentence.[70] No reporters were dispatched to the scene and there was no follow-up commentary. In March 1849, in the briefest terms, Knox quoted from his own correspondent in Newmarket-on-Fergus, regarding the 'extensive exterminations and throwing down of houses' that was in progress everywhere in the parish, 'the poor people turned out sleeping by the sides of the ditches'. Again there was neither editorial comment nor follow-up coverage.[71]

'It is indeed certain, beyond all dispute', he wrote in October 1849, with respect to remarks by the radical English MP George Poulett Scrope concerning certain clearances in the Kilrush Union, 'that immense numbers have been evicted from their holdings in Kilrush'. He then commends Scrope for refraining from 'denouncing the landlords' or ascribing to them the entire blame for the suffering caused since 'the rigour they exert is extorted from them by sheer necessity – that with many of them it is a very death-struggle for existence'.[72] The same kind of equivocation permeates his only specific reference to Marcus Keane's clearances:[73]

> How Mr. Marcus Keane may have been justified by circumstances in the system of evictions which he has adopted – and we have no doubt, reluctantly adopted – we are not prepared to say'. But we have no hesitation in saying, that the rights of property ought to be trampled in the dust rather than enforced at the sacrifice of human life. If poor people must be ejected from their holdings – (and such a course, we repeat, is often necessary) – yet, in the name of Heaven, let them not be cast out upon the world without food or shelter, and left to perish. If in these respects, a landlord or an agent does not exercise due caution by taking care that the unfortunate people are not left to starve, we really do not see how they can be held guiltless of their blood.

If we find here traces of the old, outraged, indignant Knox, they are badly adulterated by the context in they occur, emerging as no more than platitudes. His overall thought pattern by now closely follows landlord discourse, in a manner best expressed in an editorial from mid-March 1850 which is devoted to the 'moral degeneracy' now residing 'to such a fearful extent among the great mass of the people'. So many of them had been 'induced to feign destitution, and apply for public relief, while in various cases the applicants could probably have commanded more ready money than some of the gentlemen to whom they applied, and who were themselves almost pauperized'. The people were 'taught to harbour hatred, envy, and ill-will against the more elevated classes of their fellow-men', and instead of 'cultivating truth and manly independence', they were adhering to 'a low system of cunning, deception and fraud, and the mean habit of living upon the charity of their more industrious neighbours'. This 'moral destitution' (the editorial was so entitled also) had aggravated, 'to a tenfold degree the calamities under which this county has been struggling'.[74]

It is hard indeed to reconcile this verbiage with the courage and compassion Knox had earlier displayed, but the fact itself is indisputable, and in the end perhaps he was able to argue thus only because he restricted himself from venturing far enough into the countryside to witness even one eviction. Significant also of Knox's changed attitudes is that although he published material relating to the 1850 parliamentary inquiry into the Kilrush clearances, he made no editorial comment on it.

A similar regression marks Knox's attitudes towards the religious controversies that ran parallel with the clearances and which indeed in some cases were connected directly with them. Knox held the standard Protestant view of Catholicism, a negative one in which idolatry and error, corruption and the supposed degeneracy of the papal court figured prominently. We are aware of these because of occasional slips in the formal *politesse* of his editorials and indiscreet slant of certain column items. Papal difficulties in 1848 and afterwards afforded him a certain satisfaction, and his distaste for the 1850 'Romish' Synod of Thurles was not well hidden.

But these lapses were within the range tolerable to Catholic readers who were still able to read respectful accounts of Catholic ceremonies and devotional events in the *Journal*, as well as letters written by their own priests. During 1848 and 1849, however, a real confessional hostility enters the *Clare Journal*'s treatment of denominational topics for the first time. There were two major episodes here, one relating to Knox's contemptuous dismissal and prolonged wrangle in print with the *Limerick and Clare Examiner* about an alleged miracle cure at a Holy Well in West Clare in August 1848; the other a wild attack, exactly a year later, on the Society of St Vincent de Paul in Kilrush for alleged proselytizing.[75] Both attacks backfired badly, attracting widespread condemnation as well as the strong disapproval of a number of prominent Protestants, among them Colonel George Wyndham, Crofton Moore Vandeleur and Captain Arthur Kennedy.

It was in the general area of Protestant evangelical activity, however, that Knox's changing tone is most clearly manifest. In February 1847 he had repudiated in the strongest terms proposals made by evangelicals based at Exeter Hall in London to take advantage of the condition of the Irish poor in order to advance the cause of the so-called Second Reformation.[76] By the end of the Famine, however, he was defending and even promoting evangelical groups doing precisely that in many parts of Clare, and especially in the west. These developments are examined in later chapters of this book.

So at odds does the *Journal* appear in these years with the compassion and understanding we have come to associate with John B. Knox that it is tempting to reach for a single explanation and to postulate a new influence in the paper of its chief reporter, James Knox Walker, a known holder of reactionary religious and political views. It might be envisioned that Knox Walker (an unpleasant person described by one source as 'a little Orangeman with thin sneering lips and sallow face – a very disagreeable fellow') eventually became editor and gave full vent to his repellent views for some years before a reinvigorated Knox was able to wrest control from him and restore its moderate tone.[77]

But this reassuring scenario, which preserves intact our portrait of a sympathetic Knox, is backed by a few tenuous indications only, and there is no real evidence for it at all. On the other hand, contemporaries, whether supportive of Knox, antipathetic to him, or merely puzzled by his new stance, were clear that he was at the helm of the *Clare Journal* throughout, and whatever the influence of James Knox Walker on the paper, it was Knox, as owner and editor who decided policy and supervised production.[78] By the end of the Famine, therefore, John Busteed Knox, that Hurricane from the South-West, formerly such a champion of the poor, to all intents and purposes had joined their oppressors.

2

Intrepid Fire-Eater: Captain Edmond Wynne

Of all those travelling in our Famine landscape, Captain Edmond Wynne occupies it for the shortest length of time, and we seem to capture him in a kind of blur of his own physical motion. A temporary Inspector of Public Works, whose period of service extended only from October 1846 to the end of the following January, yet as he moves, or rather, gallops across the landscape, Wynne becomes strangely dominant within it. This was mainly because of a remarkable ability on his part to generate controversy and to attract the attention and approval, however briefly, of the leading relief bureaucrats and certain senior political figures to whom they were responsible. By virtue of being who and where he was at a particular time, he even came to have an impact on overall relief policies, leaving aside the incalculable effect of his arbitrary inspectorial decisions on the prospects for survival of many thousands of the starving.

In those general Famine histories in which he appears, Wynne's profile is invariably a positive one. This is because such portrayals are based on uncritical acceptance of evidence emanating from Wynne himself and his self-projection as a man of action and compassion. Two authoritative studies from recent decades that have indicated a rather different version of Wynne have yet to become part of the common awareness of Famine historians.[1] It remains to be seen from this chapter what a re-examination of the evidence regarding Wynne as a figure in the Famine landscape will produce in terms of a fresh understanding of this turbulent individual.

Edmond Wynne was a younger son in a cadet branch of a wealthy Sligo landlord family, both his parents having connections with the legal profession, his father being a barrister, his mother a barrister's daughter.[2] Destined for the British army, Edmond fared poorly in his chosen career path and managed only an undistinguished three-year stint in an unfashionable regiment, which was spent entirely in garrison duties in Ireland and England and at the lowly rank of ensign. After leaving the army with the titular rank of lieutenant (his captaincy was a courtesy title), he married into the petty gentry of north Tipperary and thereafter disappeared for nearly two decades into rural anonymity. When he surfaces again in October 1846 as a government inspector, almost certainly his appointment was secured by his brother-in-law's connections at the Board of Works.[3] We know little else of Wynne's background, apart from the fact that at the time of his appointment, he was on his second marriage, to a Wynne cousin, and that as the Famine began their family was still very young.

Wynne's appointment for the seven westerly baronies of Clare conferred on him membership of a new corps of temporary official employed by the Whig-Liberal government to police their newly instituted public works schemes. The programme was a much more extensive one than that of the Tories in the previous season and was operated by a much overhauled and expanded Board of Works.[4] Although Wynne's post was not at all a sinecure, he might still have expected to encounter what many inspectors did in the quieter parts of the country – tedious inspections of works, endless public meetings and a great deal of report-writing, a workstyle eminently suited to someone approaching middle age as he was and of as little previous accomplishment. Had Wynne or circumstances been even slightly other than they were it might easily have proved so.

By the time Wynne arrived in 'west' Clare – his remit was for territory lying approximately west of a vertical line drawn through Ennis, including districts actually in mid-county – numbers of poor people had already died of starvation and thousands were close to death from hunger; further famishing thousands again were desperate for employment that might rescue them and their children. Some districts had already seen social unrest; there had been hunger marches through towns and villages, and community blockades of corn-stores and warehouses.

In some districts, as we have seen, a limited form of agrarian insurgency had emerged, involving the regeneration of old Whiteboy/Terry Alt networks and the instigation of concerted action to prevent the outward movement of grain to non-local markets, some of it attended by physical violence. For those caught up in particular incidents this was always intense and frightening: horse-shootings, intimidation and assaults, and a number of clumsy attempts at assassination, some of them successful. Board of Works staff, newcomers to the county for the most part, and unfamiliar with the localized nature of 'outrages', tended to be affected by reports of such incidents, and especially edgy because of their disproportionate incidence on the public works, where Whiteboys were not unknown to gather in force in order to lay down and enforce wage rates or redress perceived injustice on the part of officials.

Nerves stretched as they were, engineers and supervisors leaked their mutually reinforcing fears into a Board of Works-wide consciousness through the postal network. On 24 October, Colonel Harry Jones, the head of the Board, wrote that all letters from Clare described the state of society there to be 'completely disorganized', which was far from the truth, but which the overheated imagination of his correspondents had impressed on him to be the case.[5] When Wynne arrived, therefore, he was already conditioned to expect social disintegration, violence, obstruction of his work and a great deal of fraud. Having anticipated these things, he was to find them in abundance, where they actually existed and as was much more often the case, where he imagined them into existence.

By now relief works, nearly all of them road schemes, were beginning to open all over Wynne's appointed 'west' Clare district. From the beginning, however, it was apparent that the demand for work was insatiable and that no matter how gigantic the programme would become, there would always be far more applicants than places. Wynne believed this situation was the result of a serious undercount in the 1841 census, in his district caused by the heavy concentration along its coastline of a fugitive stratum of seaweed gatherers who were not included in that enumeration. His theory was almost certainly correct, although it might have been more impressive to historians if he had not chosen to illustrate it by reference to Clondagad, an estuarine rather than a coastal parish, with a very short shoreline, little seaweed and few gatherers.[6]

In this demographic theorizing, Wynne displays for the first time what would become a characteristic preoccupation with those who were already destitute, and he was never to develop any understanding of the position of conacre men (labourers subsisting exclusively on half-acre potato plots) and small farmers, both from social strata that had been reduced by privation to an identical state of destitution. And from the beginning also, despite his succinct analysis of the actual situation, he was obsessive about fraud or 'imposition', convinced that relatively well-off tenants were being placed wholesale on works by landlord members of relief committees in order to secure their rents, leaving the really destitute without any employment. Landlords, of course, were not above such practices and certain tenants not unwilling to connive at them, but to the extent that this occurred, it was on a miniscule scale rather than on the universal one which officials insisted in believing to be the case.

But if Wynne was already brimming with suspicion when he came to Clare, we know that the relief committees were equally predisposed to dislike their new Inspector, whoever he might turn out to be. This is clear from a letter written by one anonymous committee chairman to the *Clare Journal* late in September, expressing indignation that an outsider with no local knowledge was to be given authority in his district.[7] The 'Chairman' particularly objected to inspectorial powers relating to the scrutinizing of labourer worklists compiled by his committee, whose 'resident gentry' members – clearly he was one such – 'from their daily intercourse with the people', were 'well acquainted with their wants' and 'gave their time and trouble gratis, with the sole object of procuring employment of their destitute neighbours'. To be sure, an Inspector might seek such information from stewards, gangers and country people, but these, the Chairman believes, were likely to be persons whose 'envy, hatred, malice or discontent at their own rejection by the Committee may prompt to gratify their own spleen by retailing false reports to the Inspector'. Far better, he believed, to put up with the 'trifling' level of abuse that might arise in the works programme than waste large sums unnecessarily seeking it out, much of which would wind up in any case in the pockets of jobbing Board of Works officials. From what he knew of country gentlemen, the Chairman doubted very much they would 'tacitly submit to such an insult as this inspector'.

If by his remarks the Chairman unwittingly furnishes some pretty cogent reasons for close supervision of his particular committee, still they do touch directly on the issues that would lead to difficulties later on. What is also evident from the letter is that given the strength of local feeling, a posting to the western districts of Clare would have been challenging for any inspector. When that inspector was as domineering as Wynne and as heedless of the sensibilities of the locally powerful over which he proceeded to trample, major conflict could not long be avoided.

Among the first things we notice about Wynne is how little attention he pays to the sufferings of the poor, failing even to take stock of their physical condition, which, if nothing else was a crucial factor in their ability to work. When put to it, he could certainly express sympathy with their plight and even seem convincing, but he did so at infrequent intervals and in a perfunctory manner, almost as if he were being prompted to do so. His very first report to the Board of Works superior, Colonel Jones, which was made after a brief tour of Corcomroe Barony in the north of the county, sets the tone. It begins not with references to distress, hunger or mortality, but with a nonchalant assertion of having 'met with a good many adventures', none of which, he informs the colonel with bravado, 'were sufficient to alarm a man accustomed to a Tipperary or Clare mob'.[8]

At one point in the report he tells of having found himself in the village of Ennistymon, 'surrounded by a yelling mob, headed by a priest', the collective intention being to intimidate him by numbers and aggression into paying a higher daily wage than the eight pence allowed by the Board. What he actually encountered, we can have no doubt, was the humane and scholarly parish priest of Ennistymon, Father John Sheehan, at the head of his starving parishioners, who were understandably agitated at being offered pay that was pitifully insufficient to keep their families alive, and at the harsh eight-hour days their hunger-worn bodies would have to endure, six days a week, to earn it. As Wynne presented matters, the facing down of the Ennistymon crowd was a 'very great triumph', his account designed to reassure Colonel Jones as to the calibre of his appointee. 'Altogether prospects brighten greatly', he continued, adding that the greatest difficulty he and his staff were now faced with was to maintain their principles, 'without starving some of the perverse creatures'. Assuming that this last remark was an attempt at offhanded humour, its poor taste tells much as to how Wynne viewed those whose misery he was appointed to relieve.

Relief committees first became acquainted with Wynne the day after this report was made, when he issued a circular instructing them to include on the worklists the exact number only of labourers the engineers would be able to find places for.[9] It was a curt communication, giving no indication as to how the selections were to be carried out or how the excluded labourers and their families were to survive. If it might have been calculated to raise the hackles of any relief committee, so too, had the committees known about it, might Wynne's report of two days later, which accused them of 'unprincipled behaviour' in crowding men on the works, the landowners among them accused of placing their tenants 'in proportion to the amount of taxation [they] might be expected to pay hereafter ... regardless of the claims of the individuals for relief'.[10]

On this occasion Wynne's criticism stops just short of accusations of imposition, the term he had no difficulty in using of suspect relief recipients, and which in all phases of the Famine was much in use by those wishing to repress the reality of human suffering by effectively blaming the victims. We have seen John B. Knox reaching for the term when his reservoir of human empathy had been emptied; by that time it was already the watchword for officials at all levels, its elimination their overriding concern. Later we shall see landlords, evictors and Poor Law inspectors taking refuge under its semantic umbrella.

From the first Wynne spent an inordinate amount of time combing through worklists for 'impostors' and 'unworthy' persons. 'We are getting everything our own way', he exulted on 19 November: 'This week the return will be 3,000 less than last, and I shall fully expect to strike off 3,000 more next week.'[11] Given that imposter-hunting was a bureaucratic nonsense, list revisions were at best an exercise in the relative classification of destitution, as where a labourer who might still possess a skeletal cow was displaced from a worklist by someone who had no domestic animal at all. As it happened generally, such revisions involved the striking from the lists of one set of totally destitute persons and their replacement by another, the distinction between them visible only to Wynne and certain of his colleagues.

Other comments by Wynne in this mid-November report give us an inadvertent hint as to the human cost involved in list revisions, as where he tells us that those struck off had now 'gone quietly to till their farms' or where he anticipates turning 'numbers' off the works 'who have refused to return to their former masters'. Since tillage operations did not take place in winter and farm labourers did not have any masters to return to, the fate of those struck off can well be imagined; and we can only marvel at the obtuse arrogance with which Wynne made these dispositions, as indeed at the fantasy of his concluding remark that 'altogether, we have bright prospects'.[12]

If this report is couched in the deferential enthusiasm Wynne reserves for communicating with his superiors, his demeanour towards the relief committees was very different, as instanced by a confrontation over list revisions in the Corofin sessions house a few days later. Here he supported proposals by a Tory landowner, a Colonel Synge, to strike the names of certain labourers from the lists because they still had some stock or tiny patches of land. Lengthy discussion over the men's circumstances had just ended in a compromise, a near-total capitulation by the Corofin Committee in fact, involving the retention of just one name, when Wynne suddenly declared that 'whether the Committee should retain or expunge the name', he would feel bound to use the authority vested in him to erase it anyway.[13] Committee members were left feeling angry and resentful at Wynne's bullying, none more so than the parish priest of Corofin, Father Quinn, whose attempt at insisting the poverty-stricken individual in question be left on the list was met with a furious and humiliating rebuff by the Inspector.

A week on from this again, Wynne attended the Clare Abbey Relief Committee, along with the Head Engineer, Samuel Gamble, who had also accompanied him at Corofin. Here the agenda was dominated by the issue of site invasions by frantic labourers who had failed to obtain tickets or had been struck off the lists but turned up for work anyway. When Gamble told the Committee that such men should not be paid, on cue Wynne remarked that Headquarters had forwarded him 'a large pile' of petitions received from site-invading labourers seeking payment; his judgement in the matter, he told them, would not be in doubt; they would be refused. In a didactic aside Wynne told, improbably, of having encountered a man on one works who admitted to having a weekly pension of over a shilling – which works was not specified – and he alleged with even less plausibility that there were 7,000 persons illegally on the public works in the county as a whole.[14]

Over the next months of that bitterly cold winter, Wynne's inspections would take him into relief committee rooms all over his district, as well as into the sessions houses where road presentments for additional works were being arranged and his supervision therefore required. He appeared frequently on worksites and attended court sessions where wages cases arising out of road works disputes were being heard.[15] Many afternoons were spent in the Grand Jury Room of the county courthouse in Ennis, a stone's throw from his lodgings at Row House, and just up the street from John B. Knox's office, poring over land valuations and voter lists in search of reasons to prove labourers were 'improperly' on the lists so that they could be struck off. Even for a man of Wynne's rude health, it was a punishing schedule, involving interminably tedious administration work, and entire days in the saddle on roads or cross-country, day after day, and week after freezing week.

Throughout this time Wynne worked closely with Samuel Gamble, the two men often travelling together on horseback to meetings and operating as a team during the proceedings, taking turns addressing those present and supporting each other's position on major issues. One suspects indeed that their moves at each meeting were planned out while *en route*. Gamble, whose personality was as abrupt and authoritarian as Wynne's own, seems to have been equally disagreeable to the committees. As head engineer, decisions concerning the establishment and direction of works were technically his, Wynne's role being a supervisory one. It was to Gamble accordingly that the much put-upon Father Sheehan of Ennistymon addressed an open letter of remonstrance at the end of November, which was published by an ever public-spirited John B. Knox in the *Clare Journal*.

Sheehan's grievance centred on the autocratic behaviour of Gamble's junior works engineers, whose disregard for his intimate knowledge of his parishioners was having devastating consequences for the poor, reducing his own function on the Committee to the mere compilation of worklists, which were then ignored.[16] On many occasions he had been accosted by 'streams of people' at the doors of the Relief Committee rooms, 'all expecting ... that the priest and the honourable committee (as they call it) will have their case taken up and themselves placed on the work lists':

> Among those numerous expectants there may be degrees of poverty – all may be said to be in want, but there are some invariably so forlorn as to excite pity and fears for their life, and yet when the prescribed numbers are filled up, not one of those famishing individuals can the priest or the Committee get on the works.

If Sheehan's conciliatory spirit shines through this long, courtly letter, another a fortnight later shows him abandoning this virtue entirely, as he delivers himself of a stinging attack on Gamble and Wynne. Describing the two men as 'careering about from one relief district to another to hold investigations, and correct or pretend to correct the abuses, the numberless, undefinable [*sic*] abuses of their system', he told of starving crowds meantime 'waiting in suspense for an order to get them on the works' and 'pining away by inches with hunger, wasted to skeletons, by the joint operation of cold and want of food'. In their behaviour, these two 'paid and proud officials' were constantly showing off, 'exhibiting their persons and their prowess, insulting relief committees, and exercising amongst them the air and jurisdiction of bashaws'. Wynne he singled out as 'an intrepid fire eater', who would be 'more at home in the field of Mars, enjoying the pomp of glorious war than in a committee of relief; who would be more quick at dealing out slugs and bullets than work tickets'.[17]

The naivety of Father Sheehan's apprehension of military matters and his attribution of martial valour to Wynne serve only to underscore his anger, which arose out of what he had witnessed the day before of one episode in a developing quarrel between Wynne and the north Clare relief committees. In the course of what was fated to be a protracted dispute, the Inspector was fated to meet his combative match in two landlords, Cornelius O'Brien of Birchfield and Major W.N. Macnamara of Doolin. Longstanding political rivals, O'Brien and Macnamara held both county seats in the Whig-Liberal interest, and each combined strong local following and party influence with an elevated sense of his own worth.

The dispute had begun at Corofin late in November, at a road sessions for Inchiquin barony, and which after a short time deteriorated into a slanging match between Wynne and O'Brien who held the chair in his magisterial capacity.[18] Repeated insistence by Wynne that presentments were being framed in a manner unacceptable to the Board of Works led O'Brien to lash out angrily that by the inadequacy of relief measures, the people of his district were being insulted by government and officials. When Wynne began to defend both by reference to policies and conditions, O'Brien cut across him with a loud objection to being thus lectured, asking in a menacing tone – he had been a noted duellist in earlier life – if Wynne's remarks were aimed personally at himself.[19] After Wynne had fudged his answer, a wrangle ensued over whether wheelbarrows should be produced locally or purchased in Dublin, followed by another concerning the nature of destitution and whether a man who still held on to one old cow could be considered less deserving of relief employment than a landless unemployed labourer. At the end Gamble and Wynne both refused to sign the presentments that had been voted by the meeting, thereby ensuring their rejection in Dublin.[20] O'Brien, for his part, declined to attend the adjourned meeting that followed a few days later.[21]

The row escalated at another road sessions the following week, this time for Corcomroe Barony and held in the little stone courthouse at

The Ennistymon courthouse. Author photograph.

Ennistymon, under the chairmanship of Major Macnamara, magistrate for the surrounding district. In the course of the meeting Macnamara complained of a works engineer named Millett whom he accused of grave discourtesy towards the Relief Committee, in that he had instructed check clerks not to submit worklists to its members.[22] Macnamara insinuated also that Millett was somehow involved in the corrupt appointment of certain stewards, 'bad characters' who had secured their appointments by offering gifts of poultry as bribes. 'In this country', he declared, 'a goose is now called a steward; a turkey a checkman, and a pair of chickens a gangsman'. Laughter followed the remark, redoubling when in reply to Macnamara's pointed question as to who had appointed the stewards, several voices shouted, 'the turkeys'.

Later on, Wynne caused outrage by his response to a demand by Cornelius O'Brien if he was being personal in an assertion that landed gentlemen were putting well-off tenants on the works by a rhetorical question as to the numbers of public works labourers in the district who were actually 'in comfortable circumstances'. When O'Brien replied firmly, 'no, no', to this jibe, the entire meeting and the overspilling crowd outside took up the negative as a chant. When he finally got in a word Wynne shouted that he had had 500 complaints on that score; when put to it, according to the *Clare Journal* reporter present, one James Knox Walker, he 'could not name a single individual'.[23]

A special meeting called to deal with the allegations against Millet was held the following Thursday in the same venue, in a smaller room adjoining the main chamber: Wynne had threatened to leave rather than deal with the matter before the packed crowd in the main chamber.[24] This was the meeting which gave rise to Father Sheehan's anti-Wynne tirade, as also a graphic description of the Inspector's retinue as 'a staff of officers ... vested to the chin in all the panoply of official power, and determined come what may to exercise it to the death'.[25]

Immediately proceedings began, Wynne and Gamble sacrificed Millett, allowing that he had indeed shown discourtesy.[26] Accepting the apology which the hapless Millett was obliged to tender, Macnamara made more provocative statements, elaborating his poultry-bribe allegations into the wider domestic animal kingdom, with details 'of an individual receiving a pig'.[27] Eventually, however, wrangling came to an end; face had, it appeared, been saved on both sides, and the matter settled, when as the chairman was making concluding remarks, Wynne and Gamble sprung a prepared trap, by outlining allegations that destitute tenants had been excluded from works at Liscannor by the relief committee there, whose chairman was Cornelius O'Brien, the chief beneficiaries being comfortable tenants of Major Macnamara.

Even though these allegations, like the Major's earlier porcine remarks, were essentially coat-trailing, intended to cause embarrassment rather than serious damage, O'Brien took the bait and declared that because he had criticized the Board's officers they had set out to blacken his character and that 'he regarded the affair as a foul conspiracy'. When Wynne began to reply that if O'Brien were attributing personal motives to him, he would treat them with contempt, a massive roar from the crowd rendered him unable to continue beyond that last word.[28] In the uproar, Father Hanrahan, Father Sheehan's curate, walked up to Wynne in an agitated state, telling him angrily, 'you should not be heard – don't think you'll put me down as you did Father Quinn in Corofin'. Through the tumult Cornelius O'Brien called on the chairman to exercise his magisterial powers to have Wynne bound over to the peace. Order was restored after a time, but the meeting separated in the knowledge of a clearly defined enmity between the parties.[29]

Although Wynne's version of these events is entirely reconcilable with the newspaper account, understandably his perspective is quite different. He had been insulted, he wrote to Colonel Jones, 'in the grossest possible way', but had held his temper, even when it was proposed to have him thrown out. He had been proceeding with 'the most perfect coolness' to refute O'Brien's accusations, when 'in a moment every man was on his legs', 'threatening violence, and vying with each other in abuse'. When the meeting was over, he almost had to fight his way out of the courthouse, shoving 'four or five fellows' blocking his exit. Spurning the offer of a police escort, he returned home in company with Samuel Gamble and a young Dublin journalist named Russell, the party relying for protection on an assortment of firearms Wynne kept about himself, including a rifle, a double-barrelled shotgun and three cases of pistols.

William Howard Russell, later to achieve international fame as a war correspondent, was then a callow 27-year-old correspondent for the English newspaper, the *Morning Chronicle*.[30] Having asked to observe the proceedings of a relief committee, he was unprepared for the scenes that occurred and could not have known enough to interpret them.[31] According to Wynne, who used him to back up his version of events, Russell was 'astonished' by what he witnessed and 'could not have supposed matters were so bad'.[32] Later Russell would testify as to Wynne's coolness under pressure.[33] In the meantime, the chief outcome of this turbulent meeting was another pointless investigation of a relief committee, which was abandoned when the accusers failed to turn up.[34]

As the conflict with the north Clare committees festered, Wynne was simultaneously dealing with problems twenty miles to the south, at Clare Abbey. On 5 December, an unpopular overseer on one of the works there was shot at and wounded in a Whiteboy attack. Immediately on hearing of the incident, Wynne ordered the closure of all works in the vicinity until the assailant had been apprehended, thus leaving by his own admission, over 900 families, most of them clad only in the remnants of clothing, and already on the verge of starvation, entirely without food, in the harshest weather in living memory.[35] He did so knowing full well what the consequences would be, telling Colonel Jones, indeed, that he anticipated 'sad consequences from stopping the works at Clare tomorrow'.[36] To be fair to Wynne, it was already Board of Works policy to shut down sites in the vicinity of an 'outrage', but it was a full fortnight before he 'ventured' through the parish to investigate the outcome.[37] 'Although a man not easily moved', he wrote,

> I confess myself unmanned by the extent and intensity of suffering that I witnessed, more especially amongst the women and little children, crowds of whom were to be seen scattered over the turnip fields, like a flock of famishing crows, devouring the raw turnips, mothers half naked, shivering in the snow and sleet, uttering exclamations of despair, whilst their children were screaming with hunger'.

'I am a match for anything else that I may meet with here', he continued, 'but this I cannot stand', ending the dispatch by asking when he might reopen the works.

Wynne's sense of shock may well have been genuine, but if so it is remarkable how quickly he recovered his composure; the works were not reopened until the end of the month, and by that time he was using the horrific occurrences in the fields at Clare Abbey as an object lesson for all public works labourers: at the arraignment of those accused of disturbances on works at Kilmaley, he took the opportunity to threaten 'fearful consequences' if there should be any recurrence. 'I can assure you I shall do my part', he informed the court, 'and the condition of Clare Abbey at this moment attests the determination on the part of the Commissioners to protect their officers and subordinates from outrage and insult, and the appalling consequences that must follow upon the commission of these offences'.[38]

In late December, when a works overseer was severely assaulted at Ruan, just north of Ennis, Wynne suspended the works there also.[39] Not even the 'frightful distress', which he admitted occurred in the parish as a result, would move him to recommend their resumption. In his own words, 'an example must be made'. The Ruan works would remain shut for much of January 1847, a time of indescribable suffering throughout the district and the country at large.[40]

Early in the new year the Ruan closure was linked by a strange incident with Wynne's ongoing troubles in north Clare. This occurred at yet another road sessions in the Ennistymon courthouse in January, where for much of the meeting proceedings were conducted peaceably and with every appearance of cooperation between Board of Works personnel and the Relief Committee men. In the absence of Major Macnamara, his son, Captain Francis Macnamara, and the sessions chairman, Cornelius O'Brien, were as civil as they could be to the enemy party. Wynne said little, concentrating instead on putting order on bundles of letters of application, written complaints and rolled-up petitions he had been handed by individuals in the crowd as they entered. His silence lasted until among the documents he came across a crudely written threatening notice, which he had unknowingly accepted along with the other papers pressed upon him by so many hands.[41]

Headed by a rough drawing of a coffin, and atrociously misspelled as by a near-illiterate or someone pretending to be so, the note was signed 'Captain Starlight', and it promised Wynne that if he did not change his ways he would share the fate of Pierce Carrick, a land agent murdered the previous March outside Ennis. 'They say you're an undaunted man', the pseudonymous Captain Starlight told Wynne (misspellings have been corrected), 'but I have forty riflemen, as kind as ever pulled a trigger: so go on with the works at Ruan, and quit the country, if you don't wish to go home to the mistress a corpse'.[42]

A considerable distance from his parish, and faced with a high likelihood of arrest, Captain Starlight had shown both audacity and courage; however he could not have realized how his appearance suited both opposing parties in the courthouse. For O'Brien, the Macnamaras and other Committee gentlemen, loud expressions of outrage at Starlight's 'villainy', afforded identification with law, order and respectability, counteracting Wynne's depiction of them as corrupt and anarchical. For Wynne, Captain Starlight's bedraggled notice furnished the perfect opportunity for the self-dramatization to which he was partial. From the central table, he declared impressively that if the author of the notice thought he could intimidate him or turn him away from his duty, he little knew the individual with whom

Interior of Ennistymon courthouse c. 1970. Photo courtesy Kathryn Comber/Veronica Nicholson.

he had to do. Addressing the unidentified Captain Starlight directly, he declared, 'I beg leave to inform him that I shall be on the road tonight, and happy to meet him, when he shall find me well prepared'. But 'if through any of the causes which shake the assassin's hand, he should fail to execute his purpose, or do it ineffectually, I pledge myself to him that moment shall be his last'.[43]

But Wynne was on fairly safe ground here, as he knew well. Officially ranked as the most minor form of outrage, threatening notices were essentially passive and rarely followed through; in their individual circumstances neither of the two captains, Wynne or Starlight, posed any real danger to each other, nor indeed were likely ever to cross paths. Knowledge of this perhaps accounts for such further theatrics on Wynne's part as having the courthouse doors locked in case the other Captain should still be present and solemnly walking through the chamber to see if he could identify his features among the crowd. But Captain Starlight had made his escape; the Ruan works remained closed, and the poor continued to die there of starvation and exposure to the cold.

Despite his bold showing in Ennistymon, the consistent, bruising opposition he had encountered from relief committees all over his district was beginning to take its toll on Wynne's confidence. Yet he was still buoyed by the stout support of his colleagues in the inspectorate, by Samuel Gamble and the other engineers, and by what he called 'the honest part of the County Clare gentry', that is Tory landlords such as Crofton Vandeleur of Kilrush, Major William Ball of Fortfergus, and the young squire of Beech Park, Marcus Keane.[44] Wynne, we know, had dined at Beech Park in company with Samuel Gamble; on another occasion we find him referring to Marcus Keane as a 'gentleman of high character'.[45]

If backing from such quarters enabled Wynne to maintain the momentum of his anti-imposition crusade, it also nourished a state of mind that was steadily moving from arrogance and suspicion to outright paranoia. By early January he had come to believe that all the committees in his district were engaged in a great conspiracy against him. In a letter to his brother-in-law he wrote of being under 'frightful pressure' from their 'unprincipled conduct', as they deluged him with 'lists containing thousands of names'. He had 'come to a stand-still; *shut shop* [italics in original]'. Refusing no applicant, the committees threw the 'entire odium' upon him:[46]

> I am hunted by thousands accusing me of refusing them relief, and intending to starve them. I am puzzled how to meet this move of the Committees. I am afraid they will checkmate me; however, I shall persevere to the end, only taking a little additional care and precaution, which will now be indispensable, as I fear my popularity, even among the very poor class, is at an end for a while.

Such reflections no doubt churned around in Wynne's mind as from the early days of January he embarked upon a fresh series of inspections, in many cases visiting committees he had not previously attended. As he clattered along the interminable miles of rock-hard, frost-bound Board of Works roads in various stages of construction or repair, everywhere he would have passed gangs of gaunt-faced, ragged labourers struggling to survive long days of harsh labour. He would have seen some stagger as they worked and perhaps even witnessed the commonplace occurrence of labourers dropping dead at their places. Mentioning none of this to his superiors, he remained fixated on list pruning and alleged imposition, and the fallacious notion that prosperous tenants were being placed wholesale on works to the exclusion of the destitute.

So febrile had Wynne's mind become on the subject that he was now suggesting labourers should be paid in food rather than cash; the committees, hitherto in receipt of much of the labourers' wages 'in the shape of rent, dues &c' (landlords and clergy were his targets here) would no longer have that 'inducement to be dishonest', and as to the supposed impostors, 'few men would work for food who had it of their own; many would be ashamed to work for meal who would not scruple to grasp at cash under any circumstances; the circulation of food would insure ... against starvation, while the circulation of money is a strong temptation to dishonesty'. By such means Wynne reckoned he could 'knock a third of the people off the Public Works'. In a slightly later report, he was still stubbornly maintaining that the level of employment 'if fairly and honesty distributed' was 'fully sufficient' to meet the prevailing destitution.[47]

To his superiors he brought further allegations of relief committee corruption, along with anecdotes illustrating members' inhumanity, against which his own uprightness could not fail to shine. When leaving one committee room (probably at Killard) he told of encountering a starving man, with 'nothing to cover him but the skeletons of an old pair of breeches and waistcoat', who seized on Wynne's coat 'with the grip of death', telling him that the committee had left him to die.[48] Returning immediately to the meeting in the hope of shaming the Committee members with such a sight, he failed to so do. 'It is hard to deal with such heartless men', Wynne wrote.

Although some committees escaped relatively lightly in this new round of inspections, bitter conflict erupted in others, the nature of which is well illustrated in the encounter at Kildysert on 22 January. Arriving at the committee room in company with Gamble and the Tory landowner, Major Ball, the latter announced that he had come to support Wynne in the discharge of his 'arduous and onerous duties' and that it was incumbent on every gentleman present to support the captain.[49] Wynne then began with an assertion that the Committee had repeatedly failed to respond to requests for its worklists; when told by the chairman that only one letter had been received, he wasted some words blaming the Post Office for the lapse before darkly mentioning another committee where the secretary had suppressed communications with him. But the insinuation failed to generate much of a reaction, the members clearly anxious to avoid scenes of the kind that had taken place to the north.

But as Wynne proceeded to the striking of names from the lists in his customary fashion, exasperation began to mount. For the most part those struck off were former farm servants, herdsmen or destitute smallholders, some of whom still held onto a hollow-bellied beast which they could no longer feed, and when it was suggested to Wynne that many of those recorded on the lists as having stock no longer had any, he said it didn't matter, that they still had the money from the sale.

Following a mild remonstrance from Reverend Rosslewin, the Church of Ireland rector at Kildysart, that the country would be soon be in a poor way if the people 'were thus forced to dispose of everything' they possessed, Wynne launched into a harangue in which he told of having struck some 18,000 persons from the lists in the county since his arrival; this was double the numbers that a month earlier he had claimed to have delisted.[50]

Referring to the situation in Ruan where the works were still closed, he declared that 'there was now more of the land tilled in that parish than there was in nearly all the county besides'.[51] It was a foolish reiteration of a remark repeated several times before, and it elicited a gentle reminder from Reverend Rosslewin that no tillage took place in winter. Reverend Rosslewin then spoke of the great patience shown by the people in their privations, and that they 'should not be oppressed because they were quiet', and later on remarked that if they were excluded from relief, they would take food by force, 'and they would be perfectly right in doing so'. Towards the end of the meeting, he described the public works programme as it was operated, as a system of 'the greatest barbarity'. But nothing he said was of any avail, and before the meeting ended Wynne had removed more than 200 names from the worklists.

Less than a week after the Kildysart meeting Wynne was suddenly recalled to Dublin.[52] He was replaced by a Captain Gordon, a standard product of Board of Works culture, whose approach to his duties was very similar to Wynne's, his method of determining eligibility for relief and rooting out imposition purely paper searches based on land valuations and voter lists. Regardless of the fact that these documents had been rendered irrelevant by two years of hardship and impoverishment, Gordon was content to rely on them while admitting that he had no personal knowledge at all of the circumstances of any of those he struck off lists and works.[53]

In Clare Edmond Wynne's departure was little regretted. At a road sessions in Ballyvaughan, when it was suggested a vote of thanks might be an appropriate courtesy, the level of opposition was so great that it was not proceeded with.[54] A few relief committees did pass such resolutions, but the failure of the others to do so was a glaring omission; later on Wynne was able to produce testimonial letters from just five of his twenty committees, and several of these were framed in ambiguous, half-hearted terms. And apart from the staunch and blustering Major Ball of Fortfergus, the Tory gentry had almost entirely deserted him.[55]

Although the authorities maintained Wynne had been 'withdrawn for another duty', they were without question responding to the adverse publicity attracted by his behaviour, as well as the political pressure applied by Macnamara and O'Brien. But the two MPs were not yet satisfied, their sense of injured honour leading them to press for a parliamentary inquiry. A Select Committee was accordingly appointed, which sat for several months of the summer under the chairmanship of the Whig-Liberal MP Henry Aglionby. The results of the Aglionby Committee's labours was an enormous Blue Book, which between report, minutes of evidence and appendices runs to nearly a thousand pages, the minutes alone comprising some 14,500 individual questions.[56] No sooner produced than forgotten, this gigantic document, whose report made no finding of any kind, has remained shelved since, little resorted to by historians quailing before its great bulk.

The evidence of his Clare sojourn reveals Wynne to have been a strange, erratic individual, whose attitudes and behaviour at times are such as to invite suspicions about his mental stability. His letters veer startlingly in tone from truculence to wearied embattlement, to workmanlike activity, while in several he manages to convey a humanitarian concern that is convincing until comparison is made with other correspondence of very different sentiment.[57] The views expressed across his reports abound with contradictions, all yet delivered with the same dogmatic certainty. This is nowhere more evident than in his depiction of the poor, whom in his conflict with the relief committees he presents as docile, patient and good and on other occasions as violent, treacherous and unpredictable, the majority feigning need. Thus at Clare Abbey in December 1846, he finds it regrettable that the violent actions of a few turbulent spirits has deprived the honest, willing labourers of the parish of their employment, while within days he is reporting that the inhabitants, whom he delineates as 'sullen', are as well pleased with the works closure, since it affords them the pleasure of plundering. Of the people of north Clare, meekly enduring under the oppression of the relief committee gentry in one account, he says of them in another that all the 'money in the Treasury cannot meet the wants of this frightful population'.[58]

Such contradictions are reflective of Wynne's posturing, as he creates crises and places himself heroically at their centre, at the same time displaying instinctual shrewdness in directing successive poses towards the changing needs of his Board of Works bosses and their controllers. Certainly, neither Colonel Harry Jones, his immediate superior, nor Charles Trevelyan, the Treasury head with ultimate control of relief spending, ever remarked on the abounding anomalies of Wynne's correspondence. For them the Inspector was valuable for the reassurance he brought that the public works programme, to many an organizational shambles and human disaster, was in fact administratively sound and that the difficulties encountered were a product merely of bothersome local issues. 'Captain Wynne appears to be discharging his duty right well', wrote Colonel Jones to Trevelyan on 7 December 1846, 'and it is, I assure you, a great solace to us to know that we possess a man of his judgement, discretion and firmness, whose qualities are so much wanted, and so frequently called into play'.[59] A few days later Trevelyan in turn wrote to Randolph Routh that 'Captain Wynne's undaunted spirit ... alone seems to stand between the people of Clare and complete anarchy'.[60]

Of modern commentators only Cormac Ó Gráda has placed Wynne in perspective by comparing him with another Board of Works Inspector, his colleague in the adjacent four eastern baronies of Clare, H.H. O'Brien. Unlike Wynne, O'Brien commanded respect among the population of his district, and while holding conventional views on outrage (some of his relief districts were as disturbed as Wynne's) and having few illusions about landlords or people, he did find that in general the relief committees worked well and for the most part served the needs of the poor. In O'Brien's letters there is no hint either of a county overwhelmed by crime and on the verge of social disintegration, nor of a massive level of corruption and jobbery, nor the slightest hint of Wynne's great relief committee conspiracy.[61]

Perhaps the most telling judgement on the Wynne episode comes from a comparison of his north Clare enemies, Major Macnamara and Cornelius O'Brien, with his allies among the Tory gentry. The former were certainly paternalist, reactionary and self-regarding and tainted by political association with the appalling regime of Lord John Russell – classic hack politicians, in fact, whom Charles Gavan Duffy referred to on one occasion as 'two expert jobbers'.[62] Yet neither man is recorded as having carried out a single eviction during the Famine. Of Wynne's Tory allies, on the other hand, the 'best among the gentry', including Marcus Keane and Crofton Vandeleur, as we shall see, was to engage in clearance exterminations that led to human mortality on a huge scale.

Wynne himself returned to Clare just once after he had been withdrawn. This was in late February 1847, when he made a very brief visit to justify accusations about the Kilmaley Relief Committee in his published letters of 'cruelty and oppression' in replacing destitute persons on the lists with comfortable farmers. When he proved hard-necked enough to reiterate these charges before a specially convened Committee meeting, a collective outburst of rage was the result.[63] 'It is quite impossible to convey on paper any idea of the proceedings', wrote a reporter present, 'the uproar and confusion was tremendous, and there were generally about half a dozen members speaking at one time'.

But Wynne went on doggedly through the clamour, telling the Committee that he had removed 300 unqualified persons from works in Kilmaley and – most provocatively – that the lists with which he had been furnished had been deliberately intended to deceive him.[64] He had just begun a catalogue of actual cases when a storm of protest erupted again, several members shouting that 'they were not there upon their trial and could not have their time wasted in that manner'. This was followed by the unanimous adoption of a resolution by the Committee exonerating itself of Wynne's accusations, an unfortunate move which allowed Samuel Gamble, Wynne's perpetual shadow, the opportunity of making the acid, accurate comment that by doing so the members were placing themselves 'in a very ludicrous position'.[65]

Some days after this meeting, when the Clare Abbey Committee (one of the few which had voted Wynne its thanks) demanded an explanation of criticisms they had since noticed in his letters, Wynne did not travel to refute them in person, but he did reply immediately, insisting that he had indeed found comfortable farmers on the works at Clare Abbey to the exclusion of destitute persons.[66] But his criticism was so diluted by praise of the Committee's cooperation in remedying the abuse that the members were altogether disarmed, and his admission that the Committee was 'incapable of doing injustice to the poor for the benefit of the rich' almost completely negated his original charge. Far too late, then, had Captain Edmond Wynne begun to learn the virtues of temperate speech and political discretion.[67]

3

The Poor Man's Magistrate: John Singleton of Quinville

When John Singleton returned home in mid-June 1840 after an absence of nearly two years on the continent, he and his family were treated to a public welcome by his tenants and the inhabitants of the Quin district. Early on the day of their arrival – the party were due to arrive late that night – Father Daniel Corbett, the parish priest, held a meeting in his new church so as to ensure his parishioners would turn out to greet the Singletons with 'every demonstration of respect that lay in their power'. As the family approached the parish boundaries, bonfires blazed on the surrounding hills; 'a body of nearly 1,000 men went in procession a distance of five miles' to escort the landlord's carriage to the gates of his handsome residence, Quinville Abbey, just outside Quin village, which was illuminated for the occasion.[1]

Next day Father Corbett led a delegation to Quinville to present a formal address of welcome, a wordy document which expressed 'heartfelt delight' that Singleton had at last returned to the 'bosom of his family'. His return, the address declared, brought 'renewed happiness' to that part of the country, and the returnee was welcome in his many capacities: as 'the Poor Man's magistrate; the considerate and good landlord; the good neighbour; the munificent donor to the Chapel; the benevolent friend of the poor' and the 'Liberal Protestant' unaffected by 'sectarian prejudices inimical to the general interests of the country'.

Singleton's reply to this flowery address was about twice as long and just as extravagant. Unworthy though he was of a greeting 'as unexpected as it was undeserved', he was grateful for a reception which reflected an 'overestimate of any merit' on his part; he would retain it 'with gratitude and pride'. He paid particular tribute to their 'valued Minister and worthy Chairman', Father Corbett, for his role in organizing the occasion, and ended by reiterating thanks for the address and welcome which were undoubtedly 'effusions genuine and spontaneous, emanating from the honest hearts of a generous and grateful people'.

Notwithstanding the overwrought rhetoric, which was standard to such occasions, on the face of it there seems little reason to doubt the sincerity of feeling on both sides. Singleton, from what we know, was well liked as a landlord, or at least he was not feared; and he and Father Corbett were on friendly terms, such cordiality usually being a reliable gauge of the esteem in which a proprietor was held. In addition, the tenants and inhabitants, as we meet them here at any rate, seem to have been mostly from comparatively well-off social strata in this lush agricultural parish and would have experienced relief at the safe return of a landlord who if nothing else represented a certain stability in their lives.

Singleton himself, it is clear, was glad to be home, and the only part of his reply that we need disbelieve is his expression of surprise: greeting ceremonies of this kind were customary, not to say *de rigueur*, and from the time he stepped ashore in Ireland he would have been looking forward to being welcomed in this manner. Fear and apprehension ensured that landlords who were hated by their tenants – the great majority – were also accorded such ceremonial greetings, and landlords generally, whether benevolent or unloved, sought refuge in the warmth of the greeting, regardless of whatever manipulation they had exercised to ensure it was laid on. Tenant feelings, on the other hand, could be very mixed, and such were the complexities of relations with landlords that a single homecoming ritual might encapsulate a mélange of contradictory emotions on the part of the greeters, in which liking, respect and joy were commingled with resentment, bitterness and even hatred. Some of these elements may have been present even in the harmonious Singleton family return of 1840.

Like most landlords, John Singleton's earliest antecedents in Ireland were seventeenth-century setters from England. His grandfather and namesake, of Newmarket-on-Fergus, had been tenant to the patriot-politician, Sir Lucius O'Brien of Dromoland, and on his 1776 visit, the agricultural reformer Arthur Young had been much impressed by the scientific farming carried out by Singleton *grand-père* on his 4,000 acres at Ballygireen.[2] In succeeding generations the Singletons moved to Quin, and by the mid-nineteenth century John Singleton was settled on the Quinville property, while two brothers, Hugh and Edward, were ensconced on smaller demesnes nearby.[3]

As a landlord Singleton was small scale, and from a later property return we know that his entire estate amounted to just short of 2,000 acres.[4] Much of this property was concentrated at Quinville, although we know that he owned two large farms in the Newmarket area, at Trenahow and Islandmacnavin also.[5] In west Clare there was also the isolated seacoast property at Baltard in Killard Parish.[6] His diaries show him visiting all these locations on a regular basis throughout the Famine, his track in the landscape for the most part a regular circuit linking Ennis, Quin, Newmarket and west Clare. Most of his tenants were prosperous, and only in the marginal land of faraway Baltard, nearly forty miles from Quinville, do we find him presiding over congregations of desperately poor cottiers, such as constituted the entire tenantry of so many of his friends and acquaintances.[7]

Singleton also kept much land in own hands, engaging directly in pasture farming and commercial tillage to a degree that was unusual for an Irish landlord; his diaries contain many references to livestock and to acreages under oats, hay, turnips and potatoes. Watching the weather with as much concern as the lowliest smallholder, Singleton cut and saved his own hay and turf and had them carried home in identical manner.[8] He also attended fairs and markets, in Clare and beyond, engaging with dealers and farmers in the buying and selling of horses, sheep and cattle. Perfectly at ease when rubbing shoulders with other social classes, he was as comfortable on the mail coach and other public conveyances as he was on trains, steamships, the saddle or his own carriage. Happy to accommodate other gentlemen at Quinville prior or after local fairs, he readily accepted hospitality in big houses elsewhere, while revelling in the bustle and excitement of travel between times. Of all our figures none was more of a roving disposition than John Singleton of Quinville Abbey.

Those gentry families with whom Singleton was on terms of greatest friendship – the O'Loghlens of Dromconora, the Butlers of Bunahow and the Brady Brownes of Newgrove – occupied a socio-economic position that seems approximately the same, their lifestyles as devoid of extravagance or undue frugality. Only one of the families with whom the Singletons socialized regularly, the Molonys of Kiltannon, Tulla, possessed significantly greater means, but the Molonys were notably modest and self-effacing.[9]

If all of this seems to pigeonhole Singleton with the lesser gentry, there are other indications of a loftier standing; a higher level of cultural sophistication than one might have expected in a rural squire for one thing; some rather elevated familial connections for another, and hints of wealth above and beyond that of somebody of the social position we have tentatively assigned him. In his youth Singleton had taken the Grand Tour, the prerogative of the very rich, afterwards writing an account of his travels.[10] Owner of a library of more than 600 volumes, he was passionately interested in literature and the arts, wrote (mediocre) poetry which he inscribed in a scrapbook cherished over half a century; and whenever away from Quinville, in Dublin, Edinburgh or London, invariably toured the art galleries and exhibitions.[11]

Singleton's cultural refinement fits in with someone who could claim kinship with John Singleton Copley, the early American painter and through him with the aristocratic Barons Lyndhurst of Southampton.[12] He was, moreover, much in the company of county grandees such as Crofton Vandeleur and Sir Lucius O'Brien, and although these men could not be described as friends, he was an acceptable guest at Kilrush House or Dromoland Castle. Certain of his pursuits in addition suggest an income stream significantly in excess of that which could be generated by the Quinville rental alone – his fondness for travel, for example, or the expensive remodelling of his – already very grand – mansion during the 1830s, by the Pain brothers who had just rebuilt Dromoland.[13] We can guess what these income streams might be. Singleton's farming pursuits were commercial;

like most Irish landlords we know he rented livestock farms from other landowners, although he tells us little of this directly; he may have had the use of his wife's fortune, and there are also certain commercial and industrial interests hinted at in the diaries but never explained.[14]

One factor that differentiates Singleton from most of his gentry peers relates to the attention he paid to public duty; from the earliest date we can track him in the sources, he is deeply engaged as petty sessions magistrate and *ex-officio* Poor Law Guardian, and in other positions which landed gentlemen considered to be social obligations, but which most neglected badly. None of these offices bore emolument or expense and Singleton's assiduity with regard to them reflects more than a craving for the power and patronage they conferred; so far as we are aware he did not depend for any share of his income on Grand Jury graft.

Public duties brought Singleton into working contact with classes he would have considered inferior: Catholic middlemen, town merchants and professional and newspaper gentlemen. Here his relationships display a stiffness and unease lacking in the more casual contacts of the street and market, his awkwardness often translating into a high-handed, humourlessness that caused resentment among those subjected to it.[15] As to the compassion we sometime perceive in Singleton as Poor Law Guardian, indications are that it was of a lesser degree where a particular pauper might be chargeable to his district electoral division or of a greater one (as happened on more than one occasion) where a pauper had once been his employee and was chargeable elsewhere.[16] And whatever kindness Singleton did extend as Guardian, it did not ultimately extend beyond the limits of public policy; rules laid down by statute and regulation laid down by the Poor Law were the touchstones by which his public duties were conducted.

His fellow country gentlemen thought Singleton stodgy, and among them he seems to have been an object of mild derision: one bibulous evening in October 1845, before a hotel drawing room fire in Galway, some of them encouraged him to seek the Clare county nomination; while recognizing the suggestion as a ribbing, his friends being 'half-seas over', he was flattered enough to record the suggestion.[17] For, notwithstanding an adventurous youth, extensive travel and cultural sophistication, to his equals John Singleton was amiable, worthy, conscientious and dull.

For Singleton 1845 was a good year, and his diaries over the first ten months especially furnish an absorbing record of fulfilment and personal content. At fifty-two he enjoyed good health, and in the exercise of his public responsibilities we discern satisfaction of a similar nature to that which his farming and estate activities brought him. His social life too was felicitous, a continuous round of pleasurable visits exchanged between neighbours and relatives, including luncheons, dinners and dances, often in the context of reciprocated overnight stays. Studded through the entries are expressions such as 'very agreeable' and 'very pleasant' in relation to such occasions.[18]

Above all, in this period Singleton basks in the joy of family life, his devotion to his wife Isabella evident in every reference to her, as also his love for his children: John (Johnny), whom we presume to be the eldest son, a recently commissioned young officer in the Royal Artillery; Edward, away at private school; and his 'dear' Susan, Mary and Sarah, the former already married, the latter two growing young ladies; and the pet, young Marcella.[19] The boys being away, throughout this time Singleton spends much time with his daughters, riding out with them in the morning or afternoon, shopping with them in Limerick or accompanying them to Baltard on family holidays.

Throughout 1845 he spent much time also visiting different parts of his property, engaging with tenants and supervising routine agricultural operations. Keenly sensitive to nature, he was aesthetically appreciative of all its manifestations, even the most extreme: cold sunny winter days and wild Atlantic storms are as much appreciated as pretty sunrises and dewy mornings. All of these activities, capped by his constant noticing of nature, furnish an image of pastoral serenity that is positively Virgilian, in what was probably the happiest time in the life of John Singleton.

It is hardly surprising therefore that when the potato blight first appeared, Singleton was unwilling to accept its intrusion into his existence. Only on 29 October does he refer to the failure in his diary, weeks after local and national alarms had begun to sound, a significant delay for a man so closely attuned to weather and crops.[20] His public comments are more revealing again; early in November, he instigated a resolution of the Ennis Board of Guardians petitioning the Lord Lieutenant on the necessity of protecting the nation's food supply, a vague and useless measure bearing no relation at all to the depth of the unfolding crisis. A few weeks later he was responsible for another resolution passed at a County Meeting proposing the establishment of a committee to gather information on the state of the potatoes.[21] Defending this second resolution against John B. Knox's charge that it was pointless and time-wasting, Singleton could only manage a lame, incoherent insistence that he 'did not think it deserved the name of procrastination', but that the 'true way' was to 'take time by the forelock' since 'things could not remain in their present position'.[22]

Over ensuing months little in Singleton's recorded remarks, either public or private, indicates any greater level of urgency with regard to the crisis, and his last diary entry for December looks back on 1845 as 'no bad year', although marred by 'the many croakers [and] Tory Ministers with Whig principles'.[23] Neither did the new year bring any change, and at the end of January, after delivering his son Edward to school at Stackallen, County Meath, he spent a week in Dublin, shopping and attending social occasions.[24] February was spent in leisurely mode about public responsibilities, farming operations and dinner parties, and on one memorable evening early in March he entertained a party at Quinville that included his neighbours Mrs Butler and her son James, the estimable Colonel Goldie whom we met in the Introduction, and two junior army officers, passing through the district. Most of the guests stayed over.

Late in March, however, reality intruded when, much against his inclination, Singleton was obliged to accept chairmanship of the Quin District Relief Committee. 'God knows how I wish its functions were soon to cease', he confided to his diary, 'resolutions, deputations, memorials and subscriptions the order of the day'.[25] Yet once he took on the position he paid scrupulous attention to its duties, spending long days and evenings about tedious administrative tasks, compiling lists of needy persons and subscription lists, drafting memorials for transmission to government and reports to the relief bureaucracy. In addition, over succeeding months, in his capacity as magistrate he presided at road sessions where relief works were approved. By late June as chairman of sessions for Bunratty Lower, he had already forwarded some twenty-six memorials to government for works in that half-barony alone.[26] And interspersed with these administrative tasks were tiring days on horseback inspecting works as they emerged and mediating with Board of Works personnel.

Just how much the relief programme impinged on his life during this early phase of the Famine can be determined from a trawl through his diary over a ten-day period in early summer. On Saturday 2 May, Singleton rode to Trenahow to inspect a new relief road and afterwards attended the Newmarket-on-Fergus Relief Committee, where the main business was the drafting of a funding appeal to the Mansion House Committee in Dublin. On Monday, he attended road sessions at Spancilhill, and on Tuesday the Quin Relief Committee. On Wednesday he travelled to Baltard, a five-hour journey involving a change of horses at Fanny O'Dea's Lissycasey stables, and undertaken mainly for estate purposes, but combined with an inspection of a new Board of Works coastal road at the mellifluously named Hobbawns, 'a great improvement and advantage to the fishermen'.[27]

On Friday, back in Newmarket, he attended road sessions and was much pleased at the assembly's sanction of one works adjacent to his Trenahow property. On Saturday he inspected road cuttings at Quinville, just outside his gate, noting that his neighbour and tenant, a Catholic farmer named Denis Lynch, 'our clerk', was distributing Indian meal to the poor at that spot. On Monday 11 May, he was engaged the entire cold, harsh day sifting applicants 'for food and work', half of those applying being rejected ('heartrending and difficult was the task'). The following day again he presided at the Quin Relief Committee, at which tickets were issued for seed potatoes and arrangements made for the publication of the subscription list, total funds now amounting to just over £312.[28]

If we have no reason to question Singleton's humanitarian motives in his relief work, it is not without significance that the projects on which he expended his greatest energy were all of direct benefit to himself as landowner.[29] One scheme which he pursued with tenacity was the construction of a line running six miles eastwards from Ennis towards

Quin over the great bog of Doora. A useful project that had begun in pre-Famine times with the erection of an iron bridge on the Fergus at Gore's Quay, progress had been delayed because of the opposition of poor tenants whose holdings it would divide and wreck. Singleton, however, believed the tenants' objections were orchestrated by a 'club' of his Grand Jury opponents.[30] In February 1846, he used his powers as magistrate to being proceedings under the Knox-promoted Public Works Act in order to build the road, presenting his proposal to an inhabitants' meeting.[31] His jubilation at having it 'bumptiously carried by an immense majority' despite loud opposition from rivals promoting alternative routes of benefit to them was undisguised; it also reveals, however, that not even a dreadful 'season of distress and apprehended famine' was enough to shake the edifice of works jobbery.[32]

Further delays took place before work began on the 'celebrated Iron Bridge Road', as he refers to it in a weary entry at the end of May.[33] Even so, by 25 July progress had sufficiently advanced to allow Singleton walk the entire line from Quinville Abbey to Ennis.[34] Ultimately, however, the road was destined to be abandoned in its unfinished state when the new Whig-Liberal administration came to power; it would not be completed until some years after the Famine was over.[35]

Leaving aside the question of Singleton's vested interest in such projects there is no question but that his immersion in relief operations in these months considerably restricted his other pursuits. But none of these pursuits, whether familial, social or agricultural, was entirely abandoned at any stage, and as the spring wore on he began to relax and devote more time to them. People came to visit and often to 'dine and sleep'; there were pleasant parties at home and in neighbouring houses. At the end of April he took Isabella to Cork, where she boarded the steamship *Sirius* for Boulogne to visit her mother, spending subsequent days exploring the Cork before returning to Quinville.[36] In these weeks Johnny and Edward came and went, to regiment and school respectively; there was a ball at Dr O'Brien's in mid-May and a pleasant party and dance the evening after at Quinville.[37]

By June Singleton's relief responsibilities had almost ceased, the fine weather seeing a return almost to the carefree atmosphere of pre-Famine summers. Mowing operations commenced, the sweet smell of hay wafting along fields and roads, and there were further cross-country horseback rides, this time in the company of 'dear' Mary.[38] A family visit to the Baltard house was accompanied by bathing excursions to a sunny Kilkee; there were picnics at Doon and Ballinahinch, the latter followed by a house party where Singleton danced into the small hours.[39] In July he and Isabella attended the wedding of a family friend, a Miss Barry, at the Methodist Church in Limerick, the ceremony followed by 'a splendid dejeuner', dancing again lasting into the morning.[40]

But there is an air about these various activities as they continue through the summer that smacks almost of determination, as if by engaging in them

John Singleton in old age. Photo courtesy National Library of Ireland.

the thought and reality of Famine distress might somehow be conjured away. One can, of course, make too much of this, since summer *divertissements* tended to be all-consuming affairs in any year for certain classes; but we are brought back to our original impression by the very strange manner in which Singleton wound up the Quin District Relief Committee on 11 August, by which time a numbed country had for some weeks been absorbing the implications of a second and near-total destruction of the potatoes.

Resolutions passed at this meeting thanked Sir Robert Peel and his late government (Singleton was an avowed Tory) for the 'foresight and statesmanlike policy by which their measures were guided in reference to the impending famine that so fearfully hung over this part of the British Dominions'.[41] Had Peel 'yielded to the opposition and taunts' elicited by his depiction of Irish distress, 'the additional horrors inseparable from misery and despair must inevitably have flowed throughout the entire of this extensive country'. A copy of the resolutions was dispatched to Peel, who responded in due course in suitably gratified terms.[42] In winding up the Relief Committee thus, was Singleton wilfully denying the evidence of the new, truly awful reality by drawing an adamant line under recent miseries? The suggestion that he was is strengthened by his departure next day with his family for the Limerick Cattle Show, where they spent a full week caught up in exhibitions, auctions, theatrical productions, a flower show and a glittering formal ball attended by 800 guests.[43]

But whatever mental processes were at work, it was not possible for Singleton to insulate himself for very long, and on 2 September we find him at Baltard, focusing at last on the new failure. His reflections do not, however, dwell on what it might mean for the welfare of his destitute western tenants, but on a scornful dismissal of their 'loud and general' reaction, the 'complaints and lamentations' of those who might suffer in the months to come as well as those who would 'make a pretend of it'. This last phrase, with its attribution of dishonesty to the hungry, is new in the diaries, and it is accentuated by the accompanying sanctimonious prayer, 'God help the one and forgive the others!' This diary entry clearly reflects a shifting in Singleton's attitudes, and his last comment that day that it would be the landlords rather than the poor who 'in the long run' would be 'the real sufferers' did not bode well for his Baltard tenants.[44]

In all probability it is Singleton's mutating views that we see reflected in a new ill-temper he displays intermittently as the Whig-Liberal relief measures gather pace, most notably during renewed road sessions held under their Labour Rate Act.[45] At one road sessions in Miltown Malbay in September, for example, after works proposed for a neighbouring parish were prioritized over his proposals for Killard, where his Baltard property lay, solely by acclamation of the crowd, his anger was patent: 'If I was the chairman', he told the meeting, 'I would not be put down by clamour in this kind of way.'[46] By contrast, at baronial sessions in Newmarket a few weeks later, he was exquisitely polite before a crowd that was much more unruly, and whom he addressed directly 'in feeling terms' regarding the 'awful visitation' with which Providence had afflicted them, imploring them 'to bear their privations with patience seeing that the calamity was a decree of the Almighty'.[47]

Singleton's demeanour at Newmarket is explained by the fact that this was very different territory to the prostrate West, where anything might be said to assemblies of the poor with impunity. Newmarket formed part of the heartland of the social protest which had accompanied the onset of starvation, and here Whiteboy/Terry Alt influence was to be reckoned with. We know that Singleton believed many of the Newmarket projects had been 'carried by clamour, terror and coercion', but he confined such comments to his diary.[48] He would have been aware that for a landlord to oppose popular demands in sessions court in the parish, or to raise his voice, as he had done at Miltown, would almost certainly have had the effect of drawing the dangerous attention of the 'Terries' to him.

But notwithstanding Singleton's circumspection at Newmarket, the resolutions he sponsored there were as self-interested as any previously proposed by him: that the burden of financial responsibility for works should be an imperial and not a local charge; that a tax should be imposed on absentee landlords rather than residents; and that works should be 'reproductive', that is of actual material benefit, failing which they would 'of lasting injury not alone to the landed interest, but demoralizing to the humbler classes'. Here Singleton's self-interest was disguised behind references to the needs of the 'humbler classes' and by coupling his remarks with similar demands made by those whose concerns were entirely philanthropic.

As winter approached and with hundreds already dead from hunger in Quin parish, Singleton did indeed recognize the scale of popular suffering in his diary. An entry for 24 November speaks of destitution being 'beyond anything I could predict'; another two evenings later, written after a day spent 'in comparative quiet at home', refers to 'crowds of upon crowds of poor persons' who had earlier 'besieged the place from here to Ennis', although it leaves us with the unsettling impression that he had hidden from them.[49] On 1 December, he describes a 'painful and distressing ordeal' that 'had to be passed through' in the Committee Room, that of selecting just 150 out of the thousands desperately seeking employment.[50] A fortnight later again, he writes of 'great crowds and great destitution', with 'many in want of work and the [cost of] provisions every day rising'.[51]

In addition, through the six months that follows, as the first great wave of starvation mortality scythed through the population, from time to time Singleton registers something of the dreadful scenes occurring in his immediate vicinity. Nowhere, however, is there any questioning as to why it is all happening or what it can mean. In mid-June 1847 he tells of having gone down and 'pacified' a crowd of 'hundreds of famishing and discontented people' who arrived at his gates, 'crying out loudly against the cooked food' (the nauseous mess doled out at the official soup kitchens).[52] Another group of starving people who arrived at Quinville some weeks later with the same complaint were described as 'poor, foolish and deluded people' whom he could not help because 'orders from Dublin' were 'imperative', taking it out of his power 'to relax the rules'.[53] In none of these entries is it possible to detect any emotion stronger than the wish that it would all go away.

And remarkably, through it all he still manages to maintain a schedule of social activities; among the most noteworthy diary entries in this connection is one from November 1846 when a difficult morning at the Quin Relief Committee is followed by an afternoon hunt, albeit not a very good one.[54] Many entries from the following February, during the worst days of Black Forty Seven, might have been written about a different country than Famine Ireland. On 15 February, he writes: 'Mrs and Miss Butler, James and Henry came to pass a few days with us; Captain Lindsay, Mr Tomkinson, 8th Hussars, dined with us, a dance and very pleasant party.' Two days later:[55]

Ennis again this day – our party at Quinville broke up and S[ara] and M[ary] having accompanied Mrs. Butler and Miss Vandeleur to Castlecrine – dined at Club where a rather large & gay party. Slept at Mrs. Keane's, Arthur's Row, where I stop for the assizes.

On two occasions in late spring and early summer 1847, Singleton travelled to Britain, the first time to deliver Edward to a new school in Edinburgh, the second to rescue Johnny who had foolishly run into debt in London.[56] He turns both occasions into holidays, filling his diary with excited references to the sights of the two cities and descriptions of his journeys between Ireland and Britain by mail-coach, steamer, rail and omnibus. On the London trip, he takes the trouble to travel to Westminster to catch some of the Committee proceedings in the Captain Wynne case.[57]

More extraordinary still than the continuation of Singleton's social activities is that he was able to do so, and indeed to tend to his public responsibilities and estate business, in the midst of the Whiteboy/Terry Alt insurgency, whose epicentre lay in the parishes surrounding Quinville. A closer look at some of these disturbances is therefore justified. As far back as March 1846, the house of Michael O'Donoghue of Rineanna, a prosperous farmer, was raided for arms.[58] A few weeks later, the land agent Pierce Carrick was assassinated a few miles from Quinville, and in July a servant of Singleton's Trenahow tenant was assaulted by Terries dressed in the traditional, terrifying disguise of women's shifts and blackened faces.[59] In August a party of twenty-two armed men, similarly accoutred, visited houses in Newmarket, threatening field labourers with death if they accepted wages less than 1s. 6d. per day.[60] In September, a rare Luddite-type incident featured another group smashing a threshing machine belonging to the Rineanna O'Donoghues, mechanization in their view being a threat to labourers' livelihoods.[61]

In October, on a weekday at noon, an armed group broke into the house of Croasdale Molony, a friend of Singleton's, at Kilnacrandy in Quin parish, warning him against sending corn to market.[62] Some days later, another friend, Hugh Hickman of Fenloe, Newmarket-on-Fergus, was violently assaulted in his fortified mansion. Singleton was in Baltard when he heard of the attack, and when he called on Hickman on his return found him traumatized and intent on fleeing the country; such, in Singleton's sour phrase, were the 'melancholy results' of 'all the exertions made for the relief of the people'.[63] In November, the dwelling of Dennis O'Neill of Shepperton, a Singleton tenant, was attacked by an armed party, although eventually they were driven off by O'Neill's sons.[64]

Insurrectionary violence even touched Singleton's family: in September, a corn-cart belonging to his brother Hugh was intercepted at Sadler's Cross by a party of disguised and armed men; shots were fired and the car sent back.[65] Eight months later, in April 1847, three tenants on their way to pay rent to Hugh were attacked and beaten while seven armed men stood by. The following month again Hugh was himself assaulted and badly beaten in an incident which cost him an eye.[66] In September his bailiff was shot dead.[67]

Outrage of this kind would continue to be a fact of life for Singleton and his neighbours for over a year to come, although the level of intensity fell off sharply in 1847 as the perpetrators became progressively weakened by hunger, died or were arrested and transported. Only a handful of these incidents are covered in the diaries, but Singleton would have been aware of most of them; he makes passing reference also to the vast incidence of lesser offences involving crop theft and livestock-stealing about which we know plentifully from other evidence.[68] But none of this social upheaval caused him to restrict any of his activities; his movements through the landscape continued as before; never once did he show any apprehension for his personal safety or that of his family, and unlike other landlords in troubled areas, it does not appear that he ever carried firearms about his person.[69]

A number of factors account for Singleton's relative feeling of security, among them perhaps personal courage, lack of imagination or an exaggerated belief in his popularity among the country people. A full explanation would, however, have to include Singleton's understanding of the very specific nature of rural outrage: the land agent Carrick, for example, was murdered because he was about to launch a mass clearance at Dangan, and Hugh Hickman was targeted because of wild remarks made in public against starving labourers (that they should eat grass!).[70] Hugh Singleton was a special case; a hard man, oppressive to his tenants and intemperate to the point of madness, by 1851 his property would be under the courts following his certification as a lunatic.[71] It may be indeed that Hugh was estranged from John, given the absence of any reference to him in the diaries.

John, as we know, enjoyed good relationships with his tenants and, as we have seen, was careful to avoid public remarks that might be construed as inflammatory by Terry Alt hotheads. Knowing also that it was unheard of for Terries to act against womenfolk or familial dependents, he would have been justified in feeling that he and his family had nothing to fear from their rude justice. To a great extent, therefore, after several years of famine, John

Singleton and his family had succeeded in assimilating many of its most disturbing manifestations and resourcefully remoulding in their lives around its awful presence.

Two other, very different, aspects of this process of assimilating Famine are worth exploring. The first involves charity-giving, which in pre-Famine gentry households was the province of women. With the effective abandonment by the British state of Famine relief late in 1847 and the collapse of the private effort, an increased presence of female involvement in charitable activity is perceptible throughout Ireland from about this time. Accordingly, in January 1848 John Singleton's daughter Mary was reported to be dispensing charity at the gates of Quinville, although we have no idea what form this took.[72] In March the same year a 'Miss Singleton of Quin' was granted eleven barrels Indian meal by the Society of Friends for distribution to the 'industrial poor' in her district.[73] In late October we again hear of a Miss Singleton – it is unsure if all these three are the same person – helping organize a relief bazaar in Limerick, in an account that lists all the young ladies and married women present, the context clearly revealing that the event had more to do with the world of the provincial *beau monde* than with any effective programme for relief of distress.[74]

The other aspect relates to the clientilism and cronyism that was so woven into the fabric of rural life in pre-Famine times, which Singleton was not averse to engaging in from time to time. As we have seen, he enjoyed friendly relations with the parish priest, Father Corbett, and before the Famine we see both men frequently exercising parochial solidarity in regard to jobs patronage and electoral issues.[75] The Famine, if anything, intensified this conduct, as administrative changes extended the scale of opportunity. In 1847, for example, Singleton secured the election of his tenant, Denis Lynch, Father Corbett's brother-in-law, as relieving officer for Quin district.[76] When Lynch, a competent and intelligent man, died suddenly the following January, his son, James, an eighteen-year old who was neither, replaced him, entirely through Singleton's influence.[77]

In December James was investigated for criminal negligence in a horrifying starvation case in which four adult members of two related families died, leaving the children inside with one of the corpses for nearly a week, watching as rats gnawed at it.[78] At the investigation, conducted by the Kilrush Union Inspector, Captain Kennedy, standing in for a deceased colleague, James Lynch's uncle, Father Corbett, spoke for him, although not even Singleton's influence could prevent his dismissal.[79] Shortly afterwards Singleton and Corbett succeeded in having James's brother, Daniel, elected in his place.[80] As a last remark on this clientilism as it reflects contemporary denominational and class difference, it is noteworthy that neither Father Corbett nor the Lynches, no matter how close their connection with Singleton, ever figure in the diaries as having been received at Quinville.

Through these years John Singleton never slackened in his attention to public duty, whether at the Quin Relief Committee, the public works road sessions while these lasted, the Board of Guardians or the Jail Committee. Examples of his assiduity at the Board of Guardians should serve for these other bodies also, and they are especially revealing in their contrast with the behaviour of other landed gentlemen. At one Board meeting in March 1848, disgust at the paralyzing absence of nearly all his ex-officio colleagues saw him propose that the Board should resign *en masse* and invite in paid vice-guardians: it is not certain if this was an ironic suggestion.[81] A month or so later, it was only the attention to duty of the Vice-Chairman, James Blake Butler of Glenwilliam, a friend of his and 'one or two Guardians', easily identifiable as John B. Knox and John Singleton, that Union business could be transacted at all.[82]

The kindest gloss that can be placed on Singleton's continued, even enhanced, devotion to family life, social round and public duty in these years might be that it represented a necessary psychological cushion allowing the management of harrowing experiences that otherwise might be emotionally overwhelming. A simpler, less charitable explanation might be that living as he and his family and his peers did, in a situation of socio-cultural segregation from the poor who surrounded them, past a certain point their fate was not something that exercised any significant emotional impact. Whatever the case, a continuous all-encompassing act of reality exclusion was certainly involved, one that grew monstrously with time, to the point where Singleton was able to express a sympathy for the sufferings of his destitute Baltard tenants just at that point where he was planning to eject them all.

For the Singleton family, Baltard was more than just a portion of the Quinville estate; it was a much-loved holiday destination. Situated beautifully on the Atlantic coast, it lay a short distance from Kilkee, with its more organized resort diversions. John, Isabella and the children had spent many happy summers at Baltard, and over the years it drew them back repeatedly, individually, in groups or ensemble. We encounter them often through the diaries, sea-bathing, going on picnics, walks or horseback rides along its majestic cliffs, John often combining estate business with his holiday. But it was at Baltard also that over an extended period at the end of the Famine, John Singleton engaged in the mass clearance of the poorest of his tenants in a process that was attended by all the appalling scenes and horribly prolonged human suffering common to mass evictions everywhere.

Singleton is first listed as an evictor in Captain Kennedy's *Reports and Returns* in June 1849. The reference is undated, like many of the Captain's early eviction returns, but it certainly relates to late spring or early summer of 1848.[83] Kennedy identifies ten Singleton tenants as having been 'turned out by summary eviction', in an action apparently coordinated with three of the landlord's middlemen. According to this document, among the Singleton evictees were families named McMahon, Haugh, Kelly, Gorman and Doody; there were two sets of Quinns and three McDonnells, each an indication of close familial connection and recent subdivision. The land parcels were tiny, ranging from a half to seven acres. Each McDonnell holding comprised seven acres, making them materially much better off than the others, who were clearly of the lowest cottier/labourer substratum. The 'Observations' column in the *Reports and Returns* shows that in all cases the cabins were levelled, and it reveals also something of the evictees' circumstances: John Quinn had given up his house in order to get outdoor relief; Denis McMahon had recently paid a fine; Pat Doody 'had to surrender to get relief'. In all fifty-one desperately poor persons, men, women and children, were removed from their homes and left without food or the means of procuring it.

Just one detail of the human casualty involved in this clearance survives; the case of Nancy Hoare, who along with her infant daughter, was rescued by Captain Kennedy from a crude hole in the bog of Baltard in May. We gather from a slightly later reference to persons ejected 'along the shore' that Nancy, who is not listed with the above group, belonged to that most abject class of occupier, to the extent that such a term is applicable, the coastal seaweed gatherers. Existing precariously on the sale of their harvest and squatting wherever they could, they were as invisible to contemporary bureaucracy as they are to historians; as squatters they could be removed without ceremony or legal process and did not therefore feature in eviction returns. When found, Nancy and her child had lain in the bog-hole for days – semi-comatose, sunburned, nearly naked, encrusted in vermin and hardly recognizable as human beings.[84] Given Singleton's fastidious nature, it seems likely that the newspaper publicity (the account appeared in several) may have been a source of embarrassment; his diary is silent on the incident.

Singleton next features as evictor in April the following year when he removed a further five families from Baltard. This time the detail is scantier: Simon McMahon had eight children in family, Widow Carmody had four, Michael McNamara five, Stephen Hastings four and James Galvin two – in all thirty-two persons. All had been ejected for non-payment of rent.[85] Some months later, in an abstract of Kennedy's returns, the *Clare Journal* ascribed thirty-one evicted families to Singleton to date, amounting to 163 persons.[86]

But as with so many clearances the story does not end there, and we have the evidence of his own diary (which does not mention the April evictions), to implicate Singleton in the insidious practice of 'voluntary surrenders', whereby occupiers were intimidated into giving up holding and/or cabin when the alternative of physical ejectment was put to them, often in a reasoned, amicable manner, by landlord or agent. Routinely such tenants were persuaded to destroy their cabins on the promise of a paltry sum described as 'compensation', thereby saving evictors expense and inconvenience. In the early days of January 1849, some months before his second 'official' eviction, in an entry written in Baltard, Singleton writes of 'some of the poor tenants' who were so hopelessly in arrears that he might have been 'under the necessity of evicting' them but for the fact that instead they had[87]

> given proof of their honesty and good conduct in giving me up quiet and peaceable possession of their land which could no longer be of any use to them and for the present will be a heavy encumbrance to me: burdened with rate, taxes and 3 or 4 gales of rent due. But still the poor people could do no more and fully merit the compensation (exclusive of my losses) which I propose giving to each of these poor people.

This single diary entry reveals how completely Singleton had embraced the self-deception of evicting landlords, the fiction of 'voluntary surrender' by 'honest tenants' as well as the classic rationalization that the land could be of no possible use to them anyway, and would be a major burden to the evictor, who by implication was the real victim. It cannot be a coincidence that the above reflections were made following several days spent under Colonel Vandeleur's hospitable roof at Kilrush House, whose owner was at this point about halfway through his career as exterminator of his own tenants. When Singleton tells us of an entire day spent sheltering snugly indoors during an Atlantic storm, 'chatting' with the colonel on various issues, we can have little doubt but that eviction was among the topics of conversation.[88]

It may well be that Singleton's mind had been worrying over what to do about these tenants as he headed towards Baltard after the visit and as he rode back and forth along its cliffs during the storms of the next few days – up to the point, that is, when the tenants relieved his mind with proof of their honesty. Subsequent entries reveal no sign of a troubled conscience over the now shelter-less tenants: the next day he spent at his fireside, tending a head cold, writing letters and reading Rev. J.A. Clarke's pious memoir, *Glimpses of the Old World*.[89] The following day again, 'a bitter cold and wet Sabbath day', bothered by a persistent cough, he remained comfortably in his bed and 'read, wrote and prayed'.

We learn something of what happened to the ejected tenants subsequently, from a *Clare Journal* report, which is all the more credible for the paper's renewed pro-landlord stance. Initially most of the Baltard evictees were taken in by occupiers still clinging to their cabins on the adjoining townland of Doonmore.[90] Some time afterwards they were evicted again when the Doonmore agent cleared that townlands of all its occupiers for the reason that it had become a 'pauper warren'.[91] Following this many removed to Doonbeg village where they lived 'huddled together in a few miserable cabins' for a considerable time, in such a 'state of filth and wretchedness as could not fail to induce disease among them and were there supplied with relief by the Poor Law authorities'.[92] Incredibly, they were fated to be evicted a third time, and after their expulsion from the village the survivors lay wretchedly for many months on the side of the road.[93]

The Poor Law relief afforded them during these months may have been due to the intervention of the English Member of Parliament, Edward Horsman, who arrived on the scene at the end of October. 'There on the public road from Doonbeg to Kilkee', according to the *Limerick and Clare Examiner*, 'did he [Horsman] see the old and young, men and women and wailing children, thrown out on the highway or huddled behind ditches under the drenching rain, the mothers vainly striving to shelter the helpless children under their tattered remnants of clothing'.[94]

This shocking roadside vista was visible to all passers-by, and it is highly likely that the entire Singleton ménage passed the evictees on a regular basis on their way to Divine Service at Doonmore Church each Sunday during summer and autumn family breaks. We know for certain that Singleton and his son Edward saw the evictees at about the time Horsman did, since father and son spent several days in November 'arranging new boundaries and new farms' on the reordered property. But even at that point, Singleton had not yet finished with clearances at Baltard, as we know from a diary reference at this time to 'great losses by those (and they are not few) that I shall be obliged to get rid of'.[95] In 1855, part of the cleared area of Baltard would be offered for rent as a grass farm of 200 acres, being 'well worthy of attention to farmer, speculator or capitalist'.[96]

If this all represents Famine-era estate consolidation at its worst – the ruthless removal of poor tenants and the distribution of their holdings among others adjudged more industrious, though usually just as terrified – Singleton adds another classic ingredient, the very strange, very intense contempt displayed by evictors towards their victims. At a meeting of the Kilrush Guardians a few days after this last entry, in the course of a tirade against the Poor Law rate, he speaks disparagingly of the 'present state of this wretched Union' as if he had not been a sizeable contributor to its wretchedness and with immeasurable cruelty of the poor 'burrowing behind the ditches' as if he had no connection with that either.[97]

Singleton describes Christmas 1849 as 'lovely', a 'cheerful and contented one in our family circle amid all the sorrows of the present times'. From what we have seen above, however, we can be certain that the sorrows he speaks of relate not to the roadside straggles of the sick and dying evictees near Doonbeg but to his own difficulties and those of other landlords.[98]

The new year at Quinville Abbey began miserably enough. There was no company and no *parties de plaisir* to usher it in, and the weather remained harsh, cold and windy for weeks afterwards. Following this, however there came a definite lightening of mood, presaging a great improvement in the life of John Singleton, now in his fifty-seventh year. Clouds lifted, figuratively and literally, and soon public duties and estate business returned to their old brisk routine; excursions and entertainments resumed. In January Singleton attends the Lord Lieutenant's levee in Dublin Castle; in February Colonel Vandeleur comes to visit at Quinville for a few days; in March, at the Limerick assizes, Singleton makes the acquaintance of the rising young barrister, Isaac Butt, QC, and spends 'a very pleasant and merry evening' in his company.[99] The same month at Baltard he walks among the surviving tenants at their labour, noting tillage operations in train all round: the bog where Nancy Hoare had lain with her child two years previously had since been reclaimed and was now sown with potatoes.[100]

At the end of May Singleton rode through Baltard with Colonel Vandeleur, inspecting all the recent improvements, including a sheep walk developed on ground on which tenants' cabins had so recently stood.[101] In mid-June he dined at Bunratty Lodge with the Dawsons and explored the old castle for some hours; in July while arranging for the placing of a statue to Sir Michael O'Loghlen in the new county courthouse, by chance he ran into Nicholas Westby, one of the county's absentee magnates in company with his agent, Singleton's occasional house guest, Marcus Keane.[102] By now all his turf had been harvested, and it was time for a return to Baltard for a week's holiday. 'Took a ride and walk over the lands,' he wrote on 29 July, 'tillage, and a great deal of it, very fine and most promising thank God!'[103] In August, he travelled to Dublin, and at the Encumbered Estates Court in Henrietta Street, he laid out £446 for the purchase in one lot of 'Rineen, my little farm', which he had been renting up to then.[104]

September was the high point at Quinville that year, the Singletons operating an open house for family and friends as well as their children's friends, a loose informal arrangement, in which visitors dropped in and out of the company as they pleased. The peak experience came towards the end of the month in a midnight excursion by moonlight to the medieval ruins of Quin Abbey just down from Quinville. An hour and a half was spent 'exploring the ruin inside, outside and upstairs', followed by 'a delicious walk through our own grounds', the whole experience thrilling to the participants. 'Never did Quin Abbey appear to such advantage and in such beauty to my eyes', Singleton wrote in his diary later on that morning.[105]

In most other circumstances reading of such an adventure might evoke simplicity, innocence and enchantment – and nothing else. In the context of the last obscene rages of the Great Famine all around Quin and of Singleton's destruction of the Baltard tenant community, the half-light in which it took place lends it a brooding atmosphere of Gothic horror, of a kind, however, that might have been too strong even for the darkest imaginings of a Sheridan Le Fanu or a Bram Stoker.

4

The Medical Gentleman: Dr Patrick Maxwell Cullinan

On several occasions in the later years of a very long life we happen upon Dr Patrick Maxwell Cullinan in the course of personal reminiscence. Dr Cullinan's memories, to the extent that we are aware of them, concern his undergraduate days – student pranks, eminent men he trained under and friends who achieved medical greatness. One fellow student he was happy to dwell on was Dr Charles Lever, whose fame was gained as a novelist rather than a physician; after Lever's death in 1872 Cullinan held forth at some length to a biographer on a lifelong friendship that was clearly a source of pride to him.[1] We have no evidence of Dr Cullinan sharing memories of the Great Famine at any time, although even if he never did so, the omission is not necessarily a significant one. But the absence is a great pity since the other evidence relating to Dr Cullinan's doings during the Famine is relatively strong, and it is coherent enough to allow an attempt at recreating much of his experience of that time, no matter that it has to be mined from seams that are buried deeply in the sources.

What emerges from this excavation, however, is startlingly at variance from what we might expect to hear of a skilled medical professional faced with the horrors of Famine and the enormous challenges it brought. To be sure, the one-dimensional nature of our evidence may partly account for this, but it remains striking that we hear relatively little of purely medical issues – the symptomatology of fever and its treatment or the nature of starvation-related inanition for example – and a great deal about institutional employment and emolument among medical men. Instead of collegial collaboration in the battle against contagion, we encounter cliques and competition for preferment, which for Dr Cullinan and many of his colleagues seems to have been at least as much a matter of concern as care of the sick poor. We become particularly conscious of a bitter feud that Cullinan carried on with a colleague, Dr Michael Healy, and as we read we become gradually aware of how dominant over all other issues it was among medical gentlemen, throughout even the worst years of the Famine. As they unfold in this chapter, the intricacies of the Cullinan-Healy feud reveal a great deal of the protagonists and of the Famine-era medical profession in general.

Michael Healy and Patrick Maxwell Cullinan both came of Catholic gentry stock and from families that had emerged from the Penal Laws still possessed of substantial leasehold property. Such families were notably self-regarding, particularly where, as seems to have been the case here, they cherished an awareness of ancestral status under the old Gaelic order that had perished with Aughrim. Through his mother, we know that Michael Healy was connected with the haughty O'Shaughnessys of Gort, and through them with the Catholic Church establishment, Reverend Terence O'Shaughnessy, Dean of Killaloe, being an uncle.[2] The Cullinans were descended from a minor mid-Clare sept, although the fact that Patrick Maxwell and his brother Michael both had sons called Cormac would suggest a fancied connection with the tenth-century King-Bishop of Munster, Cormac MacCuilleanáin.[3]

Latter-day Healys and Cullinans in their Newmarket-on-Fergus and Dromcliffe/Kilmaley redoubts, respectively to the north-west and south-east of Ennis, were viewed by contemporaries either as Catholic landlords or as middlemen; technically they were both. The Healys and the Cullinans were exact social equals, and they would have recognized as compeers a small number of similarly circumstanced families in their general environs. They would, in addition, have considered themselves at least as good as the Crowes of Dromore or the Keanes of Beech Park, landlord families with clearer (and more elevated) links to the old Gaelic order, and who had conformed to Protestantism under the pressures of the Penal Laws.[4] Healy and Cullinan residences were smaller than either Dromore or Beech Park, but they were commodious and sat prettily in their walled demesnes, Michael Healy being born at Manus House, Newmarket-on-Fergus, some years before Patrick Maxwell Cullinan's birth in 1806 at Shanvoy, Kilmaley.[5]

In contrast to Healy's straightforwardly Catholic upbringing, Cullinan's was more complicated, as a member of a Protestant household where at least one sibling, his brother Michael, was a Catholic. Both men would appear to have received their early schooling in John Hurley's Catholic academy in Ennis, after which Healy went on to Edinburgh University; Cullinan some years later to Trinity College, Dublin, Edinburgh's great rival as a medical school.[6] Even though Healy trained as a surgeon and Cullinan as a physician, in the provincial setting in which both men were destined to live, the distinction made little difference to their actual practice.

Healy served for a number of years as a naval surgeon on various stations and ships, 'afloat and on shore', to use his own words, before disillusion with salary and career prospects caused him to return home.[7] Cullinan returned on completion of his training, recognizing apparently that he was not destined for the eminence of classmates such as W.J. Smyth, later a famous surgeon, and with whom he once fought a muddled undergraduate *rencontre*, or William Wilde, Oscar's father, who would achieve celebrity as one of the nineteenth century's great polymaths.[8] Given their background and education, professional conceit and social pride, as they sought to establish themselves on home turf, it was probably inevitable that the close proximity to each other of two such egotistical personalities as Drs Healy and Cullinan would result in conflict.

Healy and Cullinan became acquainted just before the cholera epidemic of 1832 when they were appointed to the temporary hospital set up in Ennis in anticipation of an outbreak.[9] Neither played a significant role in the defeat of the cholera, however, since early on Healy went down with the disease, and Cullinan resigned following a dramatic announcement before the district Board of Health that from 'fatigue he was fitter for a patient than a Medical Attendant'.[10] Treatment of cholera patients was left to two even younger physicians, Drs Silver and Keane, who would bear that entire burden over the months of the outbreak.[11]

The withdrawal by Healy and Cullinan, no matter that it was justified, contributed to rumblings about the poor showing of medical men during the crisis, some of whom were alleged to have declined to attend cholera patients out of cowardice.[12] In September these rumblings assumed concrete form in an article in the *Lancet* by a military surgeon at the Clare Castle depot, who claimed doctors had *en masse* fled the district in terror during the epidemic.[13] Cut to the quick, the Ennis medical establishment promptly scapegoated, Dr Silver, the hardworking hospital junior, as the source of this information, and ostracized him for over a year.[14]

Silver, notwithstanding his subsequent rehabilitation under press and popular insistence, would always be an outsider among the Ennis medical fraternity, although ultimately he was more fortunate than Dr Charles Keane, the colleague with whom he had shared cholera duty. A member of the Beech Park family, and therefore very much an insider in terms of county privilege and patronage, the slightly built, retiring Dr Keane died in August of cholera contracted while tending to his patients.[15] The career of this gentle spirit could not have presented a more stark contrast to that which his younger brother, Marcus, then a teenager, was to carve out for himself later on.

The cholera outbreak and the Silver affair are especially relevant to our purposes for two reasons: firstly that they engendered in John B. Knox, chairman of the District Health Board, and new editor of the *Clare Journal*, such an antipathy towards medical men in general that he rarely referred to members of the profession afterwards except in terms of scepticism and derision. In time Knox was to develop a peculiarly virulent dislike of Drs Cullinan and Healy that would lead him to devote an inordinate amount of column space to their doings over the years; for us this is a particular boon since his coverage of what he saw as unseemly behaviour on the part of the two men furnishes us with the bulk of what we know of them.

The second reason why the cholera and Silver affairs are relevant is that they serve as a useful introduction to the medical establishment in Clare, a tiny community where position and institutional emolument were guarded jealously among a few senior men who also exercised a stranglehold on private practice, leaving those junior to them to scramble for future placing.[16] In all there can have been no more than forty medical men in Clare: senior men and juniors; surgeons, physicians and apothecaries, many of them serving interchangeably in these capacities.[17] In the rural districts, senior men were for the most part content with private practice; only a few of those who were resident in the county capital were sufficiently ambitious to contend for the additional institutional plums. These contending medical men, it should be stressed, had been trained at reputable university hospitals, at home and abroad, and all were skilled, intelligent and articulate.[18]

Clare's medical institutions consisted of the County Infirmary, the Lying-in (maternity) Hospital, the County Jail Infirmary and the County Fever Hospital, the latter a large purpose-built edifice constructed in 1836.[19] All were situated in Ennis, medical provision in the rural districts being confined to some twenty-three dispensaries scattered over the county landscape. From the early 1840s, the emergence of four Union workhouses, at Ennis, Kilrush, Scariff and Ennistymon, provided further opportunity.[20] With the exception of the workhouses which operated under the Poor Law, all were county institutions, funded from the cess, the annual tax raised by the Grand Jury, the administering body. By the late 1830s, the senior medical men, the 'Old Doctors' who had attended medical institutions for a generation and had always been 'tenacious of their privileges' in snapping up new employment opportunities, were one by one retiring or dying off. Behind them a small group of younger men jockeyed for position to succeed to their institutional and private practices, among whom Drs John Enright, George O'Brien, Michael Healy and Patrick Maxwell Cullinan were the most determined.[21]

Leaving aside private practice, about which we know little, success in securing institutional posts depended on the ability of applicants to cultivate relationships with Grand Jurors or Poor Law Guardians in whose hands the patronage lay. Here the political astute Cullinan was most effective, largely because he had established a valuable connection with Sir Lucius O'Brien, the Dromoland grandee and Lord Lieutenant of the County; Healy was less so because of a pompous, difficult personality that left him with the consistent support only of his influential ecclesiastical relatives.

Of the four above, Dr Enright was the first to gain an institutional foothold and by early 1840 was salaried attendant at the Lying-in Hospital and the County Fever Hospital. He did not enjoy his new position for very long, however, and died suddenly at the end of the year, his death an unexpected opportunity for Healy, to whom both his posts now passed as the most senior of the younger group.[22] In most circumstances seniority would not have deterred O'Brien or Cullinan, but these two by this time were eyeing other prizes and were content to relinquish the two posts to Healy; it was Cullinan indeed who nominated him for the Fever Hospital position. In addition, Cullinan and O'Brien now withdrew ostentatiously from midwifery in their private practices, leaving the field exclusively to Healy, supposedly in view of the limited remuneration of his two positions, but more likely to obviate opposition to their own hopes.[23]

Healy's support might now have been expected for Cullinan's application as physician to the new Ennis workhouse, which arose in June 1841. Healy, however, did not oblige, and instead put in his own bid, a lapse in professional courtesy that may have first given rise to coldness between the two men. The workhouse post was awarded according to public advertisement at £50 per annum, in the new fashion, and when Cullinan presented a tender in June 1841 in the old style, it was set aside and he was asked if he would take the post at the advertised salary. Taken aback, he prevaricated by discoursing vaguely on the 'vast amount of duties to be discharged' which 'no one person would find himself competent to perform', but accepted immediately when it was suggested that another physician might be appointed to assist him.[24] Cullinan's competence was not in question, of course, and at the end of his first year at the workhouse, the Visiting Committee was laudatory of his performance.[25]

By the end of 1845 Dr Cullinan was as firmly installed as attending physician at the Ennis workhouse as Dr Healy was at the Lying-in Hospital and Dr George O'Brien at the County Infirmary.[26] Like the other two Cullinan was also a senior salaried attendant at the Fever Hospital.[27] It is unclear if any of them yet had obtained the dispensary appointments referred to in later sources. And if individually the remuneration from these posts was low by professional standards elsewhere, when combined with private practice and incidental fees available to all qualified practitioners, the lifestyle it made possible was comfortable and gratifyingly bourgeois.

And still further opportunities beckoned for Cullinan, although discretion had to be exercised in pursuing them. When a second medical position came up at the County Infirmary in February 1846, deference towards his colleague Dr O'Brien, then doggedly resisting attempts to have him share his £400 annual salary (not an especially generous one) with another physician, dictated Cullinan should not apply.[28] But there was no obstacle with regard to the £50 per annum physician's post at the County Jail that arose in July and which an aggressive canvass secured for him. Healy had been a contender for this post but had withdrawn early in the race on the grounds that soliciting votes was humiliating and that in any case he could never hope to command the 'most sweet voices' of the twenty-three decision-making Grand Jury members.[29]

Thus matters stood just before Famine-related distress began to impact on the county's medical apparatus. Conveniently for our purposes, from this time forward in the evidence other medical gentlemen tend to fade into the background, leaving the narrative field increasingly to the interaction of Dr Healy and Dr Cullinan. Partly a reflection of the Knox's growing fixation with them, this development is indicative also of the fact that they were now

Harmony House, Dr Cullinan's residence. Author photograph.

the most prominent figures among Clare's medical community, as signalled indeed by the election late in 1845 of Dr Cullinan to the presidency of the Clare Medical Society and Dr Healy to its secretaryship.[30] Throughout 1846 and beyond Society meetings were held either in Cullinan's well-appointed consulting rooms at his residence of Harmony House in Ennis or at Dr Healy's equally plush establishment in the Georgian surroundings of Bindon Street just around the corner.[31]

It is difficult to establish with any precision how quickly and to what extent practitioners' workloads were affected by the onset of Famine. Private practice, as always, remains unknown territory, and our only indications regarding medical institutions come from incomplete workhouse and Fever Hospital statistics.[32] From the autumn of 1845, inmate numbers at the workhouse began to rise very slowly, and it was only in winter the following year that the house's original 800-place capacity was breached. At the beginning of December 1846 numbers were still hovering between 800 and 1,000 occupied places, after which they rose rapidly as external conditions became so bad as to overcome dread of the Poor Law among the destitute. Now at last, they began to flood into workhouses.[33] It was some time again before overcrowding at workhouse and County Fever Hospital saw cases and mortality soar, the increase being most dramatically manifest at the Fever Hospital. In January

1847, just eleven fever deaths took place in its wards; in February thirty-one and in April sixty-five, by any standards a major outbreak. Mortality peaked in July with a staggering death toll of 149 before it abated significantly; even so the mortality figures for January 1848 were still of the order of sixty-two persons.[34] The pattern of succeeding years would be similar, the fluctuations in mortality even more pronounced.

Staff at the medical institutions therefore would have felt a moderate increase in workload towards the end of 1846 and from early 1847 an exceptionally heavy pressure; it is difficult to imagine how they managed to cope with the demands on their skills, time and energy when the epidemic was at its height in the summer and during the periodic resurgences that were to follow. And it is as well to remember that during these extremely difficult periods as they went about their daily duties, the medical men did so at a constant, very real risk to their own lives.

We know little of the work practices of medical men during the outbreak, and most of what we can glean derives from a number of remarks made over the period by Dr Cullinan, which reveal as much about their author as they do about the medical situation. Cullinan's analysis of fever cases under his care, for example, is extraordinarily tentative, a sharp contrast with the confident pronouncements on his part in pre-Famine times when discussion was still theoretical.[35] In one report from late December 1846 regarding certain workhouse cases, he would 'not undertake to say that the disease [was] contagious in the strict meaning of that term'; in another about a week later, his remarks that overcrowding, diet and lack of ventilation were not responsible for the spread of fever were so qualified as almost to constitute a passive conclusion to the contrary.[36] So cautious was Cullinan indeed that he rarely ventured an opinion unless prompted by direct questions from individual Guardians, the Poor Law Commissioners or the central medical authorities. On one occasion early in 1847, so great was his indecision in regard to some cases that he widened the diagnostic possibilities to include cholera, whose symptoms are quite distinct: cholera would not appear for another two years.[37]

In March 1847, Dr Cullinan told the Ennis Guardians that he had been instructed by the Poor Law Commissioners to inform them that numbers at the workhouse were now in excess of capacity, as a result of which the health of the inmates was being endangered. The report which the Commissioners required him to write on the issue would be 'very indifferent', since 'there was scarcely a single healthy person in the establishment'.[38] Cagey, vague and self-exculpatory as it was, this statement amounts to what we already recognize as Cullinan-speak; having failed to mention overcrowding previously to the Guardians, by use of language that was indefinably laden with surprise and disappointment he now sought to transfer responsibility away from himself as attending physician. Much later on in the year, in November, in reply to another query from the Commissioners, he informed the Board that the state of the house was much better than for several months past and that a greater number of paupers could with safety be accepted on a temporary basis, all delivered in a manner that implied credit for himself in the arrangement.[39]

For want of data we cannot make any evaluation of Dr Cullinan's care of patients at any of the institutions to which he was attached during the fever epidemic. Cullinan was certainly a skilled physician, but the behaviours described above and those yet to be mentioned do not fill us with confidence. On another level, however, and almost against our will we find ourselves marvelling at his alertness for any income-generating professional opportunity, which the worsening crisis had in fact multiplied. During the County Assizes of July 1847, he had the effrontery to address the Baron of Assize directly during County Business to inquire if, as medical attendant to the County Jail, he was entitled to a fee for attendance at inquests held on deceased prisoners under the new Coroners Act: because of the rise in fever mortality among prisoners, inquests were potentially a lucrative income source.[40] Undeterred by an emphatic reply to the contrary, Cullinan, who had ambitions in regard to the office, then asked if coroners were to be allowed their fees.[41] Another curt negative followed.

Dr Cullinan's absorption with remuneration at this point had as much to do with defending his gains as with exploiting new opportunities, as is evident from a row that erupted at the County Fever Hospital in mid-August. This arose when a letter-writer in the *Clare Journal* alleged that the chaplains on the Fever Hospital Committee had operated a corrupt voting arrangement with the medical attendants in order to secure salary increases that had recently been sanctioned.[42] Implausible though the allegation was, John B. Knox, himself a Committee member, nevertheless gave it editorial credence, while opening his columns to those with contrary views. The challenge was taken up, not by the chaplains, but by two of the medical men, Dr Michael Healy and Dr Patrick Maxwell Cullinan.

Healy's response was a terse denial of any collusion, either on his part or that of his uncle, Dean Terence O'Shaughnessy, one of the supposedly erring chaplains: he (Healy) had not been present at the relevant Committee meeting and the Dean had left the room before the salaries topic was raised. In confining his exculpation to himself and his uncle, Healy was effectively insulting the others by an implication of their possible guilt, and it was left to Cullinan to refute the allegations which he did in his own indignant letter. His refutation is less important than an underlying general argument contained within it that medical men were badly paid for services at the Fever Hospital.[43] This was in fact true; poor institutional remuneration was a source of great grievance to the medical profession in general in Ireland during the Famine epidemics.[44]

Cullinan's letter began a protracted newspaper controversy over the issue which lasted for the remainder of the year and into 1848.[45] Arguments on both sides are inconsequential and worth dwelling on only for such

Residence of Dr Michael Healy. Author photograph.

odd twists and turns as the claim made at one point that a Freemasons' conspiracy lay behind the salary increases (a number of those involved were members of the Craft); for Cullinan's description of the original letter-writer as a 'miscreant without position or stake within society', and for a sarcastic proposal by the latter (briefly implemented) that the four junior

Fever Hospital doctors be discharged and their salaries redistributed among the four seniors.[46] Amidst the gabble, however, two facts stand out: firstly there was the understandable concern of the Fever Hospital medical men to protect salaries that were poor when compared with those awarded their peers elsewhere, and secondly the fact that the controversy was conducted, with great heat, during the worst ravages of epidemic fever yet experienced during the Famine, and almost as if nothing of the kind were happening.

For practitioners and chaplains the salaries affair came to a most unsatisfactory end at the Spring Assizes in March 1848 when the Fever Hospital Corporation, the Grand Jury-appointed oversight body, reasserted control over the Committee and reduced the salaries to what they had been before the increase. Chaplains and senior medical staff had their salaries reduced from £45 to £27 per annum; the junior doctors, who had so recently been unpaid interns, had their annual earnings reduced from £27 to only £17.[47] Incensed by the move, the *Limerick and Clare Examiner* declared it to be 'parsimonious' and 'most discreditable', indicative of a 'degree of barbarism' which it had not expected 'among persons in the rank of gentlemen'. Clergymen and medical practitioners had 'braved every danger fearlessly and chivalrously during more than one plague', while 'those grinding economists' (i.e. the landlords on the Fever Hospital Corporation) and whose own tenants 'suffered through their exactions' were by contrast 'lounging, by the fire side, eating well, drinking well, and sleeping well'.[48]

The fiscal austerity imposed by the County Grand Jury in this instance was an outgrowth of landlord fears regarding county cess, which had begun to rise as a result of advance repayments relating to the public works; reducing the cost of medical institutions was one method by which they sought to prevent it rising further. But since cess taxation was never in fact onerous during the Famine, hardly featuring indeed in the catalogue of landlord grievances at any time, there can be little doubt that the salary reductions formed part also of the gathering landlord repudiation of any and all obligations in respect of relief of distress. The *Examiner*'s fulminations therefore had a firm basis in fact, and in view of the service given by medical men and the real risks they ran to health and life on a daily basis, its characterization of the reductions as 'an act of grievous injustice' was not inaccurate either.[49]

From Cullinan's point of view, another act of injustice loomed almost immediately, this time at the Ennis Union, where in response to the deluge of new admissions, the Guardians decided to acquire an 'auxiliary workhouse', an extra building that would have to be fitted out and staffed. The decision to hire another physician and to reduce Cullinan's salary in order to help accommodate him financially was, ironically, his own doing, in that it arose after he had unthinkingly shown his workbook containing the names of 300 inmate patients attended in a single day to one of the Guardians. If his intention had been to show how overworked he was and how deserving of a salary increase, it backfired when the Guardian promptly laid down a notice of motion proposing that an extra physician be appointed, to be salaried at £40 per annum and that Cullinan's annual salary be reduced from £65 to £60.[50] During the discussion, John Singleton had not helped by suggesting – mischievously in view of the known antipathy between the two medical men – that if Dr Cullinan was unable to devote enough of his time to workhouse duties, instead of appointing an extra physician, 'they would accept his resignation, and appoint Dr. Healy in his place'.[51]

Asked for his reaction after the proposal was put formally a few weeks later, Cullinan evasively cited the 'great advantage' of two or more physicians working together, but he suggested that extra physicians were usually inexperienced men, easily gulled by malingerers and who certainly would not have been able to do what he had done the previous day, which was to send away 60 of the 310 inmates he had attended as not being ill. Warming to this theme, he seems momentarily to have forgotten where he was, as he launched into a humorous exposition of the practices 'to which medical men were in the habit of resorting in order to economize their time'.[52] One physician of his acquaintance regularly employed the stratagem of bringing 'a bottle of wine, a bottle of castor-oil and a bottle of coughdrops', into his hospital, dosing those who reported sick with concoctions from them. He believed 'it was a general practice among medical men, not excepting himself, and he did not doubt but their chairman ... could also give them some information on the subject'.

Unluckily for Dr Cullinan, the chairman was none other than Dr Healy, who had been elected to the Board some months before and happened to be in the chair on the day. Immediately and flatly, Healy denied he had ever engaged in such practices, thereby wrong-footing Cullinan with the realization of a horrible indiscretion on his part and the revelation of a profoundly callous attitude towards the suffering workhouse inmates. But Cullinan recovered from his gaffe sufficiently to deal with a barrage of questions from various Guardians relating to the proposition in hand. And at this point, when he appeared to be under the greatest pressure, he was rescued by two procedural moves made earlier, which in the midst of the clamour now clicked smoothly into place: an amendment to the original motion proposing that no appointment was yet necessary and a notice of motion proposing an increase to Cullinan's salary from £65 to £100. Against all likelihood, the salary increase was also passed in due course, and even though the Irish Poor Law Commissioners refused to sanction it, over the summer Cullinan raised the matter repeatedly at Board meetings in the hope of forcing the Commissioners to reconsider.[53]

As luck would have it, in mid-September when Cullinan's persistence seemed about to pay off, Healy wrecked his chances by insisting on full observance of the formal time-consuming procedures involved. Unmoved by Cullinan's comment that 'he did not think Dr Healy should interfere in this question since it was one in which Dr. Healy was interested', Healy replied in the same tone that he did not feel at all bound by Cullinan's opinion – that he had 'an undoubted right' to take part in any Board discussion and 'had never made an improper or an illegitimate use' of his position on the Board. After further discussion, a notice of motion was laid down that another physician be appointed.[54] Victorious for the moment, Healy now resigned as Guardian so as to be eligible for the new post; to no purpose, since it went instead to a Dr Andrew Hehir, about whom we have no other knowledge apart from his appointment to the County Fever Hospital in 1845. We presume him young, but clearly he had to have both connections and political resourcefulness to have swept the prize from the veteran Healy.[55]

A few months after this controversy had subsided, the attention of salary-preoccupied medical gentlemen swung back to the Fever Hospital on the other side of town. Here, in early December, at a formally convened meeting of the Corporation, it was the newcomer, Dr Hehir, who led the charge against the recent salary restrictions imposed by the county authorities, his complaint echoed by Dr Healy who held that the physicians' workload had tripled over recent months. Healy's support was always a dubious quantity, however, and in this case was immediately negated by an appalling betrayal of collegial solidarity, in which he told the meeting that there were too many physicians at the Fever Hospital and that the Corporation 'should have stood by the four senior men, and not have allowed them to be swamped by juniors in the profession'. This was too much for John B. Knox, present in his capacity as a member of the Corporation and who immediately retorted: 'Precisely what you did to your predecessors'.

But divided and disorganized as they were, the medical men got nowhere, and the meeting lapsed into angry recrimination regarding an individual £10 gratuity received by the Fever Hospital physicians in September.[56] Most vociferous on the subject was Crofton Vandeleur, currently engaged in the root-and-branch extermination of his poorer west Clare tenants, and so outraged at the payment that he declared his intention of setting in train a thorough overhaul of the Fever Hospital's arrangements at the next Assizes. Cullinan, for reasons we can only guess, took no interest in proceedings, his only contribution a petty complaint regarding overcrowding and leaking sheds, 'irregularities' that were 'very disagreeable' to him.[57]

Within days of the meeting its deliberations were rendered irrelevant by the arrival of a Lord Lieutenant's Order under the new Fever Act, directing that the County Fever Hospital be handed over to the Ennis Board of Guardians as a Union Fever Hospital and instructing the Guardians immediately to proceed with the election of four attending physicians.[58] For the junior medical men this was disastrous news since the seniors would be guaranteed to obtain the new vacancies.[59] And so it came about; after elections which were delayed for technical reasons until the Spring Assizes, in March 1849 Drs Healy, Cullinan, O'Brien and Hehir, all with private practices and multiple institutional employments, were elected to the new

Union Fever Hospital. Anomalously, Cullinan and Hehir now had two Poor Law Union positions each, at the Union workhouse and the Union Fever Hospital.[60]

The junior physicians cut adrift by this development had their fate postponed for a few months by the cholera epidemic of spring, for which all medical personnel were mobilized, and which for the moment put an end to their bickering.[61] The behaviour of Clare practitioners during this short-lived but horrific outbreak, it should be said, did much to rehabilitate the reputation of the profession with the public, and in the course of their attendance on patients at least three physicians in the county died of the disease. But there were nonetheless rumours of one physician who had refused to treat cholera patients, and another whose terror of contracting the disease earned him the nickname of the 'Railway Doctor' for the speed with which he dealt with cases.[62]

When the cholera had passed, the juniors were again left without employment, although the senior men did not quite escape either, since patient numbers in the Union Fever Hospital had now so declined that the Central Board of Health decided to rescind two of the four new physicians' posts, thereby precipitating new elections.[63] Of the leading applicants, Drs O'Brien and Cullinan found the financial terms of 50 guineas per annum unacceptable, O'Brien declaring he would not accept 'a lower salary than was given in other Unions', Cullinan gnomically stating that while 'he declined to assent to the salary proposed, he would not say that he dissented'. The Board promptly struck out both applications, following which Drs Healy and Hehir were declared elected.[64]

To the great surprise of the practitioners involved, these developments caused an outcry in medical circles at national level, when in two successive issues, the *Dublin Medical Press* praised Cullinan and O'Brien for their stand, predicting that next time the Ennis Guardians would 'choose the two who will undertake the duty for twenty five pounds, and when Drs. Healy and Hehir are ousted by such competition, they cannot complain'.[65] Farming out the sick poor to the lowest bidder as had been done, the *Medical Press* caustically remarked, had created such a level of public indignation and professional resistance that it would have to be reversed.[66] Doing so deprived the poor 'of their just right to the best assistance which the circumstances afford', and degraded the medical profession 'by encouraging a spirit of miserable competition', at the same time establishing 'the right of the Guardians to enforce the base and wicked practice of adjusting their arrangements for the reduction of the rates rather than for the relief of destitution'. Had the *Medical Press* been a less conservative journal, it might have expanded this last clause into an indictment of the Poor Law in all aspects of its murderousness.

As Healy struggled to justify himself before his peers through a letter in the *Medical Press*, the controversy seems to have reached a stage of constant and spontaneous mutation.[67] The Board of Health now refused to sanction Dr Hehir's appointment because he had agreed to accept less than £5 per day, and a remark made by Hehir about O'Brien's multiple employments led to a sharp retort and the inauguration of another medical feud. The weeks and months that followed brought further twists and turns, including appeals to the Lord Lieutenant (on one occasion O'Brien and Cullinan travelled to Dublin personally to meet him); the formal voiding of the Healy-Hehir appointments by the Board of Health, and the studied disregard of the order by the Guardians.[68] Only at the end of November 1849 was this particular sub-controversy settled when much to John B. Knox's satisfaction, the Lord Lieutenant issued a warrant confirming Dr Healy's appointment.[69]

To anyone attempting to make sense of its bewildering complexities it must have come as a relief when the ongoing ferment over medical arrangements at Ennis came to a fairly sudden close with the expiration of the Temporary Fever Act in August 1850.[70] Institutional medical employments now resolved themselves into a new and lasting configuration: the Union Fever Hospital was discontinued, and no attempt was made to re-establish the County Fever Hospital, whose premises would soon be allocated to a county militia revived for the duration of the Crimean War.[71] Henceforth Dr Cullinan was to continue as principal physician at the Union workhouse, Dr Hehir as second physician.[72] And as always, it would appear, the juniors were left to fend for themselves.

But the new dispensation did not bring the Healy-Cullinan feud to an end, and for a time in fact, returning order saw the rivalry stand out more sharply than ever. At this point, with so many recently added issues lying unresolved, an explosion from one side or the other might soon be expected. Clear indications of this had emerged even before this, when in January rumours had spread of a 'war of words', a 'very angry epistolary correspondence' a few days earlier between 'two of the medical gentlemen of this town', who can only be Healy and Cullinan. Remarking on the rumours in the *Clare Journal* John B. Knox lectured his readers to the effect that historically medical men had been 'proverbial for quarrelling, squabbling and jealousies of each other'; he regretted that he could not say that the profession in Ennis was exceptional in this regard.[73]

A showdown was postponed until September, however, when it was precipitated by a trouble-stirring letter that appeared in the *Clare Journal* under the pen name An Over-Taxed Ratepayer. There had been two other letters from the same source in June, both of them seeking to excite antagonism between Cullinan and Hehir by claiming that as second physician the latter was in fact doing the bulk of workhouse duties and should be paid accordingly; the third letter held that pauper numbers no longer justified the employment of two physicians.[74] Because of the inside knowledge displayed by the Ratepayer, from the start the Ennis medical men had a shrewd suspicion as to which of their colleagues was hiding behind the pseudonym, and when his identity was disclosed at a crowded practitioners' meeting in the Board Room of the County Infirmary at the end of September, there was little surprise when it proved to be Dr Michael Healy.[75]

The dramatic revelation intended by the meeting's convenors, Drs Cullinan and Hehir having fallen flat therefore, they were further put at a loss when Healy proceeded, with considerable dexterity, to spar with the allegation that he was the Ratepayer, before nonchalantly admitting he was. Pressing his advantage he neatly turned the tables on his accusers by brushing aside ethical issues arising out of his authorship and focussing the meeting's attention on the underhand methods used by Drs Cullinan and Hehir to procure the original letters.[76]

But at this point when it seemed the initiative was triumphantly his, Healy's *sang froid* deserted him and all his long-repressed resentments against Cullinan burst forth in a furious tirade. Consistently in the past, he told the meeting, Dr Cullinan had manifested 'vindictive' and 'most unfriendly feeling' towards him; all present knew of the many 'feuds' existing between them. For many years back, and while professing friendship, Cullinan was 'in secret' his 'bitterest and most inveterate foe'. Latterly he had emerged as his open enemy, having thrown away the mask. 'I don't wear a mask', Cullinan managed to interrupt, appealing to the chairman, Dr O'Brien, to halt Healy's tirade ('I am unwilling, I confess, to interrupt any statement of Dr Healy's now', the chairman said).

And so Dr Healy continued: Dr Cullinan had used all his influence with the Guardians to block his appointment to the second medical post at the workhouse two years previously, all the while professing 'the strongest assurances of perfect neutrality'. The previous year, after failing to secure the second Fever Hospital appointment – when he neither 'assented' nor 'dissented' from the terms – Cullinan had questioned Healy's competence with the Central Board of Health and the Lord Lieutenant. Again, when the Guardians sought to allocate part of the old County Fever Hospital for workhouse purposes, Cullinan had drawn up a spurious report on its unsuitability in order to bring Healy's professional character into disrepute following the latter's temporary appointment there. When the Guardians rejected the report, he had forwarded it to the Commissioners, and when their Inspector arrived to investigate, he had taken the opportunity to calumniate Healy further by blaming him for a resurgence of cholera.

Healy's recital was interrupted by denials from Cullinan, and when at one point Dr Hehir intervened to represent himself as a constant sufferer in the crossfire of the feud, Healy rounded on him by telling him his hands were far from clean, in that two years previously he had offered to work for whatever the Guardians would give him. Healy had nothing to say, however, to a remark from one of the junior physicians, Dr Whitestone – the juniors had particular reason to dislike Healy – that but for the quarrelling between the professionals Clare would still have a Fever Hospital.

In the end the meeting decided that Healy, Cullinan and Hehir should leave the room while their colleagues deliberated, and as the latter two complied they protested at the injustice of having to do so: the purpose of the meeting after all had been to investigate Healy's anonymous letters, not to address any alleged misconduct on their part. They were equally unhappy with the judgement, which involved a mild censure on all three: Cullinan for his behaviour towards Healy; Hehir for his lack of professionalism in agreeing to work for whatever terms the Guardians offered him two years earlier; and Healy for his equally unprofessional conduct in writing the letters. However, unlike Hehir and Cullinan, Healy was not displeased with the outcome and even complimented Cullinan at one point, 'giving the devil his due as a man of honour'. The meeting concluded with the formation of a new Clare Medical Association, to be governed by an important-sounding Medical Council.

But not even the catharsis of the Infirmary meeting and the new era signalled by the Medical Association was enough to heal the breach between the feuding doctors. When it erupted again at the end of 1852, however, the landscape had changed radically in many senses. Human attrition had brought the Famine to an agonized conclusion, and while the workhouse, auxiliaries and fever wards remained at a high level of occupancy, the demands on medical gentlemen had dropped sharply and continued to diminish. In May, Dr Hehir had died, as far as we know from causes other than epidemic disease, and in the aftermath of his passing, despite Cullinan's attempts to prevent it, Dr Healy succeeded him as second physician at the workhouse, for a provisional period of six months.[77]

Even though the appointment brought Healy and Cullinan physically closer to each other than either would have liked, confrontation was avoided for a time because the duties of each was distinct and their locations separate: Healy had responsibility for the 'parent' workhouse, Cullinan for a very large auxiliary called Keane's Store; in the fever wards and Turnpike Auxiliary, a shared premises, the former attended the male wards only, the latter the female patients.[78] When battle was joined again, in December, it was at a Board of Guardians meeting, and arose out of Cullinan's violent opposition to proposals to make the second physician's post a permanent one, an arrangement that would involve the reduction of his own salary from £65 to £50 per year, and the conferring of equal status and remuneration on the physician appointed, who most likely would be the sitting tenant, his deadly enemy, Dr Michael Healy.

The confrontation this time was very different from the County Infirmary stand-off, and instead of heated verbal exchanges and extempore sallies, there were prepared statements, circulated prior to the meeting, and responses that had been redacted accordingly. Even the body language, we infer, was not as agitated. Cullinan began by rereading a statement rehearsing the history of the salaries issue from his perspective, emphasizing that he had never been adequately paid for services performed during the Famine when he was badly overworked and in peril of his life; he was angered that his salary should now be reduced to the level of a newly appointed 'assistant' – by this last passing comment inflicting professional insult on Healy, a skilled and vastly experienced practitioner.

Under the pretext of exemplifying the danger of divided responsibilities, and without an accusation of any kind, the incorrigible Cullinan then managed to inculpate Healy in the recent incidence of smallpox in the children's wards and xerophthalmia in the women's section, both of which were under his opponent's care. It was cleverly and insidiously done, Cullinan having first exonerated himself and stated that Dr Healy would of course be 'equally prepared to vindicate himself', the implication being, notwithstanding his actual culpability. Our sympathy for Healy is of course lessened by our knowledge that he had not been averse to using similar tactics. Cullinan concluded by directly associating a massive cost increase in the workhouse infirmary dietary with Healy's assumption of duty there six months previously.

Aware that an angry reaction would have been counterproductive, in response Healy read a statement refuting each of Cullinan's 'insinuations', in orderly point-by-point manner. He paid particular attention to the wastefulness alleged against him in the matter of the infirmary dietary, a subject on which he knew the cost-obsessive Guardians would be sensitive. Moving on to challenge Cullinan's argument that where a lack of cordiality obtained between colleagues, a division of responsibilities would lead to 'very unseemly collisions and much confusion', he sought to prove that, on the contrary, a division of responsibilities in such circumstances would actually serve to identify any neglect that might occur. Professional men, he insisted, should be able to put aside personal rivalries in the performance of their duties, and 'although there was nothing he desired less than social intercourse with Dr Cullinan', yet 'on the neutral ground' of their common duties 'he would at all times be ready to meet him on terms of professional co-operation'.

He instanced two cases where consultation and cooperation had taken place between them, one a patient named James O'Connor who had a cancerous ulcer on his lip, the other a girl named Catherine O'Sullivan suffering from a peculiar dropsical condition. In both cases cooperation had been beneficial, and supported by Cullinan's opinion, he had operated successfully on James O'Connor, and he had transferred Catherine O'Sullivan's care entirely to Dr Cullinan. In general terms, he held that there was no reason why cooperation should not extend even further than consultations, and should Dr Cullinan's many other avocations take him from the hospital, he would gladly fill in for him.

But this ended the reasoned part of Healy's response, and it was followed by another personalized attack on his rival. Cullinan had quoted him as saying that the duties of the workhouse could be easily done by one individual, an opinion he still held, although certainly not by a man who 'in addition to extensive private practice, is engaged in the performance of duties of physician to the county gaol, of physician to the convict depot, and who holds the important office of coroner' (Cullinan had recently been elected to this office). Why, he wondered, had Cullinan earlier introduced the emolument received by Healy in his other post as a physician at the Ennis Dispensary which netted him a salary of £140 for the full year? Surely this had no more relevance than if he mentioned in relation to Dr Cullinan's claim for a continued salary of £65 per annum that he was also receiving £54 per annum as physician to the jail, a further 'large sum', as coroner, and a stipend of £10 per annum as physician to the convict depot, all paid for, added Healy, by the Guardians in their capacities as cess payers.

When the vote was taken Dr Healy was appointed permanent second medical attendant to the workhouse. He was to enjoy equal professional status with Cullinan, and each of them to have a salary of £50 per annum. Dr Cullinan, then, had lost a further round to Dr Healy and the two enemies were seemingly as bound together by physical proximity than ever they had been.

5

The Reverend Sinecurist: Henry Murphy

Like many diarists, if more than most, Reverend Henry Murphy was much concerned with the recording of weather, and each of his daily journal entries begins with a line or more of detail regarding its many variations: rain, wind, sunshine, cold, heat or humidity.[1] Reverend Murphy's climactic observations are unusually descriptive of their kind, and where they are, nuanced, as not infrequently they are towards the lyrical, it is almost as if some trapped poetic impulse is seeking to capture the essence of that individual day. But if this is indeed the case, it is the only hint we can find of a creative sensibility on the part of this unimaginative country clergyman, whose life was lived on the margins of significant events, even within the community in which he lived. Yet for all the tedium of the life which his diaries and the other documentation reveal, the minutiae of Reverend Murphy's daily round has a peculiar fascination of its own, even to the point where the angle of its perspective bears – strangely – on the Great Famine, the enormous social convulsion in the midst of which it proceeds.

When his diaries open in early 1844, Reverend Murphy had been Church of Ireland incumbent at Ennis (he was technically custodian of a Vicarial Union comprising Dromcliffe, Templemaley and Kilraghtis parishes) for over a year; before that he had briefly been headmaster of the Clergy Sons' School at Lucan; before that again he had been at Trinity College in Dublin, where he had spent an inordinately long twelve-year period in obtaining primary and Master's degrees.[2] For an ambitious clergyman with a wife and family, the Ennis curacy was not a particularly desirable posting, and certainly not one he intended to remain in for long. For one thing, although the annual tithe income of his parishes exceeded £600, a substantial sum (contributed by Catholics as well as by members of his own Church) it had to be shared with the Rector and Vicar, both of them absentees, and also with the junior curate and a number of lay impropriators.[3] For another, his principal ecclesiastical building, the Dromcliffe parish church at Ennis, was small and unprepossessing, consisting as it did of the nave of the town's venerable Friary oratory. The chancel, with its striking east window, was an unroofed ruin, the churchyard a weed-grown confusion of slanting tombstones and memorials.[4]

In the absence of a rectory Reverend Murphy rented a sprawling old residence called Green Park, just south of Ennis, where previous curates had stayed, and where he lived with his wife, Frances (Fanny), and his rapidly growing young children: Henry, Jane and Henrietta, together with a number of servants.[5] Another child, Emma, was born to the Murphys in 1845.[6] An auctioneer's inventory reveals a considerable level of material ease: the parlour and dining rooms contained suites of good furniture, the dining room boasted an elegant pianoforte, as well as sideboards and dinner table. All the downstairs rooms had Brussels carpets, fenders and fire irons, window curtains and blinds; the stairs was carpeted, with brass rods, and in the hall stood a handsome eight-day clock. The bedrooms were fitted out with dressing tables, bidets, looking glasses and free-standing wardrobes. Reverend Murphy also possessed a 500-volume library, consisting mainly of devotional and historical works.[7] Engravings purchased or won in competitions adorned the walls of Green Park's various apartments.

Reverend Murphy's clerical earnings being as meagre as they were, the domestic comfort indicated above was sustained only through exploitation of a variety of other income sources, including the stipends attaching to chaplaincies at the County Jail, the Union workhouse, the County Fever Hospital and County Infirmary, in addition to the proceeds of an extensive involvement in commercial agriculture. As well as this, although not at all in Dr P.M. Cullinan's league, Reverend Murphy was constantly in search of further revenue-generating employment: his most ambitious foray in this direction was when in September 1845, he applied for the presidency of one of the new Queen's Colleges, eventually dropping his application not because of any realization of under-qualification, but because 'a clerk [sic] would not be appointed'.[8]

But the presidency application was exceptional for Reverend Murphy, whose career aspirations were otherwise confined to Church office: while at Ennis he managed to secure appointments as Vicar of Kilmaley and Rector of Ogashin, for which there was emolument but little or no duty.[9] An attempt to add the living of Clare to these sinecures towards the end of 1844 by having his patron, Colonel George Wyndham, award it to him, failed when the Bishop of Killaloe challenged the legality of the Colonel's historical 'advowson' or right of presentation.[10]

By this time Reverend Murphy already owed Wyndham a great deal, and some years earlier the colonel had appointed him Inspector of his estate schools, thereby supplying yet another revenue stream to the hard-pressed curate. Although as an absentee, Wyndham cannot be considered one of the figures in our Famine landscape, he is of such significance to Reverend Murphy's story and at other points of the other narratives contained in this book that he merits further attention. By far the greatest owner of land in

Clare, Wyndham possessed a vast, but very fragmented estate of 37,000 acres scattered over ten of the county's eleven baronies, whose management he oversaw, in the most minute detail, from his great house at Petworth in Sussex, England, the centre of even vaster landed domains in that country.[11]

Wyndham was the illegitimate eldest son of the third earl of Egremont, who had no legitimate heirs. On entering his inheritance in 1839 he had set about a long-term programme of estate restructuring on both English and Irish properties, radically overhauling their administration and the living conditions of the tenants, into whose lives he intruded to a degree that was unusual among owners of Irish land and not very welcome to them. He would pursue this revenue maximizing programme with cold determination over succeeding decades, masking extreme and frequently inhumane methodologies under a guise of fatherly benevolence. In Ireland this involved the construction of estate schools and model farms, donations to public charities and to municipal projects and the poor, even as his ruthless coercion of unwilling 'surplus' tenants into emigration schemes passed for grand-scale philanthropic generosity.[12] During the Famine the consolidation of Wyndham land into larger units, which had begun years earlier as part of this process, would be extended in a number of strategic mass evictions, which for the most part escaped public attention or censure.[13]

On his own ground in Sussex the colonel was a depressive individual, whose dysfunctional upbringing manifested itself in many eccentric behaviours, as for example, the decades-long feud carried on with his brother Charles over fox-hunting rights at Petworth, an all-consuming obsession that he eventually resolved in one grand act of passionate intensity by the 'butchery' of all foxes in every one of the coverts.[14] His biographer and immediate twentieth-century descendant, the genial Max Egremont, acknowledged that George Wyndham was not an 'intelligent or [a] cultivated man'.[15]

In religious matters, Wyndham had a two-fold preoccupation, the first relating to his prosecution of historic rights to impropriate Church of Ireland temporalities, integral to his revenue-restructuring estate policies, and secondly a deference to the wishes of his deeply evangelical wife.[16] The first of these concerns we have seen in the failed presentation of Reverend Murphy to the living at Clare; Murphy speaks elsewhere of the colonel's proceedings in relation to twenty-eight livings, and the second may have been a factor in his attitudes during the Miltown schools' controversy which we shall look at towards the end of this chapter.[17] We can have little doubt but that Wyndham would have seen the religious and economic aspects of his estate restructuring as belonging to the same process.

For the landed gentry of Clare, unaware of the stranger side of Wyndham's personality, the enormous size of his landholdings commanded respect; his ruthless culling of tenantry and the thoroughness of his estate modernization would have elicited an approving awe, his philanthropic pose seen as an endearing condescension. For these mostly small-scale and inefficient landowners, Wyndham was a distant Olympian figure, whose rare visits to

Clare were regarded almost in terms of a divine descent, and so reported in John B. Knox's admiring *Clare Journal*.[18] Reverend Murphy, for his part, felt proud and privileged in his client status and liked to describe himself in correspondence on whatever subject as Inspector of Colonel Wyndham's Schools, a post in which at all times he displayed a meek deference towards his patron.

Even Murphy's agricultural pursuits, carried out on the twenty acres attached to Green Park (and probably on some rented conacre also), testified to his desire to please the colonel. Reverend Murphy's farming operations astonish us by their extent – on one occasion in March 1844 he speaks of employing no fewer than fourteen labourers, adults and children, at weeding and moulding up his early potatoes and in July 1845 sent twelve stone of his early crop to Ennis market and seventy-two further stone to Limerick.[19] His methods surprise us equally by their sophistication, and it is here that the Wyndham influence is most evident, since it cannot be accidental that the crop rotations employed (he mentions alternation of root crops such as turnips, mangelwurzels and rapeseed with grains such as wheat and barley) are so reminiscent of those Wyndham sought to promote among his tenants by demonstrations on his model farms, which we know Murphy visited.[20] We know also from his diaries that Reverend Murphy kept livestock, maintained a dairy and killed his own pigs.[21]

It may well be that Reverend Murphy spent more time farming than about his parochial duties, which were not onerous, involved church services for the most part, at Ennis and occasionally adjoining parishes, and an unhurried calendar of baptisms and weddings, prayers at burials and visits to sick parishioners. One night each week, he lectured on scriptural matters at the house of the devout Misses Keane in Jail Street, and we know that he regularly examined children at a Protestant school in Ennis, a role quite distinct from the inspectorial visits to Colonel Wyndham's estate schools in the west.[22] Finally, there was an ongoing involvement in certain religious organizations affiliated to the Church of Ireland, such as the Protestant Orphan Society, the Hibernian Bible Society and the Jewish Missionary Society, which are all mentioned plentifully in the diaries.[23]

On one occasion only do we catch sight of Reverend Murphy in full preaching mode, as captured in the travel book written by the wandering American Bible-reader Asenath Nicholson, who attended his Divine Service on a sunny Sunday morning in April 1845, in a church crowded with red-uniformed soldiers from the Clarecastle barracks. Mrs Nicholson does not seem to have been impressed one way or the other with Reverend Murphy's delivery – at least she does not praise his service – and she comments neutrally of the sermon (on the Last Judgement) that it was 'most solemn' and 'pointedly applied it to all classes, especially the rich, who bring up their children for this world'.[24]

Predictably, Reverend Murphy socialized most among his brother clerics, and there was a constant coming and going of clergymen and their families to Green Park. He was also received in the houses of the lesser gentry of the town and immediate environs, most of which feature in the diaries: Edenvale, Cahercalla, Greenlawn and New Hall, even if few of their owners are recorded as having visited Green Park, and those who did, infrequently; his social status of course was far too humble to have elicited invitations to the grander mansions of Kilrush House, Quinville Abbey or Dromoland Castle, which are not mentioned in the diaries. Murphy's closest social connections, however, were with two interrelated gentry families, the Pilkingtons of Water Park, Ennis and the Keanes of Beech Park, both families being committed to evangelical ideology, although in pre-Famine times, as far as we are aware, not on an active basis. Reverend Murphy's diary records happy familial gatherings at both these houses: high teas, christening parties and 'Harvest Homes', and one happy reception at Beech Park after the wedding of his young colleague, the junior curate, Reverend Charles Ward, to Miss Maria Keane, sister to Marcus Keane.[25] John Busteed Knox, a parishioner who undoubtedly attended his services on a very regular basis, does not feature in the diaries, although Knox faithfully printed a great deal of Church-related material sent him by Murphy.

Apart from his hired labourers, Reverend Murphy had little to do with the Catholic population of his wider community: contact with Catholic clergy on the other hand was frequent and the evidence suggests guardedly cordial on both sides. Like John B. Knox, Murphy was careful not to offend the aged, formidable Dean Terence O'Shaughnessy, parish priest of Ennis. He had done so shortly into his incumbency, after indiscreet remarks made at a meeting of the Protestant Orphan Society, where he had referred more than once to the need to preserve his young charges from the 'baleful [sic] influence of popery', so outraged had the Dean become as a result that he launched into a vituperative attack on Murphy in a letter obligingly printed by John B. Knox.[26] In the letter the Dean, clearly aware of Murphy's birth to Catholic parents in Lancashire, England, referred disdainfully to his convert background and his position as a 'reverend sinecurist', who so unjustly enjoyed a tithe income levied upon the Catholic population of parishes 'where your voice was never heard in prayer and your presence never felt but in the relentless exactions of what the law allows you to call your dues'.[27] Addressing the 'good sense' of Reverend Murphy's parishioners directly, the Dean had asked rhetorically if they would 'permit Mr Murphy to impair or destroy, by such indecent exhibitions, the existence of that repose from religious animosities', which now prevailed in the district.

It was a bitter response to a perceived insult and two years were to pass before the rancour generated by the incident had dissipated, when both men met in their capacities as chaplains to the County Jail and, according to Murphy, 'agreed to forget the past'; both indeed were soon promising each other full cooperation in a project to restore the east window of the Ennis Friary.[28] For what is to come later on in this chapter, the incident is a timely reminder of the sectarian passions eddying below the surface of apparent interdenominational calm in pre-Famine times.

During 1844 and 1845 then, Reverend Murphy's existence comprised a busy round of clerical duties, family life and farming activities, his movement through the landscape describing a well-worn pattern of visits paid and visits received; clerical duties performed and sick visits carried out; plantings and harvestings accomplished, and outings and sleepovers organized for the children. The routine varied little and was punctuated only by trips to Limerick and Dublin in pursuit of career opportunity. Reverend Murphy's movements were on foot, in his own car, the mail coach or Flannery's omnibus. It was a humming, self-contained little world-within-a-world, where even discordant reminders of a harsher world of social dissatisfaction brought twice yearly by the Assizes went largely hidden in the excitement of the arrival of scarlet-robed Barons, the weighty assembling of the County Grand Jury and the social occasions of Assizes Week.

The arrival of potato blight in autumn 1845 at first caused little stir in this world, and when Reverend Murphy began to dig out his main crop in mid-October, he found the tubers 'very fine' and 'very safe and good', even though he did register a 'very general complaint against a rot among the potatoes'.[29] A few days later, he speaks of 'a great outcry thro' the country about the potatoes', which was also 'general thro' England, the continent and America'. But life went on regardless, and in succeeding days, he stacked his oats, sowed an acre of red wheat, answered queries from the Ecclesiastical Commissioners on unspecified issues, bought a cow at Quin fair and drove in a funeral cortege as far as Spancil Hill, a respectable distance east of Ennis that allowed him then return home to tend his children, who had all gone down with influenza after a Harvest Home party at Beech Park.[30]

On 22 November, the potato failure intrudes briefly again in a reference to the County Meeting convened by the High Sheriff to discuss the crisis resulting from their loss; Reverend Murphy doesn't say if he attended, but we know from other sources that he was not among the speakers.[31] His priorities at this time were with harvest operations, and within a week of the County Meeting he tells us of having placed his mangolds and his field carrots in ricks and brought his Aberdeen turnips safely into the yard, leaving only the swedes still growing.[32]

After the securing of the harvests, there was little else to be done for the remainder of the year, December passing in a routine of ecclesiastical duties and meetings, the coming and going of dinner guests at Green Park and matters concerning the children. Reverend Murphy's most interested comments are reserved for the weather, Christmas Eve described as a 'very beautiful, fine day', while Christmas Day by contrast was 'a very gloomy, misty, murky, thick foggy, hazy day'. A week of storms followed Christmas, which is mentioned only for the religious duties he performs, the Reverend's greatest concern at year's end being the illness of his baby.[33]

Green Park, home of Reverend Murphy. Photo courtesy Rev. John Jones.

January 1846 opens for Reverend Murphy amidst the lulling monotony of domestic life, the only variation being an evening demonstration given by the celebrated phrenologist, Professor Alexander Wilson, who 'manipulated' the heads of Fanny and the children, the Reverend himself demurring. Some days later we find him dismissing a servant for neglecting his horse and recording a disappointing failure to have the Bishop of Killaloe appoint him to a desirable living at Toomevara, County Tipperary. A committee meeting of the County Fever Hospital held about the same time, at which Dr Healy accused the apothecary of impropriety, turned out to be no more than 'a bottle of smoke', while little Henry caused infinitely greater bother by bolting himself into a dressing room, occasioning hours of toil on his father's part before he could be released. Towards the end of the month he spent several days examining the children at Colonel Wyndham's estate school at Caherush, all against a background of cold, wet, windy, miserable weather.[34]

Reverend Murphy was out and about again in the second week of February for the commencement of agricultural operations, shaking out his manure for the early potatoes which were sowed over several weeks, a task at which he spent entire days.[35] A short interval of cold weather provided the opportunity to construct a 'car road' through his meadow, all the while normal parochial duties had to be tended to. One of these was a christening for a colleague, Dr Luke White King of the Ennis Erasmus Smith School, the ceremony followed by a pleasant evening celebration to which Reverend Murphy and wife brought wine and cakes.[36]

Mid-March brought the realities of encroaching Famine closer to Reverend Murphy than at any time since the appearance of blight. On the sixteenth, a 'squally, blustery day', he attended a public meeting called 'to supply work for the poor', the proceedings of which went unreported, crowded from the newspapers by the murder the following day of the land agent Pierce Carrick near Spancil Hill.[37] Carrick had been shot several times from behind a wall and lingered for twenty-four hours at a nearby gentleman's residence. Called out in a snowstorm early that night to minister to the dying man, Reverend Murphy was present at his death later on, in company with Dr Patrick Maxwell Cullinan.[38] Murphy was also the officiating clergyman at Carrick's burial in the frost-hardened ground of his own churchyard a few days later, a fact he records that evening in his diary, as he does the arrival in Ennis of a troop of Hussars dispatched to keep the peace in the aftermath of the murder.[39]

Reverend Murphy is less revealing about his involvement in the government relief programme, which was about this time lumbering into grudging motion. From other sources, we know that by virtue of his clerical status he was *ex-officio* member of two relief committees, the Central Committee for Inchiquin and Islands baronies, and the Ennis District Committee, both of which held inaugural meetings at the end of March.[40] Having spent the day ('a most delightful day') earmarked for the first meeting sick in bed, he was recovered enough to attend the second committee the following day; he did not participate in its proceedings.[41] His diary entry for that night, a Friday, focuses on a dinner at the house of Tom Keane, Marcus's brother, in a company which included Captain Davenport and Mr Bell, the two officers in charge of the Hussar troop, Mr and Mrs Johnson of the Bank, a Captain Hunter and a trio belonging to a prominent land agent family, Wainwright Crowe, his brother Captain Crowe and the captain's wife.[42]

There are no more references to relief committees in the diary, either under the Peelite regime or the Whig-Liberal one that followed, and it is clear that unlike so many other Protestant parish clergymen during the Famine, Reverend Murphy was not at any stage an active member on either of his committees. We know that at the end of March he did subscribe £5 to the Ennis Relief Committee which did not, it should be said, want for forceful leadership; probably Murphy's unassertive nature would have made him more of a hindrance than a help to the Committee's work in any case.[43]

On 29 March 1846 Reverend Murphy again became ill, this time with an unnamed abdominal indisposition, for which he took some 'blue pills'; when this did not work he had blisters applied to his stomach, and later again, no fewer than six leeches.[44] The illness passed within a few days, but at that point Mrs Murphy and the children came down with severe coughing which worsened as the week wore on, Mrs Murphy also having to be leeched and a blister placed between her shoulders at night. The Green Park household was much disrupted by these illnesses, and visiting clergymen had to be put up at Collins's Hotel; religious services were curtailed and rescheduled. Through it all, however, Reverend Murphy still managed to plant his oat crop and his clove seeds and to begin the sowing of his maincrop potatoes.[45]

In May the weather alternated between dark 'lowering' days with 'charming' sunny ones. For Reverend Murphy it was a pleasant time, filled with the satisfying minor routines of family and social circle. Three sequential entries towards the middle of the month capture the general mood[46]:

> Tuesday 12 May: The morning and all last night extremely wet – most charming after 10 o'clock a.m. Mr and Mrs. Vard and I drove to Quin Glebe to dine. Fanny and Mena came from Clare Glebe. John Blood Smyth came after dinner. We dropped Fanny and Mena at Clare Glebe. The aurora borealis very fine.
>
> Wednesday 13 May: A very fine day (from ½ past 12 o'clock to ½ past 1 extremely wet). J. Coffey (the Irish professor at Stackallen) came from Limerick to see me (he was an Eton pupil). I walked to Clare to bury a soldier of the 66 th. Dined at the glebe, walked home at night.
>
> Thursday 14 May: A very fine morning, a little windy. Fanny went to Limerick to purchase the summer 'wearables'. Jane, Hannah and I dined at Water Park. Had a note from Fanny to say that F. Studdert was to be home early on Saturday. She leaves tomorrow.

We look in vain in these entries, and indeed in any and all others from the summer months, for any consciousness of the distress we know to have existed in Reverend Murphy's immediate vicinity; we would be more surprised with the absence had we not already encountered something similar in John Singleton, and to an extent even in John B. Knox during the same months. Since other diarists elsewhere in Ireland exhibit a similar lack of awareness at this time, what seems to be in question is a general trend among social classes unaffected by want.[47]

The high summer of 1846 then would appear to have been a period of great personal contentment for Reverend Murphy, and we are left with very little reason for any qualifying notion of psychological retreat as we do in the case of John Singleton. In a number of cases, indeed, where Reverend Murphy's diary entries seem to group themselves in natural units or scenes, a remarkable sense of well-being emerges, most strikingly where remarks about the weather are juxtaposed with details of agricultural tasks in hand, the harmonious effect produced rather incongruous in a man so poorly endowed with imagination. One example from early June features an entry series that begins with a description of a scorching hot

Friday noontime, when a 'great change' was suddenly apparent, the day growing extremely hazy and close, a few drops of rain falling towards evening – the wheat, he tells us, 'partially in ear'. The next day he found a few of his early potatoes to be already in blossom, and the Monday following he began to mow the billowing expanse of clover and rye grass that comprised one of his meadows, a task with which he was occupied for two full days.[48]

The same sense of contentment is evident in excursions to the country, as for example, an outing some weeks later to scenic Lough Cutra, near Gort, the party consisting of Murphy, his wife Fanny and the girls, assorted clergymen and their wives, and John B. Knox's friend, the landlord Thomas Mahon. After a pleasant day spent ensemble in green and lovely landscapes, all were happily at home by nine o'clock in the evening.[49] Another pleasant interlude centres around a dinner party which the Murphys attended at Cahircalla, the residence of Wainright Crowe, on 9 July, where young people comprised the attendance for the most part: a Miss Parkinson, a young gentlemen named Frederick Morris, the Kilkee magistrate, Jonas Studdert and his cousin Fitzgerald, a young subaltern in the eighty-fifth regiment, along two of the latter's brother officers. In the evening Miss Stacpoole of Edenvale arrived, with her brother, William and a friend, a Miss Carr.[50]

Another scene again is set at the end of July, in west Clare, where Reverend Murphy was doing duty for clergymen absent on leave and availing of the opportunity of taking in the balmy loveliness of the coastline from Kilrush to Kilkee. The trip included an inspection of Colonel Wyndham's Caherush school in the company of the Kilrush incumbent, Reverend Young, where following the established pattern, he distributed 'premiums' of good clothing to the children.[51] The day following both men went to Kilrush quay to view the hissing mechanical wonder of the government steamer, *Rhadamanthus*, which had been involved in grain-carrying duties along the coast.[52] All of these places were now deeply affected by distress, no sense at all of which finds its way to the pages of Reverend Murphy's diary.

In mid-August after weeks of changeable weather, warm and close days and nights, the rain became heavy and continuous, with thundery downpours, the kind of weather that favoured potato blight, which for weeks now had been ravaging the growing potatoes all over Ireland for the second. Reverend Murphy was remarkably fortunate that his growing potatoes had so far been spared. The countryside became flooded, although during momentary respites Murphy was able to stack his oats.[53] At this point, almost simultaneously, two major developments combined to effect a major change in his life. The first of these was a decision to surrender the Ennis curacy and seek his ecclesiastical fortune elsewhere. Over the previous month he had been much in the company of senior Church figures in Limerick and Killaloe dioceses, including both bishops and the Killaloe dean, we suppose with an eye to securing a better living.[54] But it had all came to nothing, and he was now in communication with the Trustees of the Clergy Sons' School in Lucan, with a view to returning to the headmastership he had left only four years previously. The second event was his discovery, on a very wet morning of 20 August, just after he had posted a letter regarding the Lucan headmastership, that his growing maincrop potatoes, which were not due for harvesting for several months yet, were 'extensively diseased'. Early potatoes which he had been keeping for next year's seed were also badly damaged.[55]

The loss of Reverend Murphy's maincrop potatoes represented a major blow to his domestic economy and was probably the deciding factor in the decision to leave Ennis for Lucan. It was also heartbreaking for being unexpected, in that seems clear that he thought he had escaped the general destruction earlier. Only a few weeks earlier his harvested early potatoes had been healthy, and he had sold a cartload in the Ennis market for seven pence a stone, the usual high price associated with the scarce first potatoes of the season.[56] So important were the potatoes to Reverend Murphy, in fact, that his immediate reaction on learning of their destruction was to dig out all those remaining in the ground and send them into the market, unbothered apparently by ethical considerations regarding the offering for sale of diseased tubers to buyers who could not know they would be rotten by the following day.[57]

At first sight, the last months of Reverend Murphy's curacy seem little different from what had gone before – a routine of agricultural tasks and parish duties interspersed by social visits and pleasure excursions, in addition to solo trips farther afield. One notable occasion was a picnic outing he attended with Mrs Murphy, within days of learning of his harvest disaster, at the leafy demesne of Cahercon on the Shannon estuary, the party consisting of Tom, Mary and Frank Studdert, Marcus Keane and two of his friends, a Mr Bedford and a Mr Bloxham. On the way home, the group dropped in to see Miss Arthur at the aptly named Paradise estate at Ballinacally, also on the Shannon, the entire party ending the evening over tea at Green Park.[58] Murphy's last major solo outing while curate came in mid-October, when he travelled to Borrisokane, north Tipperary, on business related to his acceptance of the Lucan headmastership, when he availed of the opportunity to do some sightseeing. At Birr Castle he gazed up at Lord Rosse's 'monster' telescope and managed to gain access to Finnoe Glebe, gawping like any modern tourist at the apartments where a grisly double murder had recently taken place.[59]

But at the same time, the decision to leave lent Reverend Murphy's activities in these months a restless valedictory air, most evident in the case of his agricultural pursuits where winding-up tasks predominate – harvesting without consideration for next year's sowing and the transfer of stock to grazing elsewhere. No doubt Murphy's anxiety to depart for calmer regions was sharpened by apprehension of the mass death by starvation which was now inevitable and had indeed already begun hardly a stone's throw from Green Park, heralded by scenes of protest and hunger-related disorder from which even he could no longer avert his eyes. On Monday 5 October ('a very fine day'), he notes 'a very large assemblage of people in town', and three days later, in stormy, squally weather, records 'vast collections of people coming up from Clare', as well as the arrival of another detachment of dragoons. To read these entries is to hear the faintest echoes of what we know from other sources to have been a vast convulsive reactive movement of a hungry, frightened population at that time, involving public meetings, crowd demonstrations and hunger marches. Terrifying for the poor caught up in it, it was stressful to those who saw it, and when Reverend Murphy writes of spending the day after the second of these two entries in bed with a 'sick headache', we may postulate a psychological origin for this indisposition, just as we might indeed for those others mentioned earlier.[60] Murphy did not attend a meeting held a few days later to reorganize the relief committees under the new Whig-Liberal programme.[61]

On Thursday morning, 23 October, Reverend Murphy rode his mare thirty miles eastwards to Killaloe and placed his formal written resignation of the Ennis curacy directly into the hands of the Bishop of Killaloe. Afterwards he travelled on to Limerick where he stayed at Cruise's Hotel and arrived back in Ennis the following morning in time to attend 'a great meeting of the magistrates and clergy to consider the destitution of the poor and the disturbed state of the county'.[62] As before, he made no verbal contribution from the floor.[63]

Among the events recorded in his diaries in succeeding weeks were the dismissal of Signor Volatti, his church organist, for scurrilous remarks allegedly made about his friend Dr Luke White King, and a brief journey to Dublin where he heard the preaching of three famous Anglican divines, Gregg, Luby and Krause (the latter, Reverend Murphy comments, was 'very hum-drum').[64] On 1 December, his appointed successor, Reverend Williamson, arrived in search of a house to rent in Ennis, and a few days later Reverend Murphy had him to dinner at Green Park, in a most respectable, and no doubt, deadly dull company that included both clergymen and two of the town bank managers, Messrs Menzies and Palmer.[65]

By mid-December preparations for departure were well advanced: his children had been dispersed to other houses; his wife had gone to her mother's and the nurse and baby had been installed in a lodging house, Reverend Murphy himself being 'engaged all day preparing for my auction'. The auction took place at Green Park over two days and was much to Murphy's satisfaction ('things sold very well').[66] The house now uninhabitable, he made one last visit to the west, preaching at Kilrush and calling at Caherush school where 'reward clothing' was again distributed. The days leading up to Christmas Day and ensuing days were a flurry of farewell visits, and finally, on 28 December ('a very fine day'), Reverend Murphy left Ennis by Flannery's coach, taking his wife, young Henry and Margaret the maid, the others having left earlier. Arriving in Limerick they took the mail coach to Kildare and from there the train to Dublin. On New Year's Day 1847, Reverend Murphy was at his desk in the Clergy Sons' School in Lucan, ready to take up his duty as headmaster.[67]

Glad as he was to leave Ennis, he chose not to return for the customary presentation by his parishioners of an address of thanks but received it and replied to it instead by post. The testimonial document, to which some fifty signatures were appended, including those of John B. Knox and James Knox Walker, Marcus Keane's younger brother Henry and the Misses Keane, is lacking in the effusive warmth that was the rule on such occasions; the framers of the document may not have been on particularly close terms with their pastor. At any rate, they wrote of having had the 'privilege' of being under Reverend Murphy's ministry for several years, and now that the 'labour of love' had come to an end, they acknowledged the 'faithful manner' in which as Minister of the Gospel he had discharged the sacred trust committed to him, recognizing also his 'zeal and ability' in performing 'all the relative duties of Parish Minister'. In the new sphere of duty to which the Lord had called him he carried with him their 'sincere and most affectionate regards, and anxious prayers for the temporal and spiritual welfare' of himself and his 'amiable' family.

Reverend Murphy's longer reply combined gratitude with a certain self-inflating sermonizing; having cited the scriptural admonition that it was not 'he that commendeth himself' or was 'commended by men' who would ultimately be justified but he 'whom the Lord commendeth', he nevertheless went on to commend himself, for faithfulness in preaching the Gospel of Salvation: 'I have kept nothing back from you', he wrote, 'I have, according to the grace bestowed upon me, made known to you the whole counsel of God; and that too not only in my public addresses, but also from house to house'. He 'earnestly and affectionately' beseeched them to take care of what they had heard. '[I] would therefore in love exhort you to be followers of me, as I am of Jesus Christ', he declared, praying God 'to grant that this testimony may not rise in judgement against any, but that if there be one whose ear the sound has hitherto fallen unheeded, he may be awakened to light and life'.[68]

After his departure from Clare Reverend Murphy retained just one link with the county, his supervision of the Caherush school, which for the Inspector of Colonel Wyndham's Schools was a position that was too prestigious and no doubt too lucrative to relinquish. Twice each year he appeared in the west to examine the pupils, although it is not until October 1849 that we get any idea of the educational formation obtaining at the school, courtesy of a *Clare Journal* report of one examination ceremony. More importantly for our purposes is that the report is useful in locating Colonel Wyndham's estate schools within the colonel's grand overall design for his properties, as also indeed the specific role assigned Reverend Murphy within it.

Total enrolment at Caherush, we are told, stood at about 150 pupils, the boys' school being separate from the girls', the children taught all that was to be learned 'in the various branches of an English education', including basic literacy and numeracy skills and reading. Agricultural methods formed an important component of the boys' education, to which purpose a small library was annexed to the school, containing relevant technical works. The girls were taught domestic crafts, especially needlework, knitting and quilting, and here the reporter was much taken with one project currently in hand, the production of a 'costly and elegantly finished silk quilt overlaid with very fine net work'. A little indiscreetly perhaps he revealed this was intended as a present from Reverend Murphy to Mrs Wyndham.

The reporter was careful to inform his readers that in the area of scriptural knowledge the children's accomplishments bore comparison with those of any school in Ireland, by which was meant any Protestant school, since scripture reading did not form part of Catholic educational practice. The Caherush school, according to the reporter, was a credit to the teachers, Mr and Mrs Samuel Ball, although we know from other sources that it was Reverend Murphy, as much manager as Inspector, who was the real mover and shaker; it was he who had hired both teachers and supervised the curriculum over many years. He could not but have been pleased at the glowing picture painted by the reporter of smiling well-clad schoolchildren, happily choosing their 'reward' clothing from a selection laid out on benches by Mr Henry Elliott, the Ennis woollen draper whom he had employed to supply them.

The *Clare Journal* report, of course, was a puff piece written when James Knox Walker's influence on the newspaper was still strong, and it was designed we can be confident to counteract current negative publicity attaching to the reputation of the school's owner. For the previous week Colonel Wyndham had carried out a devastating clearance about twenty road miles to the south-east, at Lissycasey, where his agent, Reverend Murphy's friend and not infrequent dinner companion, Tom Crowe, had unleashed his wreckers on the smallholder community there, violently expelling some seventy-eight families from their homes.[69]

At least as many youngsters of school-going age were among the families evicted at Lissycasey as were at the same time filling the classrooms at Caherush, and the contrast in the treatment accorded these two sets of children furnishes a disturbing illustration of the cold ruthlessness implicit in Wyndham's estate improvement policies. On the one hand, we find him actively eliminating social strata deemed irretrievably impoverished and lazy, and on the other actively moulding the 'better' tenants and their families through basic education and agricultural training into an industrious yeomanry, rent-rich and valuation-enhancing, who could gradually be brought to civilized ways, and in time, subtly, to the truths of the Protestant religion.

The Caherush children, to be sure, were immeasurably better-off than their Lissycasey counterparts, who were left to perish with their parents by the roadside. But no matter what their level of material well-being may have been, they were present in the school only because their parents had been coerced into sending them there, not daring to oppose the wishes of their all-powerful landlord. For his part, the colonel was so pleased at the school's apparent success that he instructed Reverend Murphy to establish another one in neighbouring Miltown Malbay, which would serve a substantial Wyndham tenant body in that parish.[70] And it was this school that, almost from the moment it opened early in 1851, became the centre of a bitter inter-denominational controversy, in which Reverend Murphy would play a significant if safely distant sideline role. The dispute, in addition, reveals quite a different facet to Reverend Murphy from that to which we have become accustomed.

The Glandine dispute arose out of allegations that the teachers, Samuel and Mrs Ball, who had been transferred by Reverend Murphy from Caherush, were actively interfering with the Catholic beliefs of their young charges, and it first emerged as one of many elements in an ongoing controversy in the general Miltown Malbay area, between certain Bible-reader converts and their clerical-evangelical backers on one side, and the Miltown priests and their angry partisans on the other. Soon, however, the dramatic developments at Glandine saw the school issue eclipse virtually all other aspects of this low-level localized 'souper' conflict. This was so because of the direct physical confrontations between the larger-than-life chief protagonists, the intemperate Samuel Ball and the equally fanatical Miltown curate, Father John Fahy. It was Ball and Fahy who played starring roles in the most famous and very unedifying episode of the dispute, the mounted altercation of September 1853 in which priest tried to horsewhip proselytizer from his saddle, causing both men to tumble to the ground, Fahy ending up at the bottom of a drain and both men subsequently in court.[71]

Largely because Reverend Murphy and Colonel Wyndham categorically denied that any proselytizing activity took place at the school, historians have been inclined to tiptoe around the allegations, generating by default the conclusion that it did not in fact take place. But, in fact, a close examination of all the evidence leaves little doubt but that it did, and even if we did not have this very strongly suggestive documentation, the wider context of a district saturated with Bible societies, scripture readers and financial backing, as also Wyndham's anti-Catholicism, and Murphy's convert origins, it would have been surprising indeed if some attempt at suborning the children's religious beliefs had not taken place.[72] And there is also the fact, rarely if ever raised by commentators, that even passive exposure of Catholic children to carefully selected scripture readings, 'without note or comment', by committed evangelical personnel in a manner repugnant to

Catholic practice – which all agree took place – of itself constituted a direct act of proselytism.

It is true also to say that scholarly focus on the question of proselytism at Glandine has tended to ignore the greater context of Colonel Wyndham's great socio-economic engineering programme, of which it was a part, and in which, in classic fashion, the Bible and economic prosperity went hand in hand. At ground level, this programme was implemented by land agents such as Tom and Wainwright Crowe, and by Reverend Murphy and Samuel Ball in their respective spheres, none of them individually having much of a conception of its overall ramifications.

Reverend Murphy's limited, but undeniable understanding of his place in this scheme of things is to be found at many points of his correspondence with Colonel Wyndham and Samuel Ball, as exemplified in one letter written to Ball some weeks after the embarrassing horseback tussle, in which he seeks, timorously, to restrain Ball's aggressive tendencies which are proving destructive to all.[73] 'Now, sir,' he lectures the Glandine schoolmaster, 'I must again repeat that my sole object in the stringent caution I gave was to prevent the recurrence of such things, knowing how injurious they would be ... to the success of the good work in which we are all engaged, viz. to civilize and enlighten the population of Miltown'. His particular understanding of the need for the civilizing and enlightenment of Miltowners is amplified in another letter in which he describes them as a 'rude and barbarous' people.[74]

Reverend Murphy would continue to serve God and Colonel at Caherush and Glandine for some years, even as under pressure from the Miltown Catholic clergy attendance at both schools went into steep decline; but we leave him in a last diary entry made in June 1855 when after examining 'the few children at Caherush' and still fussing over the weather ('a very fine day') he sets off for the more peaceable and more secure living he has at last obtained at the other end of the island, in County Down.[75]

6

The Exterminator General: Marcus Keane of Beech Park

Some time after his death in October 1883, the burial vault containing the remains of Marcus Keane was broken into by night and the remains removed. Despite an intensive search by constabulary and military no trace of them was found, and even when recovered eight years later under the sensational circumstances related in Chapter 10 of this book, the identity and motivation of the perpetrators remained a mystery. To this day, however, tradition in the Beech Park area insists that the theft of the remains was a deliberate and symbolic act of desecration, carried out by local people for whom the deceased in his lifetime had been the focus of the most intense loathing and dread. For Marcus Keane was the Famine-era 'exterminator' *par excellence*, a powerful land agent and landlord who carried out a massive eviction programme in those calamitous years, causing immense human suffering and the deaths of thousands of men, women and children.

Today Marcus Keane's name, for so long etched in popular consciousness, is largely forgotten, and even in the parishes surrounding his abandoned Beech Park demesne, few tales of his deeds survive. In west Clare, where the ruin of his summer residence, Doondahlin, still broods down over the tiny settlement of Kilbaha, recollection is somewhat sharper, but relates less to clearances *per se* than to Marcus's connection with the bitter interlude of evangelical proselytism that took place there at the end of the Famine, and the concerted effort with which he was associated in coercing tenant families under his economic control into abandoning their religious beliefs for Protestantism.

But Marcus Keane's historical significance is defined much less by his proselytizing activities than by his clearances, whose scale was such as to cause mass population displacement as well as mass death and a transformation of the landscapes in which they took place. Traces of this transformation can still be found today in districts where squared-off field systems and the ghosts of eliminated homesteads and villages are still discernible to the eye. Keane's story, as that of his younger brother Henry, whose reputation in the oral tradition is more sinister again, is important both as a narrative of the Famine era and for the light it sheds on that especially grim period at its end and in its aftermath which has yet to be examined in detail by historians.

Marcus Keane was the sixth son of Robert Keane of Beech Park, a Protestant land agent with a modest property of his own. The Keanes were of mixed Gaelic Irish/English settler stock, his father's the bearers of an ancient lineage. In antiquity the Mac Catháin of Termon had been hereditary custodians of the patrimony of St Senan, the great sixth-century ecclesiastic of west Clare, in the mid-nineteenth still the object of great veneration among the people. The Keane family owned Scattery Island, the site of Senan's monastery, and all his adult life Marcus retained possession of the *Clogán Óir*, the Shrine of St Senan's Bell.[1] The Keane genealogy, however, is much more heavily dominated by landed gentry of pre-1641 English settler, Cromwellian and Old English antecedents, and by Marcus's time all that remained of the family's Gaelic cultural heritage was the anglicized surname. The sense of Irishness Marcus carried was that of Protestant gentlemen generally, one subordinate to a wider Englishness, which was much as his tenants would have seen him. Marcus did not speak Irish and his later ventures into antiquarian matters were full of egregious misunderstandings of the language and the Gaelic tradition.[2]

Although the Keanes were resident in the Ennis area since the mid-seventeenth century, it was Marcus's father, Robert Keane, who built Beech Park about 1800 and established the land agency that his son inherited on his death in 1839. Robert Keane had been held in good regard, affectionately known to the country people as 'Robert Fada' or 'Long Bob', and on more than one occasion, Marcus's critics would cite the decency of Long Bob as an instructive contrast with the evil nature of his son.[3] Marcus's older brother, Dr Charles Keane, as we have seen, died heroically tending to cholera victims in the great outbreak of 1832.

We know little of Marcus's formative years or education, nor indeed why it was he and not one of his older brothers who inherited Beech Park and the agency. He first comes to our attention in the year of his father's death when he was elected to the inaugural Board of the Ennis Poor Law Guardians.[4] Even though he was not returned at the next election, his appointment to the county magistracy soon brought him back to the Board as *ex-officio* Guardian for the Inch division.[5]

Towards the mid-1840s and into the early Famine years references to Marcus Keane in the sources become more plentiful, and perhaps surprisingly, these are all favourable, in their portrayal of what appears to be a conscientious young gentleman gradually assuming the weight of his public and estate responsibilities. In 1844, we see him first in public, giving formal testimony before the Devon Commission on landlord–tenant relations (to the effect that there was 'no need' for evictions).[6] Subsequently we come across him occasionally sitting inconspicuously on the Bench and in the first year of Famine serving, diligently, we suppose, on relief committees in different localities. He tenders well-received advice to government officials on relief administration, and as agent acts as the willing conduit of the liberality of his client landlords, contributing on their behalf to relief funds and providing employment to a hard-pressed tenantry.[7]

A letter written to the *Clare Journal* in July 1846 by Patrick Mullins of Gortbofarna, Inagh, a tenant on the estate of Nicholas Westby, one of Marcus's most important clients, attests to the agent's own benevolence. According to Mullins, Marcus Keane had rescued his large family from the 'lowest state of indigence' a number of years before and since then had repeatedly come to his assistance in difficult seasons.[8] 'So thro' Mr. Keane's kindness and assistance,' Mullins wrote, 'I have rents paid, my gardens tilled, milk to feed my children and myself. I have a horse to draw lime and sand, tho' in the year of 1843, I could not till one rood of ground'. Marcus also makes thoughtful suggestions on the topic of agricultural improvement and in January 1847 outlined a loan scheme enabling impoverished small farmers buy seed, thereby allowing them to cultivate their holdings in the next season.[9] Before a County Meeting in Ennis he advocates a scheme for organized emigration from distressed areas.[10]

As if to round off this disarming portrait of public and private virtue on the part of the young squire, there are also indications of popularity among the country people, as recorded on Marcus's wedding in November 1847, to Louisa, daughter of Nicholas Westby.[11] For Marcus, the marriage was a brilliant one that greatly enhanced his standing among the Clare gentry and his career as agent. Returning to Beech Park after the honeymoon, the young couple was greeted by a large gathering of tenants, among whom 'great excitement' was reported to prevail, 'through their anxiety to testify their esteem for their landlord and his lady, and the joy they felt at their arrival':

> A large number of them went to meet Mr. Keane, and were anxious to be allowed to draw his carriage to Beech Park, to which, however, he would not consent. On Wednesday night, bonfires were kindled in the neighbourhood, and every other means in their power were resorted to by the tenants to manifest their gratification and delight.

Charmed by the modesty of the groom and his gracious condescension towards an affectionate peasantry, the *Clare Journal* was moved to remark on the pleasure of witnessing 'such a good understanding between landlord and tenant'.[12]

The picture sketched by these sources, however, is wholly deceptive and fails to withstand even the cursory examination occasioned by puzzlement at the apparent disparity with Marcus's later behaviour. For one thing, much of the positive commentary comes from the *Clare Journal*, a landlord newspaper, whose default position, notwithstanding John B. Knox's own denunciation of gentry failings, was to present them in the best light possible. There is also the underlying fact that the very paucity of references to Marcus in this period reflects not so much a youthful diffidence as a chronic neglect of his duties towards the Bench, the Board of Guardians and the relief committees.

In addition, the plaudits of relief officials assume a different aspect entirely when the character of the two individuals in question becomes apparent: Captain Edmond Wynne, with whom we already have some familiarity, and one of his successors, the naval captain, S. Gardiner Fishbourne, men whose rigid, extreme views on relief issues mirrored those of Marcus himself.[13] One can speculate indeed on the extent to which the peculiar harshness displayed by both towards the poor whose misery they were appointed to relieve was shaped or exacerbated by conversations at Beech Park, where we know both dined at different times.[14]

Similarly, the moneys spent by Marcus on relief employment and donated to relief committees on behalf of his two most important clients, Nicholas Westby and the Marquis of Conyngham, were meagre given the enormous rental of each of these absentee magnates; and significantly, there are no references at all to relief schemes funded by Marcus himself. And whatever the short-term benefits conferred on Patrick Mullins by Marcus, it is an ominous fact that within less than ten years, no trace is found of Mullins, his family or anyone of that name at Gortbofarna or indeed anywhere else.[15]

As regards Marcus's seed purchase and emigration schemes, neither was original or practical; much of the published detail indeed was incoherent to the point of unintelligibility. And at the same time as he was setting forth these schemes, the smallholders of Clare were verging on total ruin, and the cottiers and labourers who were excluded from his calculations were dying in their thousands in the first horrific cycle of Famine mortality then sweeping through the country. Against this background, Marcus's theorizing was as grotesque as it was irrelevant, furnishing an early example of an inability on his part to empathize with, or even recognize human suffering in his immediate vicinity, no matter how obvious or now searing it might be. During the clearances this would emerge as one of his most notable traits.

The final part of this picture to disintegrate under scrutiny is the set-piece return of Marcus to Beech Park with his young bride. As we have seen with regard to the Singleton homecoming of 1840, such occasions formed part of a set of self-justifying rituals cherished by county families when celebrating family occasions, whether weddings, homecomings or the attainment of majorities. In contrast to the Singleton event, however, with its subtleties of feeling towards a landlord who was not feared, the Keane occasion is much more clear-cut; and one does not at all need to question the accuracy of the newspaper report – the 'rejoicings' of the greeters, their expressions of esteem for the married couple and Marcus's apparent modesty in not allowing his carriage to be drawn home – to realize that given the enormous power wielded by him, it would have been an unwise tenant indeed who would have failed to simulate the required level of joyous enthusiasm.

If economic power can be measured by acreage controlled, then by the time of his marriage, Marcus Keane was already very powerful indeed, more so by far than any other individual involved in landownership or management in Clare. Agent to the great Westby, Conyngham and Henn estates, as well as a number of smaller ones, the first three properties alone amounted to over 60,000 acres.[16] In 1853, Henry Keane estimated that at the height of the clearances, his brother managed between 140,000 and 150,000 acres; decades later Marcus would himself testify before the Bessborough Commission that his agency extended, even at that time, to 100,000 acres.[17] In addition to the agency, there was also the Beech Park estate, which amounted to about 4,800 acres in 1876 (some of this may have been acquired in post-Famine times), and a number of leased farms about which we know very little. Even without the agency, therefore, in his own right as landlord and middleman, Marcus was a man of prominence.[18] If one combines the power he exercised in all these capacities, taking account also of the fact that Irish land agents enjoyed an unusual level of autonomy – Marcus freely acknowledged this in his own case – then it is not to be wondered that a later, if hostile, commentator should have compared his relationship to his own and his clients' tenants as that of a tsar to his subjects.[19]

Through the early years of the Famine the Keane agency grew rapidly, and by the end of 1847 it was noticed that lesser landowners in west Clare were transferring their properties to it because of Marcus's developing reputation as 'a stringent and successful collector of rents'.[20] This drift to Keane management (the agency operated only in Clare) certainly took place in other parts of the county also: so many landlords of this level were now experiencing a sustained drop in rental income as a result of tenant failure to pay rents that the employment of a ruthless agent such as Marcus was known to be appeared to present their only means of staving off financial ruin. Such landlords could not have doubted that large-scale evictions would form part of the agent's strategy for restoring their fortunes.

In the waves of evictions that took place in Ireland in the years after 1847 no county endured more than did Clare.[21] From 1849, the first year for which we have reliable statistics, until 1854 nearly one tenth of its population experienced permanent expulsion from their homes, the Kilrush Union in the west being particularly afflicted.[22] When it is remembered that the campaign was already well under way when statistics were first collected, some idea is obtained of the enormity of the population loss and displacement involved. Staggering though the statistics are, they give little insight into the agonies suffered by the evicted; the appallingly squalid conditions in which so many died; the annihilation of entire communities, and the transformation of great stretches of the landscape to bleak, unkempt moorland, much of it remaining tenantless for years afterwards.[23]

Tenant insolvency alone cannot account for the unprecedented scale of the Famine clearances, nor the savagery with which they were carried out; and among the other relevant factors, the Poor Law itself was the most significant. Its funding tax, the Poor Law rate, carried greatest liabilities for landlords of poorer tenants, from whose rents it could no longer be recovered. Legislation passed in mid-1847 made matters worse by shifting the entire burden of relief onto the Poor Law, fuelling landlord fears that their rates would rocket upwards. In such a situation, for many the only alternative to financial ruin was the eviction of their smallholders and the elimination of each of their rate-bearing holdings.

Wealthier landlords, who were not under the same economic pressure, were drawn to mass clearance as the logical extension of estate improvement policies begun years before. For such individuals, the Famine brought the opportunity for the consolidation of smallholdings to an extent previously considered desirable but morally indefensible and in any case physically impossible given the certainty of tenant resistance. After several years of famine the poor were no longer physically capable of any effective response to landlord assault, while a massive level of tenant rent-default furnished landlords with the moral justification for mass eviction which had been lacking earlier.[24] It was not accidental that when the Clare clearances began, it was the great magnates and pre-Famine consolidators, Colonels George Wyndham and Crofton Vandeleur, who were first recorded as issuing extraordinary numbers of notices to quit. Close on their heels was the agent of the Conyngham and Westby estates, Marcus Keane.[25]

By the beginning of 1848 graphic details of the horrific results of mass evictions in west Clare were filtering through to public consciousness in Ireland and abroad, in accounts that portrayed the sufferings of evicted families, the deluging of workhouse systems by influxes of filthy and fever-ridden survivors and a frightful level of mortality among recent admissions. Among the most shocking reports were those of Captain Kennedy, the Kilrush inspector, with his descriptions of the recently evicted wandering in the hinterland, digging miserable burrows and 'scalps' in the bogs, and waiting in misery for the death that claimed thousands.[26]

One unfortunate effect of the publicity accorded the Kilrush Union was that it deflected attention from the other Unions in the county where the clearances were equally horrendous. By May 1849, according to the *Limerick and Clare Examiner*, the most unremitting critic of Munster evictors, house-levelling had reduced the Ennistymon Union also to a 'wilderness', and if in the Ennis and Kilrush Unions respectively 13,000 and 15,000 persons had been ejected already, the 'cruelty' and 'tyranny' manifested by evictors was even worse in Ennistymon, the exterminations there more 'unrelenting and merciless'.[27]

It was much earlier, however, in March 1848, that the *Examiner* had first identified Marcus Keane as a major evictor, when 'extensive exterminations' on his part had already raised up the 'odium', and 'hostility' of the country people against him.[28] Over the next two years, the *Examiner* would follow Keane's career in a mounting barrage of reportage and angry editorial

Marcus Keane in later life. Photo courtesy Katrina Vincent.

denunciation. The following general outline of his clearances during 1848 is derived substantially from that newspaper.

In February, Marcus evicted thirty families from Westby property at Annaghneal, east Clare, and had all their houses levelled.[29] Later the same month, he removed another thirty families from three townlands near Kilrush, to a total of 185 persons.[30] About the same time, in Kilmaley parish, adjacent to his Beech Park mansion, he had four townlands cleared.[31] Early in March he conducted a particularly controversial series of evictions at Meelick in south Clare. We shall return to these evictions shortly.[32]

Throughout the spring and early summer Marcus continued clearing the properties under his control, undeterred by adverse newspaper publicity or the growing disquiet of the authorities. For a time during late summer the trail becomes more difficult to follow because newspaper coverage for many weeks was dominated by the abortive revolt of the Irish Confederation; but as regards west Clare at least, the deficiency is partially supplied by Captain Kennedy's tabulations, which show that Marcus was as busy as ever in August, evicting 175 persons at Kilmacduane, west Clare, on 9 August, and 123 more a few days later in the same parish.[33] At the end of the month, he was reported to be evicting at Lissycasey, a district that to this point had escaped lightly.[34] In mid-September, he was in north Clare, where an *Examiner* correspondent wrote, his name 'sounded in my ear wherever I wandered, and [his] acts as an agent, I did not hear one man praise'.[35]

At the end of the month, Keane was back in Kilmaley: a frequent strategy on his part in carrying out heavy clearances in specific locations was to do so in different phases many months apart from each other. Here he evicted 400 individuals on three townlands, leaving 'dreadful desolation' in his wake.[36] The Kilmaley operation was especially devastating because the lands were re-let wholesale to grazier farmers, as livestock replaced human beings who according to the cold economic calculation of the evictor were without value. The Kilmaley evictees were for the most part reduced to sleeping in ditches, while those who succeeded in gaining outdoor relief 'hovered about like ghosts in the vicinity of their former dwellings until the relief ceased, and then they too, were obliged to become wanderers through the country'. Unknown numbers died.

In late October, Marcus returned to Meelick where he evicted a further eighty families.[37] In mid-November he was in Kildysert parish and at Inagh, north of Ennis a week later. It was said of him at this time that he 'prays fervently at night, and superintends in person the operation of house levelling in the morning'.[38] Almost to the end of the year, he maintained the same furious pace of eviction established earlier and elsewhere: on different dates during early and mid-December he is recorded as having carried out three separate clearance actions, the first on the Conyngham estate and the other two on Westby property in the Kilrush Union, ejecting in the inclemency of that mid-winter season family groups amounting respectively to 107, 105 and 59 persons.[39]

The above listing probably understates the full extent of Marcus's evicting activity during 1848, since so many operations were never recorded. In 1849 his eviction operations were on an even greater scale, and with ease our catalogue could be extended through that year, although to do so would serve little purpose. One indication of the energy expended by him in the campaign is that in May he surrendered his leased farms, by his own account 'not having sufficient time to devote to them'.[40]

The clearances carried out by Marcus on the Marquess of Conyngham's estate at Meelick in south Clare in March 1848 and repeatedly afterwards are of particular interest. This is not so much because of their extent or the brutality with which they were carried out, but because the controversy they aroused has left us with a body of documentation that affords us the unique opportunity of following the story from the three contrasting perspectives of the engaged observer, the investigating authorities and the evictor himself. Through this documentation we can also examine the subsequent fate of some of the evicted families which we cannot do with respect to any other comparable eviction series at this time. Most of all, Meelick tells us a great deal of Marcus Keane's work practices and his attempted rationalization of the horrors he had brought about.

Marcus's preoccupation with Meelick pre-dates the Famine clearances proper, and in March 1847 he had sixty processes served there for non-payment of rent. At the same time, assistance in the form of employment, seed and relief committee donations, 'liberally' provided by Conyngham to poor Meelick tenants in 1846, was abruptly discontinued.[41] Since we know that a number of old middlemen leases for the locality were due to expire at approximately this time, we can be sure that the withdrawal of relief was a prelude to a major consolidation.[42] In September, Marcus Keane appeared at Meelick in person and demanded possession of a further eighty tenants. By his own account, he offered to allow them to remain in their houses if they agreed to the redistribution of the lands among neighbouring tenants, but withdrew in the face of what he called 'tenant intimidation'. Around the same time, a notice had appeared on the door of the parish chapel warning tenants against taking any 'evicted' land.[43]

Matters came to a head in early March when a large group of Marcus Keane's 'levellers' or 'wreckers' arrived at Meelick and systematically cleared the property. A preliminary two-day operation saw hundreds expelled from their homes and left to fend for themselves, after which the levellers were withdrawn to other sites. A few weeks later, with further evictions pending, the *Limerick and Clare Examiner* published a description of the aftermath of the Meelick action, written by a 'special reporter' who had just returned from the scene.[44]

The special reporter's account concentrates on the fate of four evicted families, related to him by family members or neighbours, and it concludes with a table detailing the circumstances of evicted families and those awaiting eviction. The account is, naturally enough, couched in dramatic language but it does carry the power and immediacy of an eyewitness account; its reliability, as we shall see, can be measured. The first case concerned the family of Patrick Hickey, who had been served with a notice to quit under an ejectment order taken out by Keane 'nearly against the whole townland'. For a time Hickey clung desperately to his cabin, abandoning it only on the day the writ was due to be executed. Together with his wife and five children, he then sought and gained admission to the Limerick workhouse, where he stayed only a few days, before being driven thence by freezing conditions and rampant fever, which presented a greater threat to his family than the prospect of starvation outside.

Returning to Meelick the Hickeys reoccupied their cabin, miraculously left intact by the levellers. Unfortunately they also brought fever with them from the workhouse, and within days two of the children fell ill and died. Hickey was forced to scavenge materials for coffins in the neighbourhood, travelling 'no less than 20 houses to make the materials out; getting a few nails in one, perhaps, and a fragment of timber in another'. Shortly after the burial of the children, Hickey, his wife and the three remaining children fell ill. The parents died one after another, both lying dead in one bed for some time before being discovered and buried with the others. At the time of the reporter's visit, the three surviving children were still in fever.

The other three cases were equally harrowing. Inside the ruins of his house the special reporter found the family of Francis Carey, Hickey's neighbour, about to consume a miserable meal that consisted of a 'small parcel of spongy turnips and greenish tops by way of luxury'. Carey had been slightly better off than Hickey and had reclaimed a few acres of his holding, even though Marcus had refused him an outlet for his drains to a nearby stream. When he fell into difficulties after the potatoes had failed, he was refused any assistance that might have enabled him recover. Forbidden from letting his land for grazing, on Keane's orders Carey's cattle were driven off and replaced by those of other men. Forced to sell his stock at a fraction of their value, Carey fell hopelessly into arrears, and his holding was included in Keane's general ejectment.

When the levelling crew arrived, his wife, who was alone in the house and far advanced in pregnancy, firmly refused them entry, discomfiting them to the extent that they waited for Carey's return the following day before reissuing their demand. Caught between the threats of Keane's men and the promise of £5 if he himself 'tumbled' the house, Carey yielded and destroyed his own home, apart from one section of roof, under which he and his family now sheltered as they waited for the promised 'compensation'.

The third case related to a widow named Cherry whom the levellers had physically ejected from her cabin, placing her sick children on the ground outside before destroying it, one of the children dying within a short time. In the final case, a tenant named Gallagher who held 26 acres had gone to meet Marcus Keane in Limerick to offer him as much of his rent arrears as he had managed to raise. In his absence, his house was levelled and his infant children placed on the roadside. From the eviction table that follows the four case histories, we learn that some 141 persons were estimated by the special reporter to have been expelled from their homes over the two days, either by physical ejection or 'voluntary' surrender. A further 129 still awaited removal.[45]

For a short time, the Meelick clearance became a *cause célèbre* when the *Pilot* newspaper republished extracts from the special reporter's account, the resulting publicity leading to an investigation by the constabulary, carried out by Sub-Inspector Donovan of the Newmarket-on-Fergus station on 6 April.[46] Donovan's report, a remarkable survival, takes the form of a point-by-point comparison of the *Pilot* article with his own on-site observations. His report supports that of the special reporter to an extraordinary degree and in addition furnishes extra information regarding the four families that casts an even more tragic light on their situation. The surviving Hickey children were now in the Limerick Fever Hospital, and Widow Cherry's child had died in a miserable hut thrown together by her mother on a remote mountainside – neighbours would not take in the other sick children because of the threat to their own families. Gallagher, who had been secure until recently had had his house levelled; neighbours had taken in his children, and he was now living, wretchedly, in the shell of his ruined house.

If anything Donovan reveals that the special reporter's account actually understated the true extent of the tragedy at Meelick. This is evident from his review of the circumstances of those listed in the eviction table. Here he gives details of families living in makeshift huts built on the roadside or up against the gables of their destroyed houses – others huddling in cabin ruins, waiting miserably for the promised compensation. Donovan tells us of cases where ejected tenants had been taken in by relatives or had wound up on the mean streets of Limerick, and there is one truly appalling instance of a now houseless widow living with her family in a pigsty. His evidence is all the more authoritative for his neutral tone, which yet manages to convey something of the nagging terror endured by families still in their cabins but living in daily anticipation of being ejected.

Marcus Keane's justification of the Meelick clearance is found in two letters: one in the *Clare Journal* on 3 April, the other a private response written some weeks to a request for clarification by the Under Secretary for Ireland, T.M. Redington.[47] The greater part of the first letter consists of a point-by-point refutation of the special reporter's case histories. Thus Patrick Hickey, whose misfortunes had been unfairly ascribed to the Marquis of Conyngham, was not, and had never been, a tenant on the property; Francis Carey had neither been refused an outlet for his drainage nor prevented from setting the grass of his land; Mary Cherry had indeed been 'turned out', but she owed two years rent; Gallagher owed more than £70.

The plausibility of this version rests on the fact that where possible he adheres closely to technical truths. Patrick Hickey, for example, had been a tenant of the middleman who had previously rented the land; therefore, as Donovan carefully stated and Keane reiterated, he was not a 'recognised' tenant of the Conyngham estate, but technically a 'squatter', with no legal right of tenure. Similarly, Keane's assertion that only six tenants were 'turned out' at Meelick, in the sense of being physically ejected, is almost accurate (Donovan put the figure at seven).[48] But it is also hugely misleading since the great majority of those removed had been induced by threats and promises to tumble their own houses, thereby allowing the agent describe their removal as 'voluntary' surrenders. Another legalism allows Marcus exculpate himself from the fate of the occupiers of six houses whom he acknowledges were 'taken possession of': these were, like Patrick Hickey, mere 'squatters or persons who had never paid rent to Lord Conyngham'.[49]

Marcus's reply to the Under Secretary does not address the extra detail unearthed by Donovan, but with offhanded arrogance he encloses a copy of his published letter for reference. Just as arrogantly, he repeats the claim that the Meelick tenants had defaulted on their rents not because of poverty and distress but because of 'a strongly formed and general combination' against the landlord. 'These people', he says of the Meelick tenants in general, 'were holders of very small farms ... under an old and very cheap letting, a tenancy at will. The holdings were much reduced in size by subletting'.[50] Meelick then was a classic Famine-era clearance and consolidation exercise, in which Marcus Keane, eminently efficient land agent that he was, had taken advantage of the vulnerability of a once prosperous tenantry to rationalize this 'old and very cheap letting'.

Of itself, estate consolidation was not necessarily inhumane and might indeed be accepted as a legitimate long-term aspiration of efficient estate management. What makes Keane's behaviour so criminally reprehensible is that he chose to pursue it at Meelick, as elsewhere on the properties he controlled, at the height of the Famine and all at once, with fearsome brutality and indifference to the fate of those evicted. At no stage in his justifications does he engage with criticisms of his methods nor of the suffering inflicted during the evictions, and in this context the bland disingenuousness of the following passage from his second letter leaves us straining for insight into mental processes which deviate so repulsively from human feeling:[51]

> [M]any of the tenants, not only gave up possession of their own free will and threw down their houses in the absence of myself and my bailiffs, but some came to request I would not delay in demanding possession, as they were anxious to get their compensation. They appear however to have since changed their minds in hope, I suppose, of making better terms.

Marcus Keane managed his far-flung property portfolio from offices within the Beech Park demesne. We know that he employed a clerical staff and legal advisers, and in the field a small army of under-agents, bailiffs, rent-collectors, 'drivers' and 'keepers'. Of all those in his employ the single largest component were the wreckers, a multifunctional group, who carried out the actual physical task of ejecting occupiers and destroying cabins, but who were employed even more often to intimidate tenants into compliance with legal writs or highly illegal demands to leave their homes. Before long, however, the intimidatory function became redundant, as targeted populations disintegrated beyond the possibility of collective resistance; the threatening notices posted at Meelick and the 'intimidation' suffered by Marcus Keane's bailiffs in the autumn of 1847 more than likely represented a last isolated struggle of one dying community to maintain what was left of its strength and solidarity.

For the most part tenants were now so docile as to leave their cabins on the appearance of the evicting party or to agree to destroy their own houses; to surrender their land on the promise of being left in their cabins as 'caretakers', who could be easily removed later on, or to leave on the promise of a ticket to the workhouse. Evictors rapidly learned to exploit these tenant vulnerabilities in order to reduce legal costs and operational expenses. Adept though he was in all these devices, throughout his campaigns Marcus Keane still chose to maintain his wrecker/leveller force, because of their usefulness whenever large numbers of houses were to be destroyed.

He is first recorded as having deployed them when local people physically prevented his bailiffs from driving off stock at Meelick in September 1847.[52] Henceforth, this force of between thirty and forty men – Marcus himself puts their number at a precise thirty-seven – would be dispatched wherever needed. Consisting mostly of town-bred individuals, of a different culture from the rural folk whose lives they were disrupting, the tools of their trade consisted of wattles, pickaxes and crowbars, and although a later source credits Marcus with the invention of a kind of grappling hook for the removal of thatch, we have no contemporary reference to its use by his levellers.[53]

In September 1848, in one district of the Kilrush Union, a correspondent of the *Limerick and Clare Examiner* observed Keane's levellers as they went about their work, 'carrying with them implements of destruction, to demolish houses and drive hundreds to beg'. It was an astonishing sight, he wrote, 'to witness the avidity with which these wretches perform ... their revolting duty, and emboldened by a large posse of black-belted gentlemen, tear the last shred of thatch from over the fever-stricken patient or the suffering widow'.[54] Yet, notwithstanding its repeated condemnation of wrecker activities, from time to time a note of pity softens the *Examiner*'s denunciation of the levellers themselves, unhappy, starveling youngsters for the most part in their late teens, who had no other means of avoiding starvation or the workhouse than their despised occupation. In the *Examiner*'s reportage they are furtive and uneasy and not very competent in their work, partly because of the strong oblivion-conferring liquor with which their overseer supplied them.

At the end of November 1848 Marcus sent out a cartload of pickaxes and crowbars to the levellers as they set about a clearance in Inagh parish.[55] One occupier whose cabin was spared was sent into Ennistymon to procure whiskey, and 'after partaking of this preparation out of a jar without a handle', the gang proceeded to destroy thirty-five cabins, removing a total of 200 persons. In mid-December, we glimpse them again in the Cratloe area of south Clare, 'thirty or forty scoundrels from Ennis', some of them armed with fowling pieces and blunderbusses, as they seize cattle for unpaid rent, their bailiffs reportedly drunk and aggressive.[56]

On each clearance site, leveller actions were directed either by under-agents or by Henry Keane, Marcus's younger brother; apart from his fleeting early appearance in the Meelick actions, we have no record of Marcus's presence on eviction sites. Two Keane under-agents are known to us, Dan Sheedy and Basil Lukey Davoren. Of Sheedy little is known beyond the fact that he operated in west Clare and that his son, Brian, would soon become an equally loathed Keane henchman.[57] Davoren was the son of an Ennis solicitor, somewhat down in his personal fortunes when he took employment with Marcus Keane.[58] It was Davoren, a burly individual who led the drunken levellers at Inagh, flourishing a blackthorn stick, and revelling in what he called 'slaughtering houses'.[59]

Henry Keane was by far the strangest individual in Marcus's employ. Neither under-agent nor overseer, as he told a parliamentary investigation, he 'assisted' in his brother's office and on his behalf carried out more than 300 evictions.[60] For our immediate purposes, the most relevant of these was a further devastating round at Meelick in February 1849, where in the first week alone, he had twenty-seven houses thrown down on one townland and their 135 occupants scattered, 'to swell the vagrant list' of Limerick, a short distance away or perish of fever or hypothermia on the roadside.[61]

Just as the second week of house-levelling was beginning, an *Examiner* reporter who was particularly anxious to meet Henry travelled the short distance to the parish, locating him at Meelick Cross after a journey through townlands where his passage was marked by a trail of wrecked houses, with families at work constructing shelters from the debris, either within the ruins or on the roadside. Physically the reporter found Henry to be a 'fine young man', but he nevertheless cut an outlandish be-whiskered figure, with his military-style dress and a 'Jim Crow' hat tied under his chin. When the reporter arrived Henry and his 'thirty Ennis rapscallions' were setting about the removal of a family named Kinnavane from what had recently been a substantial holding.[62]

However, when the wreckers reached the Kinnavane house, the occupier, his two brothers and some local people confronted them; following a short scuffle which was watched from a distance by a pistol-waving Henry Keane, the levellers were driven off.[63] The reporter's curiosity at this highly unusual instance of tenant resistance was satisfied only when at the Kinnavanes' request he entered the house: on a pile of straw on the floor their elderly mother lay dying, her sons determined not to surrender the cabin until she had passed away in peace.

Minutes later, Henry Keane intruded into this poignant scene, entering the house without permission but without hindrance either, muttering that he would level the house if he had to remain there for a week, haranguing the older Kinnavane brother as a blackguard and telling him he would leave only when he could see the sky through the roof of the cabin. 'Kinnavane', he continued in this incoherent fashion, 'I must put your mother out; I won't stir till she is put out by the ditch side; I am the poor man's friend ... I tell you I am your friend ... I will do all in my power against you, and you have on your floor the worst of the Keanes'.

If our source for these events can hardly be described as detached, its general record is a reliable one, its presentation of Henry very much in accordance with what we know of his strange behaviour and locution from other evidence.[64] The report, indeed, is as balanced as it was possible to be in such circumstances, and it leaves unstated the obvious conclusion that Henry was blind drunk, as he often was reported to have been during clearances.[65] At any rate, having stayed all night in the cabin, Henry left at daylight, and later on that morning threatened the reporter that if he published his name or that of Marcus in connection with the evictions, 300 ejectment notices would be served immediately on 'the most respectable persons in Meelick'.[66] More extravagant threats followed in a mumbled monologue punctuated by the waving of a stick and ending with the refrain that Henry was 'the poor man's friend'.

Within a few days of this incident Henry completed this phase of the Meelick clearance, under the watchful eye of a force of police who stood by with bayoneted rifles. Their presence was unnecessary: so far beyond resistance were the tenants that 'numbers' of them pleaded with the reporter not to publish details of the evictions in order to prevent their houses being levelled. At the Kinnavane cabin, the dying widow was taken out by two of the levellers after which the house was reduced to rubble. On that day, in all nine families, totalling forty-eight persons, were ejected at Meelick, in the *Examiner*'s phrase, 'hunted like rats' from their homes.[67]

No other clearance by Marcus Keane, or indeed any other evictor, can be recreated in such detail as those carried out at Meelick, which should therefore serve as a constant reminder when we read through the raw statistical data that similar scenes attended all evictions. This is especially relevant when we look at Keane's clearances in the Kilrush Union where about two fifths of the lands controlled by him were situated – 60,000 acres by his own reckoning. It was here that his clearances were most concentrated, and it is these which earned him greatest notoriety.[68]

Basic eviction statistics for the Kilrush Union are comprehensive and comparatively accurate; from them we learn that in the period between November 1847 and the middle of 1850, some 14,364 persons were permanently removed from their homes in the Union.[69] As the full horror of these clearances began to impinge on public consciousness in Ireland and abroad, landlord alarm also began to rise: well might they react with contempt to the reportage of the *Limerick and Clare Examiner*, but Captain Kennedy's *Reports and Returns*, an official and authoritative document, was a different matter altogether. Having discussed the matter at a secret landlords' meeting, according to one source, prudence decided that any action on their part might be counterproductive.[70]

In the end, of those implicated, only Marcus Keane chose to respond, doing so by way of a formal petition to the House of Commons in which he demanded a parliamentary investigation. That he should have done so and thereby made certain of implicating himself in mass atrocity is something that remains difficult to explain and is best understood as a measure of his self-delusion.[71] At any rate when Marcus's demand was echoed, for entirely opposing reasons, by concerned journalists and philanthropists, a Select Committee was appointed, chaired by the radical MP George Poulett Scrope, with sittings timetabled for June and July 1850.[72]

Keane performed confidently before the Scrope Committee, presenting his arguments with vehemence and apparent conviction.[73] Reiterating his earlier charges that Kennedy's returns were exaggerated and inaccurate he maintained that only half the number of evictions listed had in fact taken place. Accepting that Kennedy had not exaggerated the distress prevailing in the Kilrush Union, he held that this arose from the failure of the potato crop and not any measure from the conduct of the landlords.[74] He produced specific evidence that refuted, plausibly, much of Kennedy's published evidence, and he sought to cast doubt on the credibility of individuals employed in the collection of eviction data.[75]

But however vigorously he presented his case Marcus could not deny that he had carried out evictions on a colossal scale. His justification for these is fearsomely straightforward: he had only evicted persons who had not paid their rents and who were living on 'deserted, non-productive' lands. If ejectments had not been made, and the land not 'taken up from paupers in time' and 'put into the hands of men who were capable of cultivating it and turned to some advantage', ruin and disorder would have been the outcome, as well as 'an entire failure of produce'. He also believed that 'if those people had not been removed completely from the possession of the land, and in many cases from the possession of houses, the result would be that the good tenants would leave the land and leave the country; that every man that could go would remove himself'.[76] The 'good' tenants would have left because of the plundering of their property by the 'pauper' tenants.[77]

When it was suggested to him that non-payment of rent was not the fault of evicted persons, he agreed but in an added remark implied that those he evicted were lazy tenants 'who had lived on in listless idleness from one year to another'.[78] His attitude to 'pauper' tenants was expressed elsewhere in a passing reference to the occupiers of a hut he had had thrown down, as 'eight or nine robbers' who preyed on their neighbours.[79] 'When people become poor', he declared later on, 'they very often become dishonest to supply the very calls of their nature; and when they are scattered about on the townlands, they have more opportunities of exercising their propensities'.[80]

He would not entertain the idea that evicted tenants had suffered any deterioration in their condition; they were no less or more paupers now than they had been before.[81] On the other hand, since the evictions an improvement had taken place in the appearance of the countryside, and there was now 'a better and more industrious class of men in possession of the land in the Kilrush Union than before'.[82] Neither did he accept that he had carried out evictions solely in order to improve properties, 'without consideration of the circumstances of the tenant'. 'I say', he declared, 'that there was more consideration for the feelings and wants of the poor people who were removed than there was for an increase of income'.[83]

Only once did Marcus come near to some acknowledgement of the enormity of what he had wrought in the Kilrush Union. This came at a late stage in his evidence, in a reply to a sympathetic question regarding the 'painful' necessity of large-scale eviction as a prerequisite for restoring the prosperity of the Union; gratitude towards the questioner seems to have led him to reply with a certain frankness and what resembles emotion:[84]

> Nobody has felt more than I have done the painful duty of executing those evictions. I judge that a great deal was left to my own discretion about what was to be done, and if in any respect too much was done, I feel that I am responsible for it in many of the properties, not all, but I felt that it was absolutely necessary for the interest of the country as well as the interest of private properties.

But this admission – if that is what it was – was a solitary one, an unguarded orphan amidst the half-truths, evasions and falsehoods that constitute his overall testimony. It would take other witnesses to deconstruct Marcus's version of events, and here the most damning evidence was given by one Francis Coffee, a small-time Kilkee-based land agent whom Captain Kennedy had employed in the compilation of his eviction statistics. Coffee's credentials were unique: an intimate local knowledge that was greater than Marcus's and an earlier career as evictor in the Union combined with a similar indifference to the human casualty involved.[85] Evidence given by such an individual was persuasive indeed, as where he informed the Committee that between November 1847 and June 1850 Marcus Keane had evicted some 2,800 individuals, exclusive of sixty-seven families who were allowed to remain as 'caretakers'.[86] In that period Keane had levelled no less than 500 houses, and if the caretaker families, all of them destined for eventual removal, are included, then according to Coffee, Marcus Keane was responsible for the eviction of 20 per cent of all persons evicted in the Kilrush Union.

In all this it must be remembered that Keane had been clearing properties for some considerable time before Kennedy began his tabulations and that his clearance activities extended to all the other Unions in Clare, which in their totality greatly exceeded those in Kilrush. When all this is taken into consideration, then it is clear that Marcus Keane had no equal anywhere as an evictor and that the derisive title, 'The Exterminator General of Clare', bestowed on him by the *Limerick and Clare Examiner*, was apt.[87] That it was Marcus himself more than anyone else who was responsible for calling attention to the horrors he had wrought in Kilrush, as elsewhere, was an irony that was entirely lost on him.

7

Father Michael Meehan and the Little Ark

On Sunday mornings over a five-year period between 1852 and 1857, just before twelve noon, Father Michael Meehan, parish priest of Moyarta and Kilballyowen, had his parishioners manoeuvre an ungainly wheeled shed-like structure towards the foreshore at the tiny cove settlement of Kilbaha. From inside this 'Little Ark', regardless of weather, he said Mass to reverential congregations gathered outside, numbering usually in the hundreds. This weekly ceremony was watched many times, we can be certain, by Marcus Keane from the windows of Doondahlin on the clifftop hill above, which commanded views of Kilbaha and wide vistas also across the Loop Head peninsula which as land agent he controlled almost in its entirety.

It was Marcus, at that time a promoter of evangelical ideology, whose refusal to grant a site for a new church building or permit one to be built, had led Meehan to devise his tiny mobile chapel and to deploy it on the only ground in the vicinity not in private ownership – the foreshore between high and low watermarks and the central area of the hamlet. Keane's feelings are not recorded, but it is safe to infer anger and frustration with the guile of 'Priest Meehan', as the evangelicals liked to describe the Carrigaholt pastor; perhaps also there was a level of grudging admiration for his enemy's resourcefulness.

One of the many remarkable aspects of the Little Ark affair was that it captured public imagination in the aftermath of the Great Famine when few wished to be reminded of its horrors or of the lingering miseries left in its wake. To those in the wider world prepared to receive such information it brought some intimation of what survivor populations in parts of Ireland that had been recently ravaged by Famine and eviction were still obliged to endure. To Father Meehan it brought further recognition of his advocacy of the abandoned people of the west and a renown extending far beyond west Clare. This would in turn lead to a renewal of the streams of visitors who in late years had trodden a path to Loop Head to bear witness to the sufferings of his people: political figures, journalists and philanthropists and elements even of the fashionable world, all in search of the west Clare priest and the touch of his spiritual charisma.

Great strength inheres in the Ark narrative, whose simplicity and obvious symbolism gave it tremendous appeal to contemporaries as well as to those who read of it in later times and other countries. These same qualities account for the tenacity of the Ark tradition in the west down to modern times – it has after all outlived the disintegration of the cultural world into which it was once embedded, through depopulation and social change. And behind the story, the brittle timbers of the Little Ark in its little annexe in the Moneen chapel remain the focus of enduring fascination, infused as it still is with the personality of Father Meehan as he is perceived to have been: all-wise, benevolent, passionate, determined, defiant. This larger-than-life perception of Father Meehan invites inquiry as to what kind of man he was in reality; what had he done before the Ark affair, during the Famine, for example, and how exactly the Ark story, the last controversy in which he was involved, fits into the overall pattern of his life. And even as a less heroic Michael Meehan emerges from our inquiries, he remains singular, extraordinary, in his very different way as compelling a figure in the Famine landscape as Marcus Keane, his great adversary.

Michael Meehan was born near Ennis, in 1810, a year after the birth of Crofton Vandeleur and some five years before Marcus Keane. His family belonged to the prosperous farmer class, both his parents being steeped in the traditions of Ireland's ancient Gaelic culture.[1] A paternal granduncle was Tomás Ó Míocháin, last of the great schoolmaster-poets of eighteenth-century Munster; his mother's people, the Gibsons, were well-off livestock farmers and middlemen at Kilbaha where Meehan spent much of his childhood, and where a rich Gaelic culture enjoyed one last flowering before its annihilation in the Famine.[2] The Meehans' sense of socio-cultural entitlement was similar to that of well-off urban dwellers of equivalent economic status, and not surprisingly two of his sisters were to marry into the merchant bourgeoisie of Limerick. The political and cultural consciousness absorbed by the growing Michael must therefore be seen as that of the rising Catholic middle classes, whose prosperity and self-confidence increased with every year of the new century.

At Maynooth, where he was a classmate of Father Daniel Corbett, whom we have met in Quin, Michael Meehan was an outstanding student, ordained after only three years of study. For some three years after ordination he served successively as curate in the parishes of Doora, Tulla and Ennis, before being appointed to Kilrush in 1837, a posting that may have come about as a result of an expressed preference for west Clare, where his heart always lay. Here he remained for twelve years before transferring to Carrigaholt as parish priest of Moyarta and Kilballyowen, which was to be his ultimate destination.[3]

From the first time we meet him as a very youthful curate in Kilrush, Meehan is characterized by a precocious assurance, which derives no doubt from his formation and training in addition to an unquestioned sense of his own abilities. Never content with pastoral duty alone, he found time and energy for a highly active participation in the two great public issues of the day, the non-political movement of Father Theobald Mathew for alcoholic abstinence, and the very political movement for repeal of the Act of Union. If involvement of this kind was not exceptional among younger diocesan clergy, eager for new challenges after the great triumph of Catholic Emancipation, the depth of Meehan's commitment may have been. One of the first priests to become involved in the Temperance movement, he was much beloved of the Apostle of Temperance himself, who referred to him on one occasion as the 'first-born' of his movement.[4] During 1840, the peak year of Temperance activity, he was particularly energetic, organizing or attending rallies in Cork, Limerick, Ennis and Gort, and of course, Kilrush, where the previous year he had founded a separate branch of the movement.[5]

Over a number of years the Temperance and Repeal campaigns acted in symbiosis, overlapping in terms of organization, membership and participation, both movements sweeping up priests and laity with the excitement of processions, mass open-air rallies and rousing speeches. Thus we find Michael Meehan speaking at a Temperance rally in Gort in October 1840 and a few weeks later at a Repeal meeting in Kilrush.[6] At Gort he addressed the crowd 'at great length', reportedly 'with that eloquence for which he is so distinguished', eulogizing 'in glowing terms the benevolent character of the Rev. Mr. Mathew' and concluding 'amidst loud and enthusiastic cheers'.[7] His address to the Kilrush meeting, his first political speech, was by contrast a brief one, given before a crowd of about 8,000 people, his remarks in favour of Repeal emphasizing that the agitation must at all costs be peaceful and lawful.[8]

The necessity for a peaceful approach to campaigning continued to inform Meehan's public rhetoric, even as Repeal gradually eclipsed the Temperance movement in the years leading up to the Great Famine.[9] By July 1846, well after both movements had collapsed and actual starvation had begun in many places in Ireland, Meehan's commitment to a peaceful Repeal agitation still remained, as we know from a reference in one speech to 'the [national] spirit, weaned by O'Connell from the midnight folly of rebellion' and another to the 'secret of moral power'.[10]

Yet there was a combativeness in Meehan too that is not apparent in these sources and which emerged distinctly in the period after the death of the Liberator when he had become radicalized by personal witness to Famine and the sickening performance of successive British governments in addressing it. In this period, his sympathies shifted first towards Young Ireland and afterwards to the revolutionary young firebrands of the Irish Confederation. We have no direct knowledge of his reaction to the failed Confederate Rising of 1848, but we do know that in its aftermath he was to take the most extraordinary risks to secure the escape from Kilkee of three prominent insurgents, Daniel Doyle, John O'Donnell and Richard O'Gorman, by sea to America.[11]

In regard to Meehan's participation in relief operations in the early part of the Famine, the sources are not very revealing, and this probably has less to do with his junior status in the parish than the decision by the Whig-Liberals in mid-1846 to exclude curates from membership of relief committees.[12] We do know that he was a regular contributor to relief funds and that over the space of a fortnight during the summer, along with his parish priest and the other Kilrush curates, he elected to live solely on Indian meal in order to help dispel the prejudice of the poor against this alien food.[13] We know also that on another occasion in July 1847 he intervened to calm outraged townspeople after the arrest of public works labourers following an altercation with the authorities in Kilrush town.[14]

But by this time Meehan was already fully occupied with the pastoral care of the starving, the sick and the dying. Mentally, physically and emotionally exhausting, such ministry was carried out at great risk to his own life. The demands on Catholic clergy were very heavy, as he pointed out in a letter to the English Catholic newspaper, the *Tablet*, in August.[15] 'Most of the priests have ten or twelve calls per day', he wrote, 'and must ride twenty or thirty miles to take them in':

> The physician and the humane *may* go to *some* with temporal relief; the poor priest must go to *all* with the consolation of his ministry ... There are, and have been all the summer, hovels in this barony and in every parish of it, where the sick were obliged to grope and totter to the door for turf, water, meal etc., which a charitable neighbour would bring to the threshold and no farther – the only friend that would enter there was the priest.

As this letter reveals Meehan's primary concern, with the spiritual welfare of his people, was inextricably interlinked with an acute consciousness of their physical condition, as reflected in the deceptively matter-of-fact language of a statement farther on where he regrets not having the 'wherewithal' to make his 'corporal works of mercy commensurate with the spiritual'.

Meehan was also highly conscious of the fact that for some time now landlords had been capitalizing on the helpless state of the poor to evict them *en masse*. He had noted landlord clearance in January the previous year when he had placed before the Repeal Association in Dublin documentation relating to one 'extermination' carried out on the Vandeleur estate at Tullycrine and Moyasta, townlands respectively to the east and north of Kilrush. Here in the days before Christmas, some forty-four persons had been ejected and left helpless on the roadside, in a consolidation action that prefigured those soon to take place on such a gigantic scale in the west and elsewhere.[16]

Given Vandeleur's prominence, this exposé took a certain boldness on Meehan's part; yet throughout the controversy that followed his statements are forceful, detached and assured, and devoid of any deference towards the landlord's great wealth and influence. Of equal interest is the format of this controversy: detailed charges levelled with precise information regarding named persons, their families and the size of their holdings, followed by point-by-point rebuttal on the part of landlords or their apologists, and plausible justifications minimizing the human consequences of the clearance, followed again by countering arguments from the original accuser. Over and over again, from the time Famine clearances proper emerged at the end of 1847, and into the early 1850s as they gradually petered out, in official reports, police documents and newspaper correspondence, disputes in regard to them would follow an identical pattern.[17] As regards Michael Meehan, when we find him writing of evictions early in 1848, almost incidentally he becomes one of the earliest observers to draw attention to Famine clearances anywhere in Ireland.

On this occasion, his letters were directed towards a much more sympathetic ear, the *Limerick and Clare Examiner* whose columns would soon be filled with coverage of mass evictions in the counties of north Munster. A first letter written under the pseudonym 'Hieros' gave details of the eviction of 166 persons on three widely separated townlands: Emlagh, Tullagower and Tullabrack, all owned by the absentee magnate, Nicholas Westby, Marcus Keane's client and father-in-law.[18] Keane took issue with Hieros, whom he identified triumphantly as Meehan, whose choice of pseudonym had been transparent – 'Hieros' signifying 'Priest' – rebutting his assertions with some of the misleading statements with which we have become familiar: the evicted tenants were in arrears and on departing willingly destroyed their own cabins, receiving in return a generous reward.[19]

Keane was the only evictor challenged by Meehan at this time who was willing to justify his actions, and in May when he again took up his pen to write of another clearance series in different locations throughout the Kilrush Union, involving some 118 families comprising 472 human beings, none of the landlords or agents accused saw fit to reply.[20] At this point, Meehan could not have known of Captain Kennedy's project for gathering eviction statistics (which his own letters may well have partially inspired), and his failure to write further on the subject may be due to a realization of the futility of so doing.

Although Meehan would not again contact newspapers with regard to clearances, he was soon involved in a new strategy, one that would become something of a trademark, that is, the escorting of interested parties around the scenes of recent evictions. At the end of September, one of these visitors, a correspondent for the *Limerick and Clare Examiner*, wrote of one location Meehan had shown him near Kilrush town that it was 'a most heart-rending sight to observe these poor people whose houses were thrown down, sitting on the side of the road, and by their wailings proclaiming the helplessness of their situation'.[21] At another eviction site, Meehan approached the children, 'the very personification of direful want', asking if they were hungry, and on being told by the eldest child, 'a rather intelligent girl' that indeed they were often hungry, he retrieved from his car a quantity of bread he had brought and distributed it among them. 'I have reason to know', the correspondent commented, 'that these are not the only persons he thus relieves'. People in Kilrush had told him that 'it is thus he expends on the victims of want and oppression every available shilling possesses'. Meehan, 'whose charities have ever been unostentatious', the correspondent continued, would have been displeased with his remark but 'private virtue and benevolence, amid scenes of woe and hardhearted oppressiveness, must ... produce a beneficial effect'. It is notable that the correspondent records no exchange of words with Meehan on the subject of these or other evictions.

No doubt the *Examiner* correspondent accurately characterized Father Meehan's charity-giving and his reluctance to have it publicized, although distaste at the unctuousness of the language used would have been another factor to place alongside the priest's imputed humility. But there may have been something else again at issue in Meehan's reticence, which we notice again in our next encounter with him at an eviction site a few weeks later, and where again we find him to be self-effacing.

This was during the brutal eviction of Bridget O'Donnell and her children at Garraunnatooha, in Kilmacduane parish, in November. As the pregnant, fever-ridden Mrs O'Donnell lay alongside her sick infants on the ground outside the family cabin which Marcus Keane's 'destructives' then reduced to rubble, it was Michael Meehan who anointed her. However, when she was carried to a neighbour's cabin, it is clear that he was no longer present.[22] Had he taken his departure from the eviction scene by then? And how can such things be explained? From his own account, we know that Meehan found evictions harrowing and very difficult to stomach and that the levelling of a once-sturdy cabin, the seat of home and family and security held a particular revulsion for him. In evidence given to the Scrope Committee in 1850 regarding the destruction of twenty-four dwellings in the hamlet of Tullig, in the parish of Moyarta and Kilballyowen, he would speak as follows:[23]

> I was going through the place, and I had such a horror of seeing them knocked down, that I did not like to go in. I frequently avoided the scene of tumbling down the houses. I could have frequently seen it, and people have called me to come and see it.

Such avoidance must inevitably have added guilt to the pain of recollection, a combination which best accounts for an occasional faltering in his evidence regarding evictions, and indeed his request to be recalled specifically in order to testify regarding the Tullig clearance.[24]

Does something similar underlie his rapid departure at Garraunnatooha? Certainly it would have done him little good to have witnessed the destruction of the O'Donnell home or to have known what subsequently happened to Bridget O'Donnell and her family; how after lying some days comatose in the cabin to which she had been brought, she lost the child she was carrying, as also one of her sons (to fever) some time later; and yet how, incredibly, she was alive just over a year later in December 1849, when her appearance arrested the attention of the *Illustrated London News* artist, James Mahony.[25] As we look at Mahony's sketch depicting the ragged, skeletal figure standing awkwardly between two of her surviving children, we wonder what Michael Meehan's reaction might have been when he saw it. Did he feel, as we do, the power of that image of the hunger-ravaged, distracted yet still beautiful face as it stares outwards, unknowing, at us?[26] It is quite possible, on the other hand, that when he saw the sketch, he did not recognize Bridget O'Donnell at all from among the many hundreds of dying persons he had anointed in similar circumstances over the previous few years; indeed he may not have registered her features as he anointed her outside her cabin during the eviction.

Notwithstanding the weakening of Michael Meehan's fortitude in face of the gut-wrenching emotion of eviction scenes we should not see him as neglectful in any sense of his evicted parishioners: his evidence to the Scrope Committee furnishes the strongest, most desolating testimony to the contrary. Meehan clearly is heartbroken by what is happening to his people; his exposure to their agony is deep, prolonged, despairing, his anguish at not being able to assist in any sense evident in every response he gives to eviction-related queries. It can hardly be accidental either that he did not share any eviction memories with Patrick White, the young priest who was to be his curate for seven years in the 1860s and to whom he confided so much else.

Meehan's experience of evictions was so close indeed as to enable him describe in detail the types of seaweed and shellfish on which evicted persons attempted to subsist and to differentiate among the types of shelter or 'scalps' built by them. One type was constructed against the demolished walls of houses and furnished little in the way of protection from the elements; a second was a mere hole in a dry bog, which could be very warm if covered with straw but easily waterlogged and with a 'pestilential' atmosphere inside. Yet its warmth, he told the Committee, made it the preferred option for evicted families, especially if there were children to be cared for.[27] Clearly he had been in many of these loathsome places.

Father Meehan also developed a grisly expertise in estimating, merely from the skin colour and appearance of persons exposed in this manner, how close they were to death:[28]

> The most fatal effects of starvation in the appearance of the poor people was a swelling about the face and a peculiar turn of the eye; the eye was

Bridget O'Donnell and her children. Illustrated London News.

made sharp and closed and made long; the extremities of the feet became swollen, and the upper part of the feet less swollen; they were deformed; they were not well able to walk, and they became languid and careless about what would become of them.

Asked if there were many cases of starvation like this, his reply was terse: 'A great many.' Asked if he had attended many such cases, he said simply, 'I did.'[29]

At the time he gave this evidence, Meehan was already a year into his appointment as parish priest of Moyarta and Kilballyowen. Here he witnessed scenes as shocking as any he had encountered in the vicinity of Kilrush. Indeed his very appointment to Carrigaholt, in June 1849, came about amid further mass horror and personal loss, in the great cholera epidemic of that time. Decades later Patrick White, by then a senior ecclesiastic and historian, told in his *History of Clare and the Dalcassian Clans* of hearing from Timothy Kelly, Meehan's former parish priest in Kilrush (significantly not from Meehan himself), how on learning that all the Carrigaholt priests were down with cholera, the two men crossed Poulnasherry Bay into that parish and began 'visiting from house to house people sick of cholera and famine fever'.[30] Before nightfall, according to White, they had administered the last rites to some forty dying persons, one of them being Malachy Duggan, the parish priest. Father Duggan was a famous figure in the west and had fallen ill while attending cholera cases just days before. In a scene of high drama, it was Michael Meehan, who had known him since childhood, who administered the last rites to the dying Father Duggan at his bedside in Carrigaholt village.[31] A few days Michael Meehan was appointed parish priest in his place.[32]

Meehan's new parish occupied the entire Loop Head peninsula, minus the lower part of Kilfearagh to the north-east, and it was divided into the two distinct sections of Moyarta and Kilballyown, formerly and later on parishes in their own right.[33] Smaller than Kilballyowen, the easterly Moyarta section held nearly twice its population and had suffered proportionately more during the Famine, according to Meehan because the holdings there were smaller and the sea-fishing not as good.[34] From childhood he had known the terrain in both sections intimately and understood the people there very well. He was well known to them before he became their pastor, and from some very elderly survivors who lived into the twentieth century, latter-day admirers were able to glean much information as to his appearance and bearing at the time of his appointment, when he was about forty years of age. A scholarly source based on this oral history describes him as being a little over medium height and 'strongly built, muscular, athletic'. He was 'well above the average in intellectual ability' and 'energetic and persevering'. A good preacher, he was fond of children and 'was loved by them in return'. Very active physically, he was remembered as a 'keen fowler'. A lover of music and singing he 'could play the flute and the cornet well'.[35]

It is hardly likely, however, that Meehan was able to indulge his musical or outdoor interests to any degree when so much of his time was taken up with ministering to his shattered people; the aftermath of the clearances found him still tending survivors lying huddled in roadside scalps or clinging to their cabins. He would have been aware also of those among his parishioners who escaped clearance, some of them indeed having their holdings augmented in consolidations, but almost all of them tormented by recent memories and gnawed by anxiety for the future. As they struggled to make sense of recent cataclysmic events, not surprisingly the stunned community of the Loop Head peninsula fell back on the consolations afforded by their religion and the leadership of their priest.

For his part Meehan's ability to assist his flock was limited by his own trauma and to a degree that it is difficult to measure by the narrow parameters of his priestly training. Notwithstanding all he had seen of their suffering, the safeguarding of the faith of his people and their eternal salvation constituted his real concern as parish priest, and this was something of which he was always highly aware. When therefore he perceived a spiritual threat from Protestant evangelical personnel employing the blandishments of material advantage or economic coercion, it was inevitable that he should have viewed this as infinitely more pernicious than the prospect of perishing by starvation which by his lights brought only physical death, after all. For him personally, attempts to separate one threat from the other must have occasioned psychological confusion, just as it would have added to the unacknowledged pain suffered by those among his parishioners targeted by the evangelicals.

Evangelical activities were astonishingly widespread in Ireland in the aftermath of the Great Famine, especially in the prostrate west. Although varying widely across the country according to local circumstances, common factors in this so-called Second Reformation, as we have already seen with regard to Miltown Malbay, included financial and organizational support supplied by Bible societies in Britain and the participation of certain Protestant clergy and landlord families. In the long term, of course, the evangelical campaigns were doomed to utter failure, but wherever their influence was felt they tore open great new wounds in communities which had hardly begun to heal after the years of horror and hardship.

What made matters more fraught in Moyarta and Kilballyowen was that the most powerful protagonist on the evangelical side was the very individual who bore greatest responsibility for the clearances that had left so many of the people in the dreadful condition in which they now lay: Marcus Keane, agent for Nicholas Westby who owned virtually all the land at the tip of the Loop Head peninsula. In the evangelical controversies as in the clearances, Marcus stayed in the shadows, and again it was his brother, Henry, and his brother-in-law, Rev. John Nash Griffin, a Dublin-based English clergyman who led the mission, aided by a number of convert teachers and scripture readers. For Meehan, therefore, the equation of evangelical with exterminator was unquestioning and the spiritual/material peril embodied in the Keane ménage redoubled to dimensions not far short of diabolical.

There were two evangelical *loci* in Meehan's parish, the Carrigaholt village mission of Rev. J.S. Faussett, an English cleric and the Kilbaha mission in the west. As a sizeable population centre, Carrigaholt village made sense as a base for operations; Kilbaha, a remote location, was chosen probably because the major instigators lived there at least some of the year, Marcus Keane at Doondahlin and Henry close by in a house known as The Cabin.[36] It was mainly in this ocean-bound 'little tongue of land' at Kilbaha, as Meehan referred to it, that he was called on to go to war for the souls of his people.[37]

As at Miltown Malbay and so many other locations, battle was joined over education with its crucial potential for the shaping of impressionable young minds. One of Meehan's earliest priorities at Carrigaholt had been to establish elementary schools, especially in Kilballyowen where according to Patrick White, in the ten miles between Cross village and Loop Head there had been 'neither a fixed school nor a chapel' up to then.[38] By 1851 he had 'a fair number' of schools in operation in the parish, some of them hedge schools he had absorbed into his network, with three schools operating under the National Schools system; it is unsure how many of these were in Kilballyowen.[39] From the outset it is clear that religious instruction, imparted in Irish, was an important part of the curriculum in the schools operated by Michael Meehan, who also provided pupils with Irish-language catechisms and composed prayers in Irish for use by them.[40]

It may well be that that it was Meehan's educational initiatives, with their religious emphasis, that spurred the Kilbaha evangelicals to action; perhaps also his previous history with Marcus Keane was a factor of relevance. But all we know for certain is that in October 1850, three estate schools materialized on Westby property, two of them in the far west, at Kilballyowen and Kiltrellig.[41] Staffed by Protestant converts and 'nominal' Catholics, the curriculum in these schools was heavily weighted with religious matter, mainly readings from scripture, with explications from a radical Protestant perspective. It was all done fairly overtly, the teachers frequently being not much concerned at times to conceal their intentions behind the usual evangelical mantra of scriptural reading 'without note or comment'. Westby tenants, all of them Catholic, were expected to send their children to these schools and a predictable leverage applied to ensure they did so.

We do not know exactly how all this worked out in practice, since unlike the situation at Miltown Malbay, we have no information from the evangelical side as to how the schools were operated. From the Catholic perspective, what we have is Patrick White's later highly coloured description of frightened children being forced to listen to evangelical ideology. White's description must of course be treated with the greatest caution, but given the active participation of somebody as intemperate, even as unhinged, as Henry Keane, it may not be far removed from the reality:[42]

> The children, however, soon began to open, literally, the eyes of their benighted parents. They told them things they never heard before of confession, though they were ever so familiar with it; the idolatry of the Blessed Eucharist; but above all the wickedness implied in paying special devotion to the Virgin Mother of God.

In at least one of the schools, according to White, 'a picture of the Blessed Virgin was passed along from desk to desk, to be spat upon by each of the children as a final parting with the old superstition'.[43]

Parallel with the development of the 'soup' schools, the clergyman involved, Reverend Griffin – an occasional visitor to Green Park in Henry Murphy's time – sought with great persistence to engage Michael Meehan in theological discussions in public. This the latter sedulously avoided, contriving indeed never to be in Reverend Griffin's presence on any occasion, public or private. Eventually, however, Marcus Keane engineered a meeting in the Kiltrellig schoolhouse between priest, evangelicals and the parents of children attending the schools, under the pretext of a discussion of landlord Westby's intentions with regard to estate education.

The evangelicals represented the schoolhouse meeting as a theological disputation, on Pauline or Reformation model, which the parents had independently sought, out of curiosity at the competing views presented to them; according to the *Clare Journal* they were caught 'between a desire to please the agent and an anxiety to take advantage of the only means of education afforded them, at the same time not wishing to disoblige the priest'.[44] In reality, however, the Westby tenants were far from being autonomous actors and were terrified of the Keane brothers; none would have dared approach them on any issue whatever. Most were survivors or beneficiaries of land consolidations, and all lived in dread of causing offence to either Marcus or Henry, which might have consequences of the kind they had witnessed over and over again. Docility and extreme deference were qualities expected of such tenants; self-assertion of any kind would have brought immediate chastisement.

At the meeting, which took place on a Friday in early September 1851, Michael Meehan and his curate Father Michael McMahon faced Reverend Griffin and Reverend Charles Ward, Henry Murphy's old junior curate. The meeting was moderated by Marcus Keane, brother-in-law to both evangelical clergymen, and was attended by a crowd of about 100 people. In the *Clare Journal*'s genial report, the discussion was carried on 'with much earnestness and good temper' on both sides for three hours before being adjourned to

Father Michael Meehan. Photo courtesy Diocese of Killaloe.

the following day when it was renewed for an even longer period.[45] Michael Meehan's version of the meeting was very different: the tenants present were cowed and silent, and the 'disputation' consisted of a constantly frustrated attempt on his part to deflect his opponents' biblical rant with straight answers as to what was happening in the schools. At the end of the meeting, as the parents were leaving, he called out to them, asking 'could they any longer doubt that the school was a trap? How could they, even if their lives were to be taken from them send their children to be instructed where there was no disguise on the resolve to root out their religion?'[46]

These were hard, harsh questions, and not at all to Meehan's credit, since he knew full well that these devout Catholic parents were perfectly aware what kind of school it was to which they were sending their children, and that the alternative, of removing them, would open up such a prospect of suffering as to make it no choice at all. Remarks made by Meehan some time later indeed show that he well understood the bribery/intimidation pressure the agent was heaping on them in terms of 'squaring boundaries between the tenants, giving out bog and other privileges, pulling down houses [and] applotting the compensation allowed by the landlord'. He even acknowledges the parents' dilemma in a famous Munster proverb: 'when your hand is in the dog's mouth you must draw it out as smooth as you can'.[47]

How aware was he then of the extra weight his parting words at the Kiltrellig meeting was adding to the burden already borne by the parents? By any standards his language, as reported from other sources at this time, was terrifyingly extreme: 'Kill, boil, eat them if you have to do it', decades later Patrick White would quote Meehan as saying to the parents on another occasion, 'that will be but destroying their bodies, but don't sell their immortal souls'. In White's version, Meehan had said this 'in bold metaphor': the modern reader can only flinch at the crudity of the language used.[48]

As a result of Michael Meehan's efforts, most of the parents withdrew their children from the Westby estate schools, but when some continued to send their children there, his language escalated again, and on Sunday 28 September, after Mass at Cross Chapel, he denounced them from the altar. Unfortunately, the only detailed account of this denunciation is the *Clare Journal*, which is based entirely on evangelical sources and which presents it as an old-style 'priest's curse', uttered allegedly after Meehan had solemnly quenched the altar candles and rung the altar bell, the formal Church ritual preceding excommunication.[49] Part of the alleged curse – about half – runs as follows:

> May the devil be their guide on the right and on the left, lying and rising, in bed, and out of bed, sitting and standing within and without, may all misfortunes attend their families and labours. And any person or persons sending their children to this school henceforth, may they be struck blind and deaf so as never to see any to their children again; and may the children sent to this school go wild. May they never leave this world until they be such examples as that the marrow may come out through their shinbones.

A fearsome curse indeed – if we can believe Meehan ever spoke thus. Among the reasons for scepticism are the suspicious precision of the language, which the evangelicals insisted was a verbatim rendition, and the fact that any transcription would have necessitated the presence of a spy in the chapel to record it, which could not have gone unnoticed and in any case would have compromised any moral integrity to which the evangelicals might otherwise have laid claim. More than likely, the curse was confected and translated – with a deal of scribal help – by Henry Keane who had been hanging around the chapel before Mass until he was asked to leave.[50]

Needless to say Michael Meehan denied he had cursed anyone or that he had performed any candle-quenching, bell-ringing ritual; the *Clare Journal* report he decried as a 'gross and vile misrepresentation' of his actual remarks, which he said were taken from Scripture and applied 'according to the scope and purpose for which they were written'.[51] However, even if we ignore the impenetrability of this last statement, there were other prevarications and inconsistencies in his explanations, and certain inadvertent admissions also, that reveal that whatever about the so-called curse, whatever he actually had said had been uttered with great deliberation and in the harshest terms possible, the intention being to frighten an already deeply anguished group of parents into obeying his instructions to take their children out of the Kiltrellig school.

Controversy over the alleged curse continued for about a year, the evangelicals gleefully citing their version in their tracts and in certain British conservative prints, Michael Meehan defending himself in Catholic publications in Ireland and Britain, and engaging where he could in verbal counterattacks on the evangelicals and their cause.[52] For evangelicals Meehan became the 'Cursing Priest', and Rev. Griffin singled him out for attack at a meeting in Exeter Hall, the home of extreme evangelicism, in London, one evening in May 1852, where he read out the 'curse' to an audience that was appropriately shocked to hear it.[53]

Even though Meehan's altar denunciation saw further pupil withdrawals from the Westby schools, in November the evangelicals were claiming a total enrolment of thirty-five Catholic children, which is consistent with Meehan's own disparaging reference of a few months later to 'the children of eight or nine pauper families' (not for nothing was Meehan a strong farmer's son).[54] The following June when the newly appointed Bishop of Killaloe, Dr Vaughan, trailing an impressive clerical entourage, swept into the parish to spend a weekend bolstering lay and clerical morale, Catholic sources were admitting there were still twenty-one children spread over the three schools.[55]

Aside from the schools' issue, it seems that the total number of converts made by the evangelicals in Meehan's parish was very small, and at the height of the campaign amounted to less than 100 persons, a tiny fraction of the overall parish population of 9,300.[56] But damage to the community is not to be assessed purely in terms of numbers, and for every convert and parent of a soup school child, there were many more tenants who had been subjected to the severe annoyance of evangelical public ranting, of intrusions into their houses which they were powerless to stop, and religious lectures as they paid their rents, all of it endured 'before the poor got time to breathe, after these terrible years of cholera and famine and death, still fresh in their fear-worn memories'.[57] For this hitherto devoutly monolithic Catholic community, in addition, conversions represented a sort of breach in nature, the fears and impotent rage of its members with regard to what the agent and his evangelical acolytes had imposed on them transposing into an intense, undying hatred of the converts, between the few motivated by religious feeling, those stimulated by 'avarice', to use Meehan's words for material advantage, and the great majority who had been acting under coercion.[58] The parish consumed itself with internal bitterness, traces of which subsisted long after the evangelical campaign had faded away.

Two incidents illustrate the continuing community bitterness with particular vividness. In the first, a convert youth was jeered at by a crowd who shouted 'souper, souper' after him and threw stones at him, as he drove his ass-and-cart through the street of Carrigaholt during a fair in the summer of 1854.[59] At the trial of three of his tormenters, sixteen to eighteen-year-olds like himself, at the Kilkee Petty Sessions soon after, the young man's incidental comments to the court reveal much as to the context of the incident: 'My mother was turned out of her land; Mr. Keane gave her leave to re-build a hut upon it; I was not a Protestant until after the hut was built by leave of Mr. Keane.'

The second incident took place the following year, just after the sudden death of the four-year-old son of Reverend Faussett, the most indefatigable of the evangelical clergyman. When travelling through Cross village on his way to choose a grave at Moyarta cemetery, Faussett, father of eleven other children, was hooted and pelted with heavy stones. Returning the next day to Moyarta, he found the grave had been half-filled with stones, apparently by young boys, one of whom had defecated into it.[60] Reverend Faussett's account of this revolting incident is permeated with sorrow, bewilderment and bitterness, and if the incident broke his spirit, as seems likely given that we hear no more from him, he surely can be added to the human casualties of the souper conflict.

Thus did the souper wars in the west grind on through the early 1850s, a low-intensity struggle comprising petty and nasty episodes of the kind described above; there were sordid squabbles over alleged workhouse proselytism – unedifying bedside tussles over the last wishes of dying soupers and an endless deadening tedium of pamphlet and newspaper argument and letter-writing. Towards the middle of the decade, however, the sources show the evangelicals as increasingly beleaguered, as reflected in the ascending stridency of their anti-Catholic rhetoric. Evangelical embattlement is especially noticeable in a deeply personalized loathing for 'Priest Meehan', the 'Cursing Priest', whom they had so badly underestimated. And behind their verbal glorying in the fury incited by their endeavours as a reflection of success in rocking Romish designs, the attrition of the years inevitably told.

Even before the evangelical campaign in Ireland fell apart suddenly in the mid-1850s, for reasons that had more to do with the movement's international ambitions as with their Irish troubles, it is likely that many local evangelical groups were already at the end of their tether.[61] As funding and logistical support from British sources evaporated, the unease of mainstream Protestants with regard to evangelical methods turned to passive opposition; the support of landlords and their womenfolk, which had been significant, died away. By the time of the second of these two incidents, it was in fact all over. In west Clare Marcus Keane seems simply to have lost interest, moving on from active promotion of the evangelical cause as he had earlier moved on from estate consolidation. His brother Henry disappears almost entirely from view.

But none of this was predictable in the early 1850s when Michael Meehan was faced with the onslaught of an aggressive and richly resourced evangelical campaign. It must indeed have seemed unstoppable when over it had suddenly loomed the juggernaut of Marcus Keane. It was in this dark period that Meehan decided to take battle directly to the evangelicals, by forging a pastoral presence for that portion of his beleaguered flock right at the epicentre of their mission at Kilbaha, the hub of Keane influence, and where most of the converts, the waverers and the parents of soup school children lived.

Approaches to landlord Westby for a site for a chapel were thwarted by Marcus Keane, and when Meehan quietly acquired a double cabin from two tenant families emigrating to America and knocked the internal walls together into a temporary chapel which he named St Patrick's, he was evicted as soon as he was identified as the new tenant. It was Marcus Keane himself, or so it was believed, who with his bare hands, had overturned the basic wooden altar Meehan had set up in this makeshift chapel, when his wreckers superstitiously refused an instruction to do so.[62] Little daunted, for a time Meehan attempted to say his Sunday Masses in the open air, on public ground near the foreshore, sheltering altar books and sacred vessels from wind and rain, firstly in a kind of tent and then by an arrangement of carts strategically placed so as to offer some protection. However, neither expedient was enough to prevail against the elements on this exposed Atlantic peninsula, as often cold, wet or savagely wild as it might be fine and tranquil.

The solution Michael Meehan arrived at, the construction and deployment of a mobile chapel on wheels, with which we began this chapter, was ingenious. As propaganda it was of an extraordinary subtlety. Initially Meehan referred to this slatted wooden structure – it measured six feet by five by eight feet high at the apex of its pitched roof and there were glass windows on each side and an open back, with wheels attached to short projecting shafts – as a 'kind of sentry-box'. But even after various alterations were made it resembled nothing so much as a bathing box of the type used in nearby Kilkee to protect the modesty of respectable ladies attiring themselves for immersion in the ocean.[63]

The choice of the term 'Ark' for the structure, seemingly by Meehan himself, was inspired; through it the mundane bathing box was miraculously transmuted into sacred object. Now suffused, however indefinably, with biblical association, the box-become-Ark instantly appropriated from the evangelicals all the Old Testament resonances they had taken for granted as their exclusive property. With the further refinement of a diminutive, the Little Ark acquired an extra layer of meaning, a homely simplicity exemplifying dignified resistance on the part of the disempowered to landlord tyranny and religious oppression. The evangelicals, who recognized a propaganda coup when they saw one, made only sparing reference to the structure in their publications, as a 'band- box' or 'show-box', sometimes attempting a tone of satirical dismissal, but never, of course, using the term the 'Little Ark'.[64] There was little they could do when from the cramped interior of his Ark Father Meehan celebrated Mass in all seasons, with a kind of discreet ostentation, for nearly five years of Sundays between 1852 and 1857.

But we should be careful not to characterize the Little Ark story as a mere exercise in propaganda. The dilemmas of the Kilbaha poor, their sufferings at the hands of agent and evangelicals were very real: Michael Meehan, a complex and flawed individual, subject to the prejudices of class and clerical estate, was yet a genuine leader of his people, fighting on their behalf for the last resource remaining to them; what he – and nearly all of them – would have seen as their prospect of eternal life. The reconstruction of the human dignity of Michael Meehan's parishioners, which is all the modern observer sees, was inextricably linked up in the minds of Michael Meehan with his loftier spiritual objectives. And in exchange for the leadership of Father Meehan, for all his sometimes coercive methodologies, in the matter of the Little Ark as in his wider devotion to their interests, which all acknowledged, this otherwise lost people returned an unstinting love. Only incidentally then was Meehan a propagandist.

All of these things invest the story of the Little Ark and the unskilled pictorial efforts with which it has been represented with a deep poignancy, one that embraces all those involved in the evangelical imbroglio, including the soupers and even the hot-collared evangelical clergymen caught up in the treadmill logic of their silly, self-damaging mission. Through the entire story we have difficulty only in feeling sympathy for Marcus Keane, thirty-something squire of Beech Park, wealthy, brilliantly married, and father to a much-loved young family, yet cold, and pitiless with regard to those his socio-economic power made his near-helpless creatures.

Legal challenges to the presence of the Ark as a public nuisance succeeded only in fuelling the publicity surrounding it, especially when such transparent expedients were defeated, as they all were.[65] Hooting attacks by soupers while Mass was being said only confirmed the picture of actual persecution and lessened sympathy for these unfortunates.[66] Drawings of the Ark were circulated in Ireland and abroad, the publicity resulting, as we saw at the outset, in another influx of wealthy and well-meaning visitors, the philanthropically genteel, to the west to view conditions for themselves and to meet the famous Father Meehan. A substantial inflow of funds followed for the building of a chapel of ease at Kilbaha, Meehan's ultimate goal and dream.[67] When he was offered a site by his cousin Peter Gibson at Moneen, at a location considerably outside Kilbaha village in 1857, Marcus Keane did not interfere. Immediately the site was granted, it was encircled by a boundary wall, inside which the Ark was placed pending the building's construction. As the walls began to rise, Father Meehan set out for Britain in search of funds with which it would be built.

The new church was dedicated to the Virgin Mary in May 1858, in an ecclesiastical ceremony replete with triumphalist ritual, the occasion presided over by two Catholic bishops and a host of clerics of various ranks. As celebrants and worshippers walked in procession into the fine new church, they reportedly passed and lingered near Father Meehan's little wooden Ark, which had been placed near the front door, an appropriate symbol for the victory of the humble and the meek.[68]

8

The Cabin-Tumbling Warrior: Crofton Moore Vandeleur

When Captain Wynne was beset by his imagined and self-created enemies, Crofton Moore Vandeleur was one of those to whom he turned for testimonials of character and service. This Vandeleur did indeed supply but in a manner that contrived somehow to withhold full approval and to include also an implicit note of censure. In his testimonial letter to the former inspector, which was very brief, Vandeleur referred to Wynne's 'straightforward conduct' in implementing his brief and in 'putting down jobbing' wherever he found it, his praise, however, going no further than that. The 'really destitute in many cases' were indebted to Wynne's exertions, but the implication of the full sentence was that there were many cases where they were not, doubt being further increased by the added clause, 'whatever others may say'. Wynne had carried out his duty 'with great forbearance and good temper', but this was only 'as far as my observation went'.[1]

Whether Wynne found any comfort in this less than wholehearted endorsement, its effect must have been to remind him that despite the power he had recently wielded among landed gentlemen, in the overall scheme of things his had been a lowly place, no more than that of a mid-level, temporary state functionary. The reminder was not accidental, but it was not so much a deliberate snub, for which Wynne was not of sufficient account, as the instinctive controlling reflex of an individual with a very elevated self-image: that of Crofton Moore Vandeleur, the great magnate of west Clare; Lord of the Manor of Kilrush, Colonel of the County Militia, Deputy Lieutenant of the County, Chairman of the Kilrush Board of Guardians, owner of nearly 17,000 acres of land including the town of Kilrush and possessor of multiple business interests abroad.[2]

If to Vandeleur's indifference towards his former ally are added other problematic attributes we will note as we go along, we might think to have discerned a pattern in the attitudes of this aloof, forbidding figure that would lead to his transformation into one of the worst evictors in Ireland by the end of the Famine, a man whose actions would lead, directly and indirectly, to the deaths of thousands of poor people, including more than a thousand recent occupiers on his own estate. However, such character traits that we adduce in Vandeleur do not mark him out particularly among his fellow landlords and were common in many who did not carry out mass clearances. And at the time his letter to Wynne was written, in March 1847, his persona was still that of the improving landlord, a dynamic modernizer of his extensive properties and his town of Kilrush, and a man interested in the welfare of his county. In addition, even his Catholic detractors could not deny that churchgoing Protestant though he was, Vandeleur was free of bigotry: in 1838 he provided a site for a Catholic parish church in Kilrush town, formally laid the foundation stone the following year and contributed to the building fund.[3] Evangelical theology held no interest for him either, and he would refrain pointedly from any involvement in the sectarian ferment that swept up many Protestants at the end of the Famine, although perhaps genteel disdain for the social origin of many of the activists was also a factor here.[4] If we are to understand Vandeleur then, we shall have to look further and for longer.

Crofton Moore Vandeleur properly belonged to the landed gentry, but he also had strong connections to the nobility through his mother's family, the Moore earls of Drogheda.[5] On his father's side he was descended from a Dutch merchant named Maximilian Vandeleur who had settled in Ireland in late Tudor times and whose progeny had abandoned trade for a higher-status landed lifestyle.[6] The territorial base carved out by one Vandeleur branch in west Clare by 1700 from the disintegrating behemoth of the Thomond domains was essentially the patrimony that Crofton inherited when he attained his majority shortly after his father's death in 1828.[7] By that time little of the family's Netherlander heritage remained apart from the Vandeleur surname and the derisive political soubriquet, 'the Dutchman', which opponents were wont to throw at him during electoral contests.[8]

Shortly after taking over control of the Kilrush estate, Crofton began gathering to himself the administrative and social impedimenta appropriate to a Lord of the Soil. In 1831 he became a magistrate and the following year served as High Sheriff of Clare; during his term he married Lady Grace Toler, daughter of the second Lord Norbury (the first had been the notorious hanging judge).[9] In subsequent years, Crofton served regularly on the county Grand Jury, of which in his capacity as Deputy Lieutenant of the County, he was frequently elected foreman. In 1841 he became the first chairman of the Kilrush Board of Guardians and two years later assumed command of the moribund Clare county militia, a position which allowed him assume the title of colonel which he would insist on for the remainder of his life.[10] The county militia remained moribund.

Attempts to add a county seat to these honours in 1835 and 1841 failed dismally, and on both occasions he was easily brushed aside by the Whig-Liberal candidates, Cornelius O'Brien and Major W.N. Macnamara, whom

Captain Wynne was to fatally antagonize years later, and whose victory over Vandeleur was ensured by a skilful, practised marshalling of the Catholic vote.[11] But these were setbacks to be expected and in time to be overcome, and on the eve of the Famine, among Clare landlords, only Sir Lucius O'Brien of Dromoland surpassed Crofton Moore Vandeleur of Kilrush House in terms of wealth, public profile, political influence and social prestige.

Despite its great size Vandeleur's landed fiefdom, all of it situated within the Kilrush Poor Law Union, was an isolated one, remote from the great metropolitan centres of Europe for which the Harrow- and Cambridge-educated Crofton had such a fondness and for which he habitually abandoned Kilrush for portion of each year, sometimes for a year at a time. Much of the land was poor and unreclaimed, a great part let out in old middleman leases which at the time he entered into his inheritance still had periods of years yet to run.[12] The largest proprietor in Kilrush Union, Vandeleur was the only landowning magnate to be technically a resident, the others having their landed base elsewhere. By far the dominant landed figure in the west he ruled over a numerous and varied tenantry that included lesser landowners, middlemen, comfortable tenants, smallholders and cottiers.

During the 1830s and early 1840s, Vandeleur invested a great deal of time and money in the modernization of his west Clare domains. Though hampered as so many other landlords were by middleman leases from a thorough consolidation of farms and holdings, there is some evidence of a piecemeal attempt whenever the expiration of such a lease allowed the eviction of the 'squatter' subtenants. It was this tendency that lay behind the clearing of one entire townland, Carrowdotia, in 1836, where about thirty tenants and their families, living on holdings that ranged from the very small to the miniscule, were ejected: accounts of the sufferings of those evicted in this small clearance operation are virtually identical to those of Famine times.[13]

During this time Kilrush town offered much greater scope for Crofton's developmental enthusiasms, and in the years leading up to the Great Famine he lavished attention on it, building literally, on foundations laid down by his father. New streets were formed, which he named after family members, and had lined with substantial new premises, to be occupied by landed or professional gentlemen, shop-owning merchants or owners of other commercial enterprises.[14] Public buildings such as the Catholic chapel, the market house, fever hospital and courthouse also contributed to the civic adornment of the fast-growing town.[15] Even the workhouse, which was built in 1841 on high ground at Broom Hill, was an embellishment to a town which one admiring visitor characterized in that year as 'rising rapidly'.[16]

The extent of Vandeleur's ambition for Kilrush can still be seen in present-day Frances Street (named for his mother), a broad thoroughfare designed as an impressive approach to what was intended should be a bustling waterfront; by the early 1840s large, handsome buildings flanked the street on both sides, and down at the end several warehouses already stood on recently completed sections of new quay, which easily accommodated the Shannon steamer and the twenty or so coastal vessels customarily moored there. In addition to developing the port facilities, there was a long-term project to secure the Atlantic Packet Station for Kilrush. But even as things were, the prospect from the Creek was imposing, with views across the deep-water anchorage, and just offshore, the sheltering mass of Scattery Island with its venerable monastic ruins.[17]

If one were to judge by ceremonies held in December 1841 following the launch of a schooner built at Vandeleur's new shipyard – the timbers came from his oak woods, the ship was named *Lady Grace* after his wife and launched to the music of his own brass band – the 'Colonel's' relations with his town tenants were warm.[18] At an evening function held later in a hotel named the Vandeleur Arms, he listened to congratulatory speeches by several favoured shopkeeper tenants. One speaker contrasted present-day Kilrush with its appearance only a few years previously, attributing all the positive changes to Crofton's 'laudable undertakings' for promoting its 'commerce, trade and shipping'. Another asked rhetorically, 'Is there in Clare, gentlemen, a better landlord? Does he not set his lands for the value?' In returning thanks, Vandeleur told the gathering that he 'did not wish to call any of them his tenants, as that was too cold a term for the interest he felt in, and the attachment he had for them, which was every day increasing'.[19] But it is noteworthy that Crofton granted leases to very few of these 'friends', whose conditions of tenure left them subject entirely to his mercurial whim.[20]

But at least some of the time, the town tenants basked in the warmth of the colonel's benevolence, unlike the smallholders and cottiers of the hinterland of whom he intended to rid himself whenever the opportunity presented, and as he had shown earlier in the case of the Carrowdotia tenants. Vandeleur's attitude towards poor people in general is revealed in comments made to the Whately Commission on poverty at Kilkee in 1835.[21] Initial remarks to the sub-Commissioners indicate a laudable acceptance of moral responsibility towards the aged and infirm poor, those 'bowed down to the ground by old age and infirmity', who should have 'their comforts and their wants' seen to.[22] By contrast, his attitude towards beggars was one of rigid intolerance: it was 'absolutely necessary' that an end be put to vagrancy, which was 'injurious to the morals of the poor'. In Kilrush he had often noted the 'bad consequences that result to those who give lodgings to beggars, as they carry about disease and frequently rob the poor people'. All the petty larcenies lately committed in the town, he stated, where perpetrators had been brought before the magistrates, were the work of strolling beggars.[23] In fact, very few beggars came before magistrates at any point, and Vandeleur's concern with those who afforded them lodging is perhaps the first significant indication of the direction of his thinking.

Because Crofton Vandeleur was so often absent from his estate and town he was never fully in touch with what was happening there and had little real knowledge of his tenants' lives, none at all probably of the poorest occupiers. But absence made no difference to decision-making on Vandeleur's part, and there is no question that he allowed his agent, Francis Fitzgerald, anything of the autonomy allowed Marcus Keane by his clients. Fitzgerald is hardly mentioned in the sources, and we cannot doubt that he was anything more than a vehicle for the transmission of Vandeleur's instructions.[24]

At home in Kilrush in the aftermath of the harvest disaster of 1845, at the November County Meeting which we have mentioned several times already, it was Vandeleur who shaped the opinion of the meeting by his expressed view that the damage done to the potato crop across the country was being much exaggerated and that the crisis was in all respects a manageable one.[25] If this view was partly due to ignorance of conditions in his own backyard, a more relevant factor was Vandeleur's deeply conservative resistance to any large-scale use of public money that might have tax implications for himself. And because of Vandeleur's great influence among his fellow landlords, it is not stretching the evidence to attribute a great deal of gentry complacency and inaction regarding relief measures at this time to him.

Once the relief programmes got under way, however, Vandeleur's record was creditable enough, or so it would appear at first glance, both on the level of private charitable contributions and involvement in relief administration. A personal donation of £40 to the Kilrush Relief Fund in April 1846 seems liberal, as does a further £50 the following month, not to mention a massive £600 given towards relief works involving the deepening of the Kilrush creek and the building of a quay wall.[26] Again, in January 1847 we find him donating the smaller sum of £10 to the Kilrush Relief Committee towards its newly opened soup kitchen and a further £40 about the same time whose purpose we are not told.[27] No doubt there were other unacknowledged contributions, and in addition we know that later on he would be a significant donor to the funds of the Kilrush Conference of the Society of St Vincent de Paul.[28]

The *Limerick and Clare Examiner*, however, was not impressed by Vandeleur's charity giving and was churlish enough to point out that his donations to the Kilrush Relief Committee were miniscule in the context of an estimated annual income of £20,000, as compared to a recent donation of £20 by the Kilrush parish priest, Father Timothy Kelly, whose annual income of just £300 was expended for the most part in charity.[29] Hardly an unbiased source given its delight at any opportunity to slate the man it referred to as the 'Carpet Militia Colonel', the *Examiner*'s views were nevertheless not without foundation.[30] The paper indeed could also have argued, although it did not do so at the time, that Vandeleur's apparently munificent donations in the creek and quay projects were chiefly of benefit to himself as owner of Kilrush; doubly so since the sums advanced were matched by similar sums from the British Treasury, in financial arrangements that constituted a remarkably cost effective means of improving his own property.

As Chairman of the Kilrush Relief Committee, like John B. Knox and John Singleton in their respective districts, and for all we know Marcus Keane, in these early days, Vandeleur proved energetic in the organizing of public subscriptions, the drafting of lists of labourers and the application of pressure on government agencies – routine and tedious business that need not detain us.[31] His relief duties became more onerous still after administrative changes introduced by the Whig-Liberals in the autumn of 1846 assigned him as Vice-Lord Lieutenant of the county the responsibility of reorganizing its relief committees. Here we find him vetting requests for assistance from a restructured relief network and directing aid towards where he believed it to be most urgently needed.[32]

Because of our hindsight of Vandeleur and his later activities, as we search through all this documentation we find ourselves on the alert for instances that might reveal at least some degree of sympathy with the situation of the poor at this earlier point. Two documents initially seem promising in this regard, both from early 1847: in the first of these, dating from January, Vandeleur informs the Relief Commissioners of the extreme difficulty of purchasing affordable food of any kind in the district and urges them in very strong terms to supply the deficiency.[33] In the second, at a landlords' meeting in Ennis in February, we find him criticizing, apparently for humanitarian reasons, the very public works system which he had helped operate, having witnessed 'the hale and the strong become rapidly feeble and emaciated through lack of sustenance', the average labourer toiling for wages that 'could not possibly give half sustenance to himself and family for a week'.[34]

The trouble with the first of these documents is that its tone is dictated by its fund-seeking objectives and it is accordingly filled with a heightened urgency, as calculated to elicit a positive response – little specific warmth or concern for the starving need attached to it. The apparent sympathy of the second document emerges very differently in subsequent remarks by Vandeleur which roundly criticize the public works labourers and the soup kitchen ration recipients, in the latter case since 'it was well known that whenever anything was given gratuitous [sic] the whole country would flock to it'. A close reading of the second document indeed reveals that for Vandeleur, the issue was not one of human suffering, but of the cost to landlords of feeding an entire starving people; in this connection he tells his audience 'his greatest fears had reference to his neighbours rather than himself', and he 'did think that any landlord would be discouraged from improving his estate as long as he laboured under the apprehension of its being overrun with paupers'.

Because of his wandering propensities Vandeleur was active in the relief programmes on an intermittent basis only. During times when he was resident in Kilrush we encounter him at relief committee meetings, on the magisterial bench or as foreman of the Grand Jury at the Assizes. On a handful of occasions we meet him in crowd situations in public, where he takes a forceful and effective hand. In May 1847, for example, on his return from yet another foreign excursion, he came on a demonstration by a crowd of angry and starving labourers just discharged from the public works in Kilrush town, led by an individual who directed their movements by blowing a horn. Using his magisterial powers, Vandeleur called out the constabulary and had the horn-blower arrested, exercising a finer judgement afterwards, however, by allowing the labourers disperse without any interference.[35] A month later he again defused a potentially explosive situation in the town when he took it upon himself to rescind an order made by the district Relief Inspector, a Captain Hill, who had insisted on dispensing cooked meal from the town soup kitchens. Unable to resist Vandeleur's (probably illegal) intervention, after his departure Hill returned to the old method, thereby sparking off a street riot.[36] Months later, the Kilrush Guardians would vote Vandeleur thanks for his exertions for relieving the poor during the previous season and in the same resolution censured Captain Hill.[37]

We glimpse Vandeleur again in public in the sultry weather of late summer, this time not in a relief context but in that of an electoral campaign, as he becomes actively involved in promoting the candidacy of his fellow Tory, Sir Lucius O'Brien, for a county seat in the general election of that year. In the attempt to displace his north Clare Whig-Liberal enemies, Messrs O'Brien and Macnamara, Vandeleur threw himself furiously into the campaign and participated in many of the tumultuous scenes that took place at Ennis just prior to polling.[38]

Much later in the year, in a lowering and leafless December, we see him once again, this time in the company of the new union inspector, Captain Kennedy, in the middle of agitated crowds milling around the Kilrush workhouse, clamouring for outdoor relief. By now Vandeleur and Kennedy had taken stock of each other, each impressed by what they saw of the other's competence and decisiveness. Cooperation in putting down crowd unrest on this occasion – quite ruthlessly – did much to enhance a cordial working relationship and developing friendship between the two men.[39] The ultimate fate of the Kennedy–Vandeleur work and social connection, so auspiciously inaugurated, will be taken up in the next chapter.

During 1847 Crofton Vandeleur had been to the fore in the re-evaluation process taking place among Irish landlords, the results of which were soon to manifest themselves in estates all over the country. This is evident as early as the February landlords' meeting, where his remarks succeeded in planting in the anxious minds of his fellow proprietors the nightmare scenario of the emergence on their estates of pauper warrens, vast concentrations of the incorrigibly idle and permanently destitute, which would wreck their fortunes and engulf them in poverty, and 'the improving landlord made to suffer for his slovenly neighbour' whose tenants might overspill onto his property.[40]

At that point the preferred solution among Clare landowners was still a massive programme of government-sponsored emigration, a measure whose 'beneficial tendency' Vandeleur proclaimed at the same meeting.[41] When instead government opted to shift the entire burden for relief of destitution to the Poor Law, landlord thinking mutated rapidly towards mass eviction. And again it was Crofton Moore Vandeleur who led the trend, in Clare as almost certainly in landlord circles in other counties.

We have seen Vandeleur dabbling in multiple eviction in his early years as Lord of the Soil in Kilrush, and on the eve of the Great Famine he did so again, in an operation that was on approximately the same scale as the Carrowdotia evictions. This was when in April and again in December of 1845 he evicted large numbers of smallholders from the townlands of

Crofton Moore Vandeleur in later years. Photo courtesy Clare County Archives.

Tullycrine and Moyasta.[42] In the April operation, twenty tenants and their families were ejected, in the December one eight more, the total number of victims amounting to approximately 100 persons. At both locations, those evicted were very poor occupiers, and although technically squatters, all were solvent and rent-paying.[43] It was the aftermath of the December phase of this clearance that attracted the attention and condemnation of Father Michael Meehan the following month.

Of all of the pointers towards Vandeleur's destiny as exterminator the Tullycrine and Moyasta evictions represent the strongest to date. But it does not seem likely that any decision on wholesale clearance had as yet been made at this point, and probably it would not be until the new government relief policies began to be implemented. But as chairman of the Kilrush Board of Guardians and owner of the greatest property in the west, Vandeleur was uniquely placed to apprehend, from a landlord's point of view, the potential implications of the new policies and to formulate the two logical strategies to be applied in order to cushion their impact on the finances of Kilrush landlords such as himself.

The first of these was boardroom-based: entrenched resistance to increases in the annual rate, savage cost-cutting at the workhouse and a rigid policing of pauper admission; the second an unprecedented level of mass eviction of poorer tenants and the annihilation of their tax-bearing holdings. In regard to the first of these, it is perhaps significant of an approaching resolve or a passive decision by default that over the summer, as chairman of the Kilrush Board of Guardians, he made little attempt to ensure that sufficient accommodation would be provided for the flood of destitution that inevitably would descend over the workhouse once the emergency soup kitchen network had closed: only about 300 extra places were created, instead of the several thousands that would be needed.[44] Implementation of the second strategy would await only the appropriate moment.

Vandeleur may have been mulling over these issues throughout the summer, which for once he spent at Kilrush, a great deal of the time aboard his yacht, *Caroline*, sailing along the coastline and the waters of the Shannon estuary. Early in September, following an Atlantic storm, *Caroline* was reported missing and Vandeleur, his crew and a party of friends aboard were feared lost. When the yacht appeared at Kilrush Creek a fortnight afterwards, there was great excitement, and to show their happiness at his safe return the inhabitants of the town and vicinity came in delegation to greet him; bonfires were lit on the streets, flags decorated buildings and the town was illuminated at night. It was all done in a spirit of mingled relief and joy on the part of the various participants and also, without any shadow of a doubt, fear of the consequences of not doing so.[45]

Within weeks of his miraculous delivery from the sea and the celebrations that followed Vandeleur embarked on the systematic mass eviction of his very poor tenants, beginning with the serving of some 300 notices to quit on smallholdings and individual cabins in the townlands of Leadmore, Carnacalla and Caherfeenick (the first two in and near Kilrush, the third some miles away near Doonbeg).[46] These were not the subtenants of middlemen whose leases had just expired, but Vandeleur's own direct tenants, as would be the case with most of those he was to evict subsequently. Mass clearance being a new phenomenon and west Clare a remote location, no further data survives relating to the evictions carried out on the basis of these notices, and it would be a whole year later before the press noticed any actual clearances by Vandeleur, by which time his reputation as a consolidating evictor was already well established.

But details even of this second wave of evictions in the early autumn of 1848 are scanty, and all we know is that they took place on the townlands of Carnane, Carnacalla and Monmore on foot of some forty-six notices to quit served on tenants some time previously and that as the wreckers executed the writs the 'wailings' of the evicted were sufficient to 'arrest the passersby'. The actual wreckers on this occasion consisted of a small group of labourers, among the few still employed by the Board of Works at the Kilrush docks project, whom Vandeleur obliged – highly illegally – to leave their construction site to physically eject the families and destroy the houses, tasks they were reported to have carried out with the greatest reluctance.[47]

The *Limerick and Clare Examiner* to which we owe these details made a great point of comparing the supposed humanity of John Ormsby Vandeleur with the inhumanity of his son: John Ormsby, many had told him, 'never disturbed a widow in her holding [and] scrupled to heap affliction on those already stricken heavily by the hand of Heaven'; Crofton, on the other hand, 'excludes from house and land so many widows and orphans as do not satisfy his own or the judgement of his agent'. It was to the children of some of these evictees that Michael Meehan distributed bread when he escorted the newspaper's correspondent around the site, as we saw in the previous chapter.

Significantly, this clearance operation was not included in the otherwise comprehensive data compiled by Captain Kennedy for the Poor Law Commissioners, which also omits further actions by Vandeleur a month later at Kilkee and Doonbeg, where thirty houses were destroyed and their occupiers scattered.[48] But Kennedy does include other evictions by Vandeleur about the same time, which are not mentioned by the *Examiner*: the 137 persons evicted at Leadmore, Carnacalla and Monmore on 10 October, the 196 ejected a few days later at Ballyerra and the 33 at Tullycrine on the same day.[49] From Kennedy's *Reports and Returns* we also read of a further 123 persons evicted by Vandeleur at Moyarta and Banemore at the end of the month.[50] On 14 November he is recorded as having cleared some 109 persons from Tiernaclohane, Cloncullen and Carhue (Kilmacduane); at Banemore on 5 December he had another 93 persons evicted.[51]

Vandeleur began 1849 with another massive clearance, and on 9 January he ejected no fewer than 196 persons from farms at Leadmore, Carnacalla, Ballynote, Monmore, Moyasta, Banemore and Dysart.[52] By now his clearances had assumed such proportions as to delineate him as a major exterminator, of a type that was now becoming widespread in Ireland: hundreds of tenants had been thrown out on the side of the road, most of them during short and dark autumn and winter days, where they were exposed to the inclemency of the weather; their homes had been destroyed, their holdings extinguished and the lands amalgamated. Vandeleur's wreckers had returned to the same townlands again and again to carry out evictions, thereby maintaining tenants' terror at an excruciating level. It was at this point that philanthropic visitors and journalists from other regions and from Britain began to appear in the west to see what Vandeleur and other evictors inspired by him had wrought; and in February after a tour of the Kilrush Union, a reporter for the *Galway Vindicator* referred to Vandeleur as a 'cabin-tumbling warrior', a description that was repeated afterwards and headlined by the *Limerick and Clare Examiner*.[53]

After a gap of some months, on 10 May Vandeleur had seventy-three persons evicted from Caherfeenick and Clashmore.[54] On 9 June he returned to Caherfeenick to expel a further seventy-five persons.[55] In August, heedless of the damaging publicity of Captain Kennedy's newly published *Reports and Returns*, he destroyed a large number of houses in the vicinity of Kilrush town.[56] In September he was again at Tullycrine where he evicted five families, amounting to some thirty persons.[57] At Knock about the same time he had a further thirty persons removed from their homes.[58] Although Vandeleur would evict again, in 1850 and afterwards, and on a major scale, the Knock operation appears to mark the end of the phase of frenzied activity in his clearing activities and the expending of the rage and aggression that had driven them. It had taken little over a year on his part to bring about this gigantic scale of physical damage and human suffering, which literally became carnage in that a large proportion of the evictees died subsequently.

Remarkably, we do not possess a single eyewitness account of an eviction by Vandeleur or a description of the aftermath, and only in a few cases do we know anything of the circumstances of evicted persons. We do not know exactly what were the calculations that led his wreckers to return repeatedly to the same townlands or on what basis they weeded out certain tenant families as opposed to others. Neither do we know how much of the organizational work was done by his agent, Francis Fitzgerald, or to what extent Vandeleur involved himself directly in planning evictions. We do not even know if he was ever present at an eviction; although the Galway journalist mentioned above spoke of having seen him personally take a hand in one action, this is so uncharacteristic that one suspects him to have mistaken an under-agent for the landlord.[59] Many of the clearances, in fact, took place during Vandeleur's absences, some as he sailed in *Caroline* along the coast in the early autumn of 1848 and, undaunted by his recent maritime misadventure, gave over sailing time to the hunt for the escaping Young Ireland insurgents, Richard O'Gorman and Garrett Doherty – more time indeed than Michael Meehan gave to helping them escape.[60]

But if Vandeleur paused his clearances for a time after the Knock operation, seven months later, in April 1850, he was still dealing with the enormous fallout from what he had previously done, the greatest problem being that so many of the evicted were still in the neighbourhood, many having been taken in by neighbours. Vandeleur's way of dealing with this problem was to instruct all his surviving smallholder tenants in the Kilrush electoral division not to shelter evicted families, under pain of being evicted themselves.[61] Although evictors commonly made such prohibitions during the Famine clearances it was rare for them to be done overtly as Vandeleur did in this case, by the serving of the tenants with a formal printed notice.[62]

The absence of concern on Vandeleur's part that this action might attract adverse publicity is explained by his response when indeed he was condemned for it. This was to produce a detailed memorial signed by his town tenants, 'the most respectable men of all creeds and classes', to which he declared the printed prohibition was a response, its aim being to save them from an 'influx of strange paupers'. He had been happy to oblige his town tenants in this matter, he said, since 'it could not be supposed that a proprietor could submit to have the paupers of all the neighbouring electoral divisions shipped on him and his tenants without a struggle'.[63]

Forty names were attached to the memorial, which on the face of it seems a damning indictment of the callous intolerance of the respectable townsfolk of Kilrush, and not just their landlord. Its main demand was that Vandeleur ensure that the new Vagrant Act be rigorously enforced in the town, since Kilrush had become 'a receptacle for the straggling beggars of the several parishes of the Union'. The streets were 'swarmed', the shopkeepers 'beset', property 'rendered insecure', the industrious 'interrupted in their legitimate pursuits', because of the 'importunities' and 'begging practices' of 'such hordes'.[64] The language of the memorial, however, fits in too neatly with Vandeleur's specific obsessions, and his eagerness to publish it is equally suspicious: familiarity with the manipulative *modus operandi* of many landlords will recognize the probability that the memorial had been confected by Vandeleur, and the town tenants coerced into signing it, compliance ensured by their helpless tenurial position as occupiers without leases.[65]

And if Vandeleur had not admitted to himself or anyone else that it was his own actions in evicting tenants that was responsible for the spoiling of his town with 'hordes' of the suffering poor, there were others there to remind him of the fact. One of them was the English philanthropist, Reverend Sidney Godolphin Osborne, who travelled to west Clare late in 1849 to view conditions for himself. Osborne came of aristocratic landowning stock in England and was possessed of a sense of entitlement that was greater even than Vandeleur's, whose wide domains and wealth did not impress him and whom he declared he knew of only as an 'evictionist'. When Osborne stated, somewhat obliquely, that 'management of the Union' was as much responsible for the crowding of the town by 'these poor wretches' as the refuge given them by the smallholders, he was referring directly to management of the Board of Guardians by its chairman, Crofton Moore Vandeleur.[66] The *Galway Vindicator* was more direct in its declaration that the houseless crowds swarming in Kilrush were 'not unlikely to be a portion of the tenantry formerly belonging to his mightiness, Colonel Vandeleur himself'.[67]

The attitudes revealed in the episode of Vandeleur's 'ukase' – the *Vindicator*'s phrase – afford the clearest view we have into the moral abyss constituting the mental processes of exterminating landlords, whose depths are fathomable only after reading of the actual state of the 'vagrants' so despised by the colonel, as in the following exactly contemporaneous description by an *Examiner* correspondent.[68] All approaches to the workhouse, the correspondent noted, 'were lined with one dense mass of skeletons with shrivelled limbs and gloomy aspects – poor creatures scarcely conscious of existence'. Turned away from a crammed workhouse these silent crowds returned to the town centre, and the following morning were 'strewed like dead corpses around the market house, writhing in all the agonies of pain and hunger'.

In mid-June, just before he left for London to attend the Scrope Committee inquiry into the Kilrush Union, Vandeleur began another assault on his destitute tenants, taking out ejectment orders this time in the Dublin courts – he may have learned this cost-saving technique from Marcus Keane, who pioneered it – against scores of occupiers, affecting in all about 500 persons. Townlands through which his levellers had repeatedly rampaged were once again afflicted with mass expulsion and destruction: Carnacalla, Monmore, Caherfeenick, Banmore and Tullycrine, in a fresh wave of clearance that caused one Kilrush resident to ask rhetorically when would 'the Moloch of landlordism cease from its cruel labours?'[69]

In London Vandeleur attended the Scrope Committee every day it sat, over a period of nearly two months: not a summoned witness he went before it voluntarily and returned willingly for follow-up questioning.[70] Like Marcus Keane he delivered his evidence forcefully and with a level of conviction that had we no other source we might accept at face value as that of a justly aggrieved landowner whose honourable and often kindly actions had been horribly misrepresented, rather than the narcissistic delusion that it was in reality. To read Vandeleur's evidence is almost to come under the spell of his self-delusion, and so convincing is his constructed image of himself as a wronged man that we find ourselves rereading all we have learned of his conduct in order to reassure ourselves as to its veracity. Only when we have done so and again reread his Committee evidence do its contradictions appear clearly and its facile rationalizations fall apart.

Vandeleur gave his testimony in a detached, reasoned manner, his responses altering only when the integrity of his constructed self-image is threatened by close questioning. At such points we find him straining to conceal a developing hostility towards Captain Kennedy, the chief witness, towards whom the Committee showed respect; he makes no attempt to conceal his contempt for the journalist James Shannon, one of Kennedy's data-gatherers, nor his violent antipathy towards newspapers such as the *Freeman's Journal* and the *Limerick and Clare Examiner*.[71] His loathing of the *Examiner* is intense and intemperate.

The earlier part of Vandeleur's evidence was given over to a defence of the Kilrush Board of Guardians and an indictment of the alleged inefficiency of the Vice-Guardians who replaced them between March 1848 and November 1849. In effect this was an apologia for himself, since his dominance over the Kilrush Guardians was so great that he effectively *was* the Board. On occasion he is so revealing as to use the first-person singular when referring to decisions that should have been the collective decision of the Board. Using the chairmanship to ride roughshod over discussions, he had of himself decided Union business on crucial areas of its operation, from admissions policy to the striking of a rate. Supine, lazy and unintelligent as its members were, the Board was grateful to be relieved of these responsibilities, and even Captain Kennedy had been so admiring of Vandeleur's management of Union business as never to pay attention to his personalized decision-making let alone oppose it.

The Scrope Committee, to be sure, did hear one witness who was critical of Vandeleur's Boardroom dominance; this was Cornelius Doherty, the only elected Kilrush Guardian to give evidence, who in referring to the period after the Board was restored in November 1849 spoke of Vandeleur's habit of ruling on the admission of paupers without reference to other Guardians.[72] In December Vandeleur had ended a sub-committee system established in his absence for the purpose of speeding up relief applications, on the grounds that 'some of the Guardians were acting too liberally in the way of giving relief'. His action led to delays lasting all day and evening when it was first implemented, at the end of which half the applicants had not been heard, according to Doherty, the remainder returning home late in the night, 'a distance of probably 10 or 12 Irish miles, with their little children upon their backs'. But Doherty's evidence was lost in the general avalanche of information with which the Committee was inundated, and it was never referred to again.

But Vandeleur's own evidence reveals an unquestioning belief in his right to rule the Board and Union thus. 'I have stayed myself constantly from 12 o'clock in the day till eight o'clock at night ruling the books', he asserted of the period mentioned by Doherty, 'and after ruling the books the whole day, and perhaps going through 2,000 or 3,000 [relief applications], I would get 200 admissions'.[73] In the breathtaking presumption of this statement we get to the heart of the horrors of the late Famine period in Ireland. Here we have the multitudes of the destitute poor, in advanced stages of physical deterioration, being screened for relief purposes by the landlord who was the major contributor to their condition, directly and indirectly, as evictor and inspirer of evictors, the individual who as a major taxpayer had the strongest vested interest in rejecting them, admitting openly to having refused all but the tiniest minority. And far from seeing anything untoward in this, Vandeleur was prepared to place it on record before a parliamentary investigation, not as the appalling admission it was, but as a proof of how hard he had worked and how seriously he approached his responsibilities as chairman of the Kilrush Board of Guardians.

Notwithstanding this ironclad sense of righteousness, the longer Vandeleur's testimony went on the more threadbare it became, and by the time he began to speak of the clearances the partial truths and embellishments of his earlier testimony had given way to outrageous falsehood. Clearances, he told the Committee, had been exaggerated; those that had taken place in Kilrush Union were of small account compared to those carried out elsewhere (we know the Kilrush clearances to have been unique in their extent and in the consequent human casualty).[74] The total of 833 persons he was alleged in Captain Kennedy's *Reports and Returns* to have evicted, up to mid-1849 was a grossly inflated figure and the details were full of errors, which he spent some time in adumbrating. Finally he admitted to having evicted half the numbers asserted by Kennedy, unconcerned that even this number constituted a horrendous admission of human destruction. These evictions he held had been 'absolutely necessary', and it would have been 'utterly impossible that the country could have progressed or that improvements could have been carried out, or that either rates or rent could have been paid in the Union', had they not taken place.[75]

Preposterously, he maintained that the very poorest occupiers he had evicted had somehow secreted funds away during the period they had not paid their rents, and so had been able to emigrate (emigration among Kilrush evictees we know to have been negligible).[76] When asked what happened to those who did not emigrate he replied that some had rented smaller farms and some had become ruined; pressed further he allowed that two-thirds of those expelled had become paupers.[77] Asked if sickness and death had been the lot of any of the evicted he replied, 'not that I am aware of' and added, lamely, that there was sickness at the time of the cholera (The vast majority of Kilrush evictees are known to have died subsequently).[78]

Because of the clearances, Vandeleur held, 'the land has lately got into the hands of a much better class of tenants, who are of more industrious habits, and who are not embarrassed with the debts and the liabilities which the former occupiers were'. He believed that the Kilrush Union was in a much more wholesome state at present than it had been for some years.[79] And in the strange surreal world inhabited by Vandeleur – and indeed John Singleton as we have seen – it was he and other landlords who were the real victims of the clearances. 'I may say', he declared at one point, 'that in many instances the landlords have barely lived'.[80]

In the end Vandeleur's evidence was demolished in a few sentences by Francis Coffee, the land agent/civil engineer/surveyor who minutes before had made short work of Marcus Keane's testimony. We should not idealize Coffee, who was neither a morally committed individual nor a sympathetic one. As a land agent, he had been an evictor, of considerable culpability in the Kilrush Union, the very individual in fact who cleared and destroyed the village of Tullig and caused such anguish to Michael Meehan.[81] His work in collecting eviction statistics for Kennedy was purely a professional undertaking for which he was paid a fee, and no doubt he would have performed an equally professional service if he had been asked to carry out evictions by the Inspector.[82]

But Coffee's local knowledge, technical competence and professional manner made him the perfect expert witness, his testimony supported, dramatically and authoritatively, by a great map, multicoloured and inscribed with details of the 2,700 separate evictions he had identified in the Kilrush Union between November 1847 and the end of June 1850.[83] Coffee also submitted a list of seventy-six significant evictors, together with details of each eviction, meticulously executed and annotated. Coffee's evidence established beyond doubt that Vandeleur had evicted 180 families, to a total number of 1,001 persons, a significant update from Kennedy's *Reports and Returns* of mid-1849.[84] When to this is added evictions carried out before the arrival of Kennedy in Kilrush, those done while the Committee sat, and those done subsequently, there can be little doubt but that the total number of Vandeleur's evictions and his victims significantly exceeds that with which Coffee's evidence indicts him.

A year after the Scrope Committee's proceedings had ended, late in July 1851, Crofton Vandeleur, Lady Grace and their children arrived home from London, where they had been specifically to view the Great Exhibition, a 'short period of relaxation', according to a piece communicated to the *Clare Journal*, 'from the arduous duties which they have been so actively and incessantly discharging during the present trying times'. While in London, the Vandeleurs had done the social rounds, visiting 'numerous' friends in the 'Court Circle'; Miss Vandeleur had been presented to Queen Victoria. The 'amiable family' were now returned in order 'to cheer and aid a suffering district by their benevolent exertions'.[85]

Reverend Sidney Godolphin Osborne's reaction to this piece of Vandeleurian posturing, if he saw it, is not recorded. Much earlier Reverend Osborne had himself been to the Great Exhibition, in March when it had first opened, and in one of his famous 'S.G.O.' letters to the *Times* he had compared the splendours of the Crystal Palace where it was held to the appalling sights he had so recently witnessed in Kilrush, declaring that 'as a Christian and a subject of a Christian government', the comparison made him feel 'utter disgust'.[86]

Throughout the spring and summer the combative clergyman maintained a barrage of criticism in his *Times* letters; Vandeleur and the Kilrush Guardians in turn discussed S.G.O. and drew up memorials refuting his allegations, while the *Clare Journal* weighed in editorially and indignantly on their behalf.[87] Osborne's culminating letter came three weeks after the return of the Vandeleurs to Kilrush, in reply to critical comments made by Crofton at a Board meeting.[88] In this remarkably vituperative letter, Osborne contemptuously referred to Vandeleur as a 'militia colonel ... although of a non-existing regiment, who yet ever paraded the title', and as an 'evictionist ... wanton in the exercise of his power', and as 'a man who only seeks his own ... who calmly works the Poor Law with such imbecility as to make "relief" another name for death'.

Scornfully, he advised Vandeleur to retire as Chairman of the Board of Guardians, a position for which he had 'neither the talent nor the temper' and to seek 'some more worthy field of employment than this one', the chairmanship as he managed it being 'from some cause on another, a scene of weekly death disgraceful to our whole land', and in which he was a 'cruel failure'. 'In a short time', he told Vandeleur, 'you and I shall be alike forgotten', except perhaps 'in the record of the few in which a relentless war was raged on a wretched famine-stricken peasantry',

> when the government not alone connived at much illegal razing of their dwellings, but held them to be *supported* by law ... when they *died* in *fifties* per week in the workhouses ... I say in the record of these years of Irish horror and English disgrace by some future historian our names may perchance figure on the same page. It is nothing for either of us to boast of, for the reader will turn in horror from its revelations.

Reverend Osborne's violent attack was provocative to say the least, and it posed a clear challenge to Vandeleur, who was wise enough not to take it up; we have no record of any response on his part. But Osborne's remarks made no difference to Vandeleur's outlook or behaviour. As late as March 1853, in the last days of the Famine clearances, we find him again serving ejectment notices against tenants in Moyarta, Ibrickane and Clonderlaw baronies, preparatory to one further round of large-scale evictions.[89]

9

The Most Charitable Officer: Captain A.E. Kennedy

Our initial impressions of Captain Kennedy are derived from the *Illustrated London News* sketch in which he features, and the few lines accorded him in histories of the Great Famine. From these we imagine the Captain to be relatively young but mature beyond his years; energetic and decisive yet reserved and austere. And we imagine him compassionate towards the poor and unfailingly courageous in confronting their landlord oppressors. The impression is one that lingers even after we have delved in the sources, partly because we are reluctant to relinquish an image that in its way is as clear-cut, as strong and as satisfying as that constructed for Michael Meehan, and partly also because a good deal of it remains true.

But nothing human is quite so simple, and notwithstanding the work of modern historians, most notably Ignatius Murphy, the first to accord him scholarly attention, our re-evaluated Kennedy differs in many senses from the picture above, in some ways markedly so. For on one level, he was almost a caricature of the class structure that produced him, with a controlling temperament and a level of social prejudices that made him almost a carbon copy of Crofton Moore Vandeleur; on the other hand, he was often troubled, struggling with a conscience that told him – weakly at first – that the horrors he daily encountered held a very different causation to that which colleagues and official culture ascribed to the shortcomings of the actual victims. That his conscience prevailed was not a foregone conclusion, and that it did lends the Kilrush Inspector a human credibility that is in many ways more impressive than the more heroic image.

Kennedy spent two years and eight months at Kilrush, about the same period as each of his military tours and the career postings that came afterwards. The Kilrush sojourn, however, was pivotal in ways the others were not, and apart from the changes it wrought in him personally it effectively altered the direction of his life. But that was for the future, and when he arrived by coach in Kilrush in November 1847, all that was apparent was a former military man adapting to civilian life in the role of a Temporary Union Inspector, at a time when a major famine crisis was once again gathering, one that in the west would be as bad as any so far experienced.

Arthur Edward Kennedy was the fourth son of a well-connected County Down landlord, Hugh Kennedy of Cultra.[1] A career officer who saw service in several British army regiments over a period of nearly twenty years, his lot during that time had been a succession of uneventful garrison postings in Britain and Ireland. The most interesting point of his career seems to have been a Canadian tour where he had had some contact with the native Indian population but as far as we know he never saw combat. All Kennedy's commissions were purchased, his captaincy in 1840 fairly late in his career. Kilrush was his second appointment with the Poor Law; earlier he had served as inspecting officer in the Kells Union under the Soup Kitchen Act.[2] This *curriculum vitae* was very similar to that of scores of Kennedy's fellow Temporary Inspectors, and among his new colleagues the youngish captain (he was thirty-eight) did not stand out, either in his service values of duty and discipline or, as will become apparent, in his perspective on the poor.

A generous salary of £439 per annum, topped up by whatever military benefits and private income were available to him, allowed Kennedy a lifestyle in Kilrush commensurate with his breeding and background.[3] After a short period of rooming in one of the town hotels, he rented a large house at Cappagh, a hamlet south-west of the town.[4] This he filled with good furniture, and with china, glassware, hangings and drapes, books, clocks, barometers and other fittings.[5] Having fitted out his house in this tasteful manner, Kennedy then sent for his wife Georgina and his young daughter Elizabeth. A second daughter would be born to the Kennedys while they were in Kilrush.[6]

Very soon after his arrival, the captain's spare military figure, invariably attired in dark frock coat and tall hat, had become a familiar sight in and around Kilrush; on foot by himself, or with wife and children in the family horse and car, or riding between Cappagh and the workhouse on its northerly eminence overlooking the town. Kilrush was a fine town, although for gentlefolk enjoyment of its fine precincts had of late been marred by the slow-moving presence of ragged gaggles of the hunger-worn poor, listlessly perambulating the streets, leaving individual corpses to be found, as they regularly were, like litter, on the flag-ways in the mornings.

Such sights would not have shocked Kennedy; several years of famine had rendered them familiar in most Irish towns, although the numbers involved might have surprised him. Kennedy would certainly have noticed how impressive the streets and buildings of this geographically remote town were, and he would have noted the handsome market house that dominated the central square and around which pedestrian and wheeled traffic flowed. One street he would have travelled frequently led eastwards from the square, in an opposite direction to the waterfront, shortly coming up against the high stone walls enclosing the wooded demesne in which, amid lawns and gardens, stood Kilrush House, the home of Crofton Moore Vandeleur.

As we have seen, by virtue of their respective Poor Law offices as Chairman and Union Inspector, Vandeleur and Kennedy were thrown together immediately, and from their earliest meetings an easy cordiality developed, born of mutual admiration, background and age (Vandeleur was a year older).[7] Almost certainly social visits were exchanged between Kennedy and Vandeleur families, who would also have worshipped on Sundays together in Kilrush's Church of Ireland parish church. For the Inspector, whatever difficulties he might have expected to encounter in his work, the friendship and support of Vandeleur promised to help make manageable, and to ensure also that interludes of leisure would be enjoyed in pleasant company and surroundings.

The day after arriving in Kilrush, Captain Kennedy inspected the Union workhouse and made the acquaintance of the Board of Guardians, both the ex officio, or landlord Guardians, and the elected members, for the most part farmers, middlemen and shopkeepers. His first report to the Irish Poor Law Commissioners opens with the inspection and meeting, and taken with his second one a week later, both brisk documents designed to impress, shows him launching vigorously into his responsibilities; identifying problems, imposing solutions or making forceful recommendations as to how matters might be resolved.[8]

The Guardians he finds congenial and encouraging; yet they and the rate collectors display a 'want of activity and energy' in their respective duties. The Master was elderly and incompetent, his neglect the cause of irregularities within the house that were 'numerous and culpable'. Blunders had been made in collecting the Poor Law rate; the paupers were undisciplined and unclean, and there was one grave lapse where a side-gate to the adjoining fever hospital allowed visitors access to afflicted patients, thereby facilitating the spread of contagion. Almost as an afterthought, Kennedy tells the Commissioners that twenty-one persons had died in the workhouse of smallpox and fever in his first week as inspector.[9]

As regards the rural hinterland surrounding the workhouse, it would be a long time before Kennedy was able to find his way around its geographical sprawl, and a claim made in February 1848 that he had already 'acquired an intimate personal knowledge' of its 'people and localities' was premature and not a little arrogant.[10] For this was an enormous area, comprising perhaps a fifth of Clare's land mass, running west of a line drawn from Mullagh to Kildysert villages and tapering down to land's end in the long triangle of the Loop Head peninsula. Much of it was roadless terrain through bog, unreclaimed or marginal land; the county roads, where they existed, had been largely wrecked during the public works phase of famine relief.

One of the poorest and most populous Unions in Ireland, Kilrush had already suffered atrociously through starvation, fever and the massive casualty of government relief programmes, its teeming pre-Famine population of 82,000 souls significantly reduced by starvation and fever mortality, very little by emigration. For the moment the Union was *terra incognita* to the new Inspector and for perhaps a year after his appointment his knowledge of it would be a superficial matter of villages, squalid hamlets and isolated crossroads, where the indigent poor assembled for relief assessment.

In these first weeks, therefore, Kennedy concentrated on policing the workhouse, addressing irregularities and inefficiencies wherever he found them. Daily he inspected each department in the house, arranged for additional inmate accommodation and organized a tightening up on the collection of the rate; pauper labour was mobilized in preparing land about the workhouse into a garden and in gravelling of the yards up to then 'ankle-deep in mud'. Rate collectors and workhouse staff were called to account.[11] By the end of his second week, he told the Commissioners, the Guardians were 'less desponding' than before, more efficient and 'cheerful', and they now gave willing support to his efforts at bringing 'general discipline, cleanliness and regularity' to the house.

Twice in these first two reports Kennedy mentions that 6,000 notices to quit had been recently served in the Union, but these references are as oddly offhand as those relating to workhouse mortality.[12] We find the same lack of curiosity on his part when he was first presented with the human fallout from clearances, as well as a puzzling inability to connect consequences with causes. In his second report, for example, he describes, with evident shock, the condition of about 200 persons applying for admission to the workhouse as 'a tangled mass of poverty, filth and disease', the sufferers being 'in all stages of fever and small-pox mingling indiscriminately with the crowd, and all clamouring for admission'. Their misery and want, he tells the Commissioners, 'baffle description', adding that when he arrived home after a day spent processing the admissions, he was covered in vermin.[13]

How strange then that he makes no remark at all as to what or who could have been responsible for such 'an appalling sight'? A diligent inquiry of the kind for which he would later become noted would have revealed that the only relevant ejectment notices, those in respect of Leadmore and Carnacalla townlands in and around Kilrush, related to properties owned by Crofton Vandeleur, the genial Chairman of the Board of Guardians. Instead we find Kennedy praising the Chairman who had stood with him and one or two of the Guardians all day, and 'regardless of personal danger, examined and admitted [the applicants] to the house or hospital'.[14]

If these failures of discernment can be understood in terms of the flood of impressions bearing on Kennedy's mind in these early days, overloading his ability to process them all, they still bother us: they are the first discordances in our perception of the Inspector. Rapidly they would be followed by others, until we become aware that we are dealing not just with the new Inspector's initial impressions, but also with a set of pre-existing attitudes and prejudices through which they were filtered.

What disturbs us most about Kennedy as we read through sources such as these is a pronounced hostility towards the poor; and it is this perhaps that most clearly defines him as a servant of the Poor Law. The central notion here was the belief found virtually everywhere among his colleagues that the poor were degraded persons, who observed few moral standards, their most deplorable failings being dishonesty, passivity and exceptional craftiness. In this highly judgemental perspective shared widely across respectable society as a whole – we have already seen examples aplenty in the case of several of our figures – unless resisted these combined vices would lead to a massive and unnecessary expenditure on relief, permanent habits of social dependency and a ruinous level of taxation. Kennedy, like all Poor Law inspectors, was resolutely determined to prevent this.

For a time Kennedy's anti-poor attitude became even more pronounced as he began to travel along the densely populated seaboard of the Kilrush Union and became aware of the awesome depths of the poverty of its people, 'a turf-digging, seaweed-gathering, fish-catching, amphibious population; as bad fishermen as they are agriculturists'. In such contemptuous terms he describes them to the Commissioners in November 1847, and as people who were without 'any regular mode of gaining a living', and who were 'inert, improvident, and utterly without foresight'.[15]

Had he been more aware he would have realized that none of this was true, and that the combination of turf-digging, seaweed-gathering and fish-catching represented in fact an extremely resourceful adaptation by the poor to the conditions of their existence, and that far from displaying inertia they were exceptionally active; far from being irregular, their 'mode of gaining a living' formed an endless, very regular and repetitive cycle of backbreaking work, all of it dictated by the need to survive. Without the exceptional foresight they displayed, in normal times, they could not have survived. That their activity yielded such poor results was a function of their poverty and illiteracy and exclusion from a technical knowledge that might have improved their lives. Neither were the poor, as Kennedy declared in another remark, 'content on the lowest scale of existence'; they were merely accepting of a reality in which they had no possibility of changing.[16] The collapse of the elaborate subsistence structures on which they had existed in pre-Famine times meant that by the time of Kennedy's arrival, large numbers of this most vulnerable class had already suffered and died.

Bureaucratic rigidity combined with this opprobrious attitude towards the poor in Kennedy's early investigations into the deaths of persons for whose relief the Poor Law held legal responsibility. Doggedly we find him insisting, often against the evidence, that such persons had died of causes other than Poor Law negligence, usually their own foolishness. Thus in December, regardless of a police inspector's report, the certification of a physician and the verdict of a coroner's court, he concludes that fifty-year-old John Reidy, of Kilmacduane, had not died of starvation, but was a long-ailing, 'delicate' man, who died rather of disease, 'aggravated by want'.[17] Likewise, Denis

Clohessy also of Kilmacduane, who died in January 1848, 'was constantly destitute of most of the necessities of life', but was 'undoubtedly in possession of sufficient [means] to prevent death'.[18] Sixty-year-old Timothy O'Keeffe of Bresla, who died in February, after being struck off the relief lists for fraudulently claiming rations for his two children, might well have died of starvation, but because of the fraud, the Poor Law was not accountable.[19] Similarly, 35-year-old Mary O'Brien, from Kilmurry, a young woman who died in March shortly after entering the workhouse, had indeed perished of starvation, but having refused an offer of admission the previous Christmas, the Poor Law was not liable legally or morally.[20]

At times Kennedy's concern with exculpating the Poor Law authorities became a reflex that led him into circular reasoning and absurd distinctions. The best example here dates from January 1848 when after encountering an emaciated man bringing his two dead daughters in a cradle to a cemetery – the family had been in receipt of outdoor relief – he rationalizes their situation to the Commissioners. Reflecting on the undeniable fact of the two dead children and the physical condition of the father, who had made 'no claim of a want of food', Kennedy held that neither starvation nor disease was in question, but rather 'a protracted insufficiency of food'.[21] In his remarks, there is no questioning of the monstrous nature of a system purporting to relieve the destitute but under which such enormities proliferated.

Some glimmer of understanding seems to inform his next sentence, however, where he states that want of food and 'long privation' had 'broken down the constitution of the people, and made them an easy prey to the most trifling ailment'. If such a comment can be read as indicating a private ambivalence with respect to the Poor Law, at no point does he express it openly, never asking, for example, why starving persons would emphatically and repeatedly refuse to enter the workhouse, and why they would often allow themselves die rather than submit to its horribly oppressive and dehumanizing regime. Published remarks on his part reflect only resentment and anger, and at very best a level of condescension towards the poor.

Kennedy's attitude towards evicted persons was no different, his anger at the ragged and filthy family groups and larger parties who arrived at the workhouse gates mounting with the increased frequency of such arrivals in ever more advanced stages of decrepitude and ill health. In describing the first evicted party he met (mentioned already) Kennedy refers to the parents as being possessed of the 'sagacity of animals', in allowing their children to descend to such a level. Subsequent accounts would replicate over and over biting denunciations of parents; animal comparisons would feature again. And in March 1848, after another clearance resulted in a further surge in relief applications and in one day the dumping of 'three cart-loads of half-comatose creatures' outside the workhouse, many of whom could not walk, 'some in fever, some suffering from dysentery, and all from want of food', 'the most appalling cases of destitution and suffering', we find mingled with his pity, the symptoms of exasperation and contempt.[22]

Kennedy's greatest frustration with the occupants of the three carts lay in the fact that regardless of their physical state, when they realized they had been brought to a workhouse, many refused to enter, despite his encouragement to take a look inside first so he could 'demonstrate the utter groundlessness of the prejudice against it'. He is careful, however, to neither inquire into the 'prejudice' nor make any comment on it in print: his reticence is understandable, given that both he and the Commissioners to whom he wrote of this incident shared an unstated awareness of the extent to which the Poor Law depended on it in order to keep inmates numbers at a manageable level.

Kennedy's prejudicial commentary on the poor reached a peak in April when the workhouse was engulfed in the greatest wave of destitution yet experienced, when on one Board Day, some 300 persons arrived at the gates. As before, his words of sympathy are laced with revulsion for the 'mass of helpless, hopeless and revolting misery' he gazes on, among whom there abounded 'impostors' who 'came dressed for the occasion'; that is relatively well-off persons, who supposedly attired themselves in rags in the hope that outdoor relief was about to be granted.

Kennedy was as vocal in regard to 'imposture', 'imposition' or 'abuse' as any other official, and he pursued it with the zeal of a medieval cleric in search of heresy and heretics. He discovered it among relief applicants, among admittees to the workhouse, most often by humiliating body searches, which revealed pitiful sums of money secreted on about their persons, forlorn hopes of future independence from the Poor Law machine. In one case, Kennedy comments with mingled triumph and indignation of an illiterate fisherwoman, who was found to have woven a string of dried mackerel into a belt around her waist for consumption later. He even discovered it in his next-door neighbour in Cappagh, a well-off widow, with a 'good house', let at high rent during the summer and a farm stocked with cattle and poultry. Clearly misinterpreting a remark on her part, and without at all considering the absurd improbability of someone in her position seeking relief of any kind, he concluded that 'the strictest scrutiny' was necessary, since 'the shamelessness of all seeking relief would be amusing, if it were not melancholy'.[23]

Kennedy's abuse-phobia was most pronounced in regard to outdoor relief, that is assistance afforded needy persons, whether in cash or in cooked food, without imposing on them the obligation of entering the workhouse. Under the Poor Law Amendment Act of 1847 such assistance could be offered to able-bodied persons only when workhouses were overcrowded and only under the most stringent conditions. By November 1847, the aged and infirm were being allowed outdoor relief, as were disabled persons and dependent widows with children; by December, Kennedy was advising the Commissioners that it would soon be necessary to extend it to the able-bodied, a suggestion that was favourably received.[24] But he refrained from pursuing the matter, even after the arrival of the Commissioners' sanctioning

Sealed Order just before Christmas, the reason being a crowd demonstration outside the workhouse which convinced him that the demand for outdoor relief was being artificially stimulated.[25]

Christmas came and went, and in the teeth of what he acknowledged were catastrophically deteriorating conditions, still he withheld his recommendation with regard to outdoor relief to the able-bodied. Naturally enough his obduracy made him unpopular, to the point where along with Colonel Vandeleur he was threatened with death in a Whiteboy notice posted at the Colonel's gate on New Year's Eve 1847.[26] Kennedy in fact held out for an astonishing two months further, until finally the Commissioners themselves stepped in to remind him that 'one of the main objects of a Poor Law is the preservation of human life, and the Commissioners rely on you making such arrangements as will prevent the possibility of death from starvation in Kilrush Union'.[27] Though gently phrased, towards an officer in whom the Commissioners held particular trust, Kennedy was very definitely being given an instruction, and it was thus that Kilrush, the most afflicted Union in Clare, became the last one to sanction outdoor relief to the starving, so-called able-bodied class of pauper.

These months also feature other instances of insensitivity, even inhumanity, on Kennedy's part towards the starving poor. In January and February 1848, while inspecting recipients of outdoor relief in coastal parishes, he reveals that he has obliged these sick and infirm people to parade before him in all their misery. Of the several thousands he saw, those, that is, 'whose state would admit of their attending', constituted a 'fearful array' who must have endured much just to be present. 'Their constitutions', he wrote, 'are irretrievably broken by protracted privation, and the most trifling ailment will bring them to the grave'. He expected one-third to be dead by the summer.[28] Did Kennedy not realize that his mode of inspection had to be the cause of great additional suffering to these unfortunate people, many of whom had travelled long distances to be present? His letters reveal no such realization.

And through it all he expresses astonishment at 'the lying and deception' among the people, innate traits, he clearly believes, rather than stratagems resorted to in the struggle for survival. Aged and infirm parents, sent by their families towards the workhouse to take the pressure from the remainder, are 'abandoned' by their children; wives whose husbands have gone to America to make money to send home for their families are 'deserted' by them.[29] Instances of cruelty or callousness are seized on as indications of inherent tendencies, and isolated incidents are taken as typical; the man, for example, who would not go near his seriously ill wife for fear of catching fever, or the woman who caught fever and was thrown out of her lodging along with her illegitimate child.[30] Typical of the generalizations to which he was prone with regard to such cases was that made in regard to the latter incident, that 'the inhuman conduct of the poor towards each other when stricken by fever or dysentery is incredible'.

But even as we absorb all this evidence of fraud-hunting zealotry, coldness, insensitivity and prejudice on the part of the Kilrush Inspector, we never quite lose sight of the other Kennedy, who is indeed emotionally affected by what he witnesses and who does feel compassion towards famine and fever victims; even at the height of his tirades against them there is never a time when such feeling is entirely absent. The contradiction gives us reason to believe that for much of the time Kennedy was at war with himself, and that the rising vehemence of his anti-poor rhetoric in early 1848 reflects an internal struggle of conscience that was approaching crisis point.

Since Kennedy's Poor Law correspondence survives in excerpted form only for the summer and autumn of 1848, we cannot follow whatever process is involved for any length. But these extracts, and further material published during the autumn and after, are notable for a striking change in tone. It is not so much that the level of human sympathy expressed for the poor has significantly increased, although it certainly has, but that it is so much more manifest due to the fact that the anti-poor rhetoric and the shibboleths of abuse and imposition have altogether disappeared. The patience of the poor under their many afflictions increasingly appears as a motif in Kennedy's writings, and by January 1849 he was conceding that men 'are called able-bodied here who would not be so designated elsewhere'.[31] When he came to give evidence to the Scrope Committee eighteen months later, nothing remained of his earlier attitudes.

This change of attitude on Kennedy's part is traceable ultimately to four main developments: the absence of Crofton Vandeleur from the Broom Hill boardroom from late January and his subsequent departure from Kilrush; the dissolution of the Board of Guardians in March; the granting of outdoor relief to the able-bodied in April; and about the same time, the decision to begin collecting eviction statistics. Vandeleur had been ill for much of January and in early February, along with his family, left Kilrush for Dublin, 'to recuperate from his travails as Chairman of the Kilrush Board of Guardians', according to one favourable source. The family stayed away until June, and when they returned, to be 'hailed with loud manifestations of joy and gladness', the Board of Guardians no longer existed.[32] Very soon after Vandeleur decamped once again from Kilrush.

According to Kennedy, the immediate effect of Vandeleur's departure was that conduct of Union business fell apart, and disorder returned; more significantly for the Inspector, however, was that henceforth he was liberated – permanently as it turned out – from the Chairman's insidious influence.[33] And when in succeeding weeks Guardian performance continued to deteriorate, in March he acted decisively on his own initiative to have the Board dissolved for gross neglect of its responsibilities, a fate that had already befallen one-third of all Irish Poor Law Boards. Two Vice-Guardians replaced the dissolved Kilrush Board, and until November the following year, in conjunction with the Inspector, they ran the Union as a three-man team.[34] During this period, for the first time in its short history the Union was managed efficiently, even if in many respects the poor did not feel the benefit of the change.

Now that it was safe to leave workhouse management to others, Kennedy began to travel deeply into the Union hinterland for the first time, his main task being the policing of outdoor relief to the able-bodied, whose introduction he had so vigorously resisted. More than anything else, it was his travels through a clearance-scarred landscape that made him realize their full horrific extent, as he began to come to terms with the unpalatable fact that men known to him and liked by him were centrally involved in this hideously omnipresent destruction of lives and property. It was thus that a precise knowledge of the dynamics of clearance was forced on Kennedy, making it impossible for him to ignore landlord culpability any further.

The main result of this new knowledge was the compilation of an exhaustive catalogue of evictions throughout the Union, the task that most consumed Kennedy in his time as Inspector. The decision to collect statistics was fraught with the danger of antagonizing powerful landed interests, represented by such as Crofton Vandeleur, the Marquis of Conyngham and Colonel George Wyndham, to name the most politically influential magnates; and it was arrived at in the most tentative and careful manner; it is impossible indeed to tell from the documentation whether the proposal originated with Kennedy or with the Commissioners.[35] But the purpose of the exercise is very clear: to determine if landlords were illegally dumping their evicted tenantry on the Union. Whatever humanitarian impulse was involved, it was not the first priority.

It was about this time that Kennedy begins to appear in the public prints as a benefactor. On 30 March, the *Clare Journal* told its readers that the 'philanthropic exertions of this gentleman in the cause of suffering humanity were deserving of the highest praise', while on 5 April the *Limerick Chronicle* was referring to the 'great improvements' already visible at Kilrush workhouse under Kennedy and the Vice-Guardians.[36] Henceforth, praise would be showered on the Kilrush Inspector from all directions, first in the provincial papers, and then the national prints, irrespective of their individual political stance.

If we except the newspaper coverage of Guardian or Vice-Guardian meetings where he features, the body of references to Kennedy is not that extensive; there are long gaps, reflecting times when he would have been in-country or temporarily seconded to other Unions, and there are few for the high summer of 1848 when the Confederate Rising crowded other coverage from the public prints. Each reference we have, however, is laudatory and comes with internal indications of a much wider knowledge and appreciation of the Inspector's humanitarian virtues. Much of the evidence is anecdotal and tends to emphasize Kennedy's generosity towards afflicted persons on the one hand, and his fearlessness for his own personal safety on the other.

Incidents in the first of these two categories feature Kennedy at eviction sites, giving sums of money, invariably silver rather than copper, to the heads of evicted families; shillings rather than pence to surviving relatives of deceased destitute persons at coroners' inquests and distributing sums liberally to poor people he meets in the street. Late in October 1848, for example, when faced outside by a great crowd of starving young women and men, 'deserted' by spouses in the search for work, placing as many as he could on the lists, he emptied his purse to those remaining, all of them persons outside the Poor Law's legal definition of relievable destitution.[37] In December, he gave a seller of goats' milk a loan of ten shillings to clear a debt for which his goats had been seized; when the man repaid the money, Kennedy was so struck by his honesty that he forgave the debt.[38] In May 1849, before questioning an evicted woman during a clearance investigation in Killofin, Kennedy first handed her 'some silver' to enable her obtain milk for her skeletal infant, who appeared as if 'sent forth from the grave for human commiseration'. At the sight of the money, the woman 'burst into a flood of tears'.[39] On hearing her story Kennedy gave her more money for her children. Anecdotes of a similar kind and testimonials to his kindness by reporters, local correspondents, the Society of St Vincent de Paul, coroners and even policemen followed Kennedy down to his last days in Kilrush.[40]

Turning to Kennedy's fearlessness, since taking up his appointment he had been constantly in the midst of fever-ridden crowds, returning home often covered in vermin and ignoring the obvious health dangers this involved. In April 1848 during a fever outbreak which killed sixty-three persons in the workhouse in one week alone, the *Limerick Chronicle* praised Kennedy ('a most active and attentive officer') for the courage and composure he displayed by his daily fever hospital visits, which had the effect of calming the nurse tenders who otherwise 'would before now be frightened away by the awful mortality'.[41]

In acting thus Kennedy exemplified the general run of Union inspectors who, whatever their other faults, were notably courageous; within weeks of each other indeed, in the winter of 1848–1849, two successive Inspectors at the Ennis Union died at their posts of typhus, Kennedy substituting each time on a temporary basis.[42] However, his own behaviour went far beyond what was expected of Poor Law officers, reaching a level of recklessness, as where he approached fever-stricken persons in the street, touched their bodies or physically lifted them onto carts for transportation to the workhouse.

The earliest example we have of this tendency comes from May 1848, when he rescued Nancy Hoare and her child, recently evicted from John Singleton's property at Baltard, from the foul roadside shelter where they lay. Climbing down to reach the comatose pair he came into close physical contact with them, and the accounts suggest lifted them himself out of the pestiferous hole before sending them to the workhouse. Already at this point he was reported to have rescued thirty-nine people in similar circumstances over the previous two months.[43]

The following April while inspecting cholera hospitals at Carrigaholt and Kilkee at the height of the epidemic, both he and the Union physician, the equally self-careless Dr Foley, were 'all but obliged to place a poor man in his coffin when his widow and sons "stood far off", understandably hesitating to endanger the remainder of the family with this dreadful disease'.[44] 'I candidly acknowledge', wrote a reporter some months later, 'I have shrunk from approaching some of the hospital huts this gentleman has been seen to enter for the purpose of examining the condition of the fevered and deserted inmates.'[45]

One Sunday afternoon in spring 1849, when promenading along the Square Road in Kilrush, Kennedy came upon a young man who had collapsed from hunger and cold, and past whom several persons had already hurried.[46] Placing 'his hand on the poor man's bosom to try whether there was action in the poor man's heart', he had him sent to the workhouse. This, according to our source, was just the 'latest of the almost countless instances in which succour has been personally rendered by the every unshirking and prompt benevolence of Captain Kennedy'. In June the same year, he rescued a dysentery-afflicted woman named Ellen Lynch from a cowshed where she and her young son had lain after eviction from the adjacent cabin, while standing 'ankle deep in manure' as he tended to her.[47] In August he came across another recently evicted widow, this time with seven children, five of them in fever, lying together in a hollow near a bank just outside Kilkee. Placing three of them in his own car, he had the remainder removed 'from the unwholesome couches and the exposed position on which they were remaining'.[48]

In June the *Limerick and Clare Examiner*, which credited him with saving hundreds of lives, paid Kennedy a tribute that gives us some idea of the general esteem in which he was held. It also conveys something of the self-destructive impulse inherent in his salvaging of the afflicted and abandoned:[49]

> He has often raised the diseased starveling in his own arms from the ground; he has handled corpses that no other man but the physician and himself would venture to approach. He has examined the bodies of the destitute, though infected with cholera and other dangerous maladies, and has habitually visited the wards of the hospitals when most crowded, and most filled with the vitiated atmosphere exhaled from the poor. If ever the purest and most exalted benevolence were personified in layman, it is in this officer ... and a manliness of spirit that disdains modifying the truth in deference to any one, constitutes him the ablest, most effective, and yet the most charitable officer connected in any rank with the administration of Poor Law.

Can we see in the extravagance of the alms-giving of this 'most charitable officer' and the recklessness of his physical-touch rescues an expiation of the guilt generated by his earlier anti-poor rhetoric and behaviour? Does it represent to any extent the hidden internal turmoil of a loyal Poor Law officer who is unable to admit to himself that far from addressing the needs of the poor, the organization he serves is in fact the major contributor to their suffering, an active as well as an indirect cause of mass death by fever, starvation or clearance? Is there some sort of Freudian death wish involved, a subconscious throwing away of his own life in view of the mass death all around him? We can only speculate about such things, and all we can say for definite is that the evidence points to a level of dysfunction in Kennedy's behaviour during this time.

Our speculations on this issue are strengthened by the manner in which Kennedy exposes not just himself, but those he loves; his wife and even more so, his seven-year-old daughter, Elizabeth, to the same risks.[50] 'Miss Kennedy', as the sources invariably refer to her, is first mentioned by the *Limerick and Clare Examiner* in October 1849 as being of a similar humane character to her 'excellent' father, despite her extreme youth. She is reported as having begun to 'give practical effect to the parental inculcations and the example she is set', and under her 'immediate and attentive superintendence', 200 suits of clothing were 'purchased and made up' for distribution 'among the ragged, thinly vested poor'.[51] According to a slightly later report, Miss Kennedy had traversed the Union, aided by the 'amiable and charitable mother whose virtues she inherits ... conveyed from house to house ... and hut to hut, by a father who never wearies in the service of the poor ... distributing her bounties; carrying comfort to the trembling; virtually bestowing life to infancy and age ... But for her, death would have laid its icy hands on many a shivering being'.[52]

Captain Kennedy and his daughter Elizabeth. Illustrated London News.

Inevitably, Miss Kennedy became part of her father's growing legend, and as accounts of her doings spread from local to national prints, she became a character in her own right.[53] When thirty-three starving persons, who had just been rejected by a cost-cutting Kilrush workhouse regime, were drowned while crossing Poulnasherry Bay late in November, the bodies were recovered days later in a naked state, with the exception of one dead child who, we are told, wore a dress given her a few days earlier by Miss Kennedy. In Kells, County Meath, a poet was moved to apostrophize her in verse:[54]

> Fair Child, and is it left to Thee,
> Young as thou art in years
> To soothe the pangs of Misery,
> And dry the mourner's tears?'

A few days before Christmas Miss Kennedy acquired a brief international celebrity when the *Illustrated London News* published the sketch which shows her dispensing charity clothing, under the watchful eye of her father, to a group of ragged women and children from a sidecar. More than any other document it is this drawing, combining philanthropic father with charitable daughter, which has fixed the image of Captain Kennedy as a significant figure in the Famine landscape.

Elizabeth Kennedy makes a lonely little figure in the drawing, which was accompanied by text informing readers that the misery of destitute children had so affected her that 'with the consent of her parents, she gave up her time and her own little means to relieve them', giving away her own clothes and purchasing materials with which she 'made up clothing for children of her own age'. Encouraged by her father and 'some philanthropic strangers, from whom she received sums of money', she devoted herself 'with all the energy and perseverance of a mature and staid matron to the holy office she has undertaken'. The reporter hoped that the drawing would 'immortalize the beneficent child, who is filling the place of a saint, and performing the duties of a patriot'.[55] So indeed it has done.

But a degree of media flummery attaches to this saintly portrayal of Miss Kennedy, and despite its undoubted poignancy the drawing has more than a hint of Victorian sentimentality about it: no observer had the poor taste to point out that no matter how precocious a seven-year-old might be, she could not have been anything but a disastrous liability in any kind of relief operation. Nor did anyone have the nerve to posit a level of parental irresponsibility in the placing of a vulnerable child in such proximity to fever-ridden persons. But in any case, Elizabeth's celebrity was a thing of a few months only, and after the *Illustrated London News* sketch, there are only a few further references to her, making us suspect that she had perhaps been whisked away to safety by a mother finally gripped with terror for her little girl's continued health.

At the time Elizabeth and he posed for the sketch artist, Captain Kennedy was coming to the end of his great statistical project, the recording of all evictions in the Kilrush Union since November 1847, the date he had assumed his responsibilities as Inspector. By this time, however, the Kilrush Union was again under Guardian control, the landed interest again dominant, along with their middlemen client-tenants and the equally subservient business folk of Kilrush town.

Kennedy might have expected antagonism from the Board, which had not fared well in his published correspondence or his *Reports and Returns*, and no doubt certain Guardians were seething at the stream of well-connected visitors he had conducted through the Union who had all carried away very negative impressions from the experience.[56] In the event, however, Union business was resumed tranquilly, to which the absence of Colonel Vandeleur from the early meetings was undoubtedly a contributing factor, as also a very poor attendance on the part of *ex officio* Guardians, maintaining a long-standing and dismal record. The residue of elected members was so inept – a 'body of farmers and shopkeepers', as Kennedy had once described them, people of 'presumption and absurdity' – as to welcome direction by a strong hand such as his.[57] At the first meeting of the restored Board indeed we find Kennedy, knowing well those with whom he had to deal, giving a patient assurance 'of his ready and earnest assistance if the Board would only help themselves'.[58]

Neither was this situation immediately affected when Crofton Vandeleur returned to his Chairman's seat in the boardroom on Broom Hill in December. And even when Vandeleur signalled his resumed dominance over the Guardians by proceeding to dismantle the relief structures erected over the previous eighteen months, Kennedy did not rise to the provocation. In succeeding weeks, in fact, the growing antipathy between the two men was manifest on only two occasions, the first when Vandeleur hounded James Shannon, the journalist whom Kennedy had employed during the compilation of his eviction tally, from the boardroom; the second a sharp interchange between Chairman and Inspector on the general nature of evictions.[59] On the first occasion, an unmistakeable insult, Kennedy neither intervened nor commented, and on the second refrained from pressing his point.

We can account for Kennedy's inaction here in a number of ways; as a reluctance to be drawn into pointless argument, such as might only serve to add to tensions, or as part of his old landlord's son's reluctance to recriminate with members of his own class, or again because he felt engagement was outside his remit as a servant of the Poor Law. But whatever the reason, since Kennedy never showed his true feelings, when a year later Crofton Vandeleur himself declared that his relationship with Kennedy had been one of occasional differences of opinion but had been generally a cordial one, he was not necessarily being untruthful.[60]

But of course Vandeleur was also being disingenuous, and we know that for some considerable time he had been actively subverting Kennedy's influence by newspaper propaganda and the use of political connections. Under a surface amiability he undermined Kennedy whenever he could and schemed for his removal from Kilrush. An attack on Kennedy by the Tory *Dublin Evening Mail* in late December was probably instigated by Vandeleur, who a few weeks later travelled to Dublin in order to 'work heaven and earth' to get rid of the troublesome Inspector.[61] In the course of his visit he was reportedly 'the convivial guest' of the Lord Lieutenant, Lord Clarendon and also of the Poor Law Commissioners, Kennedy's superiors.[62]

A working relationship of some kind was maintained between Kennedy and the Kilrush Board of Guardians through the winter and the first six months of 1850, which became more frayed with the passing weeks. After the Scrope Committee hearings, even this was no longer possible, no more indeed than Kennedy's relations with the Union's landlords. Kennedy was the first witness to give evidence, and he was the only one to be recalled repeatedly to the Committee Room throughout its sittings, elucidating evidence he had previously given and fielding queries based on the testimony of others. In this way the entire investigation came to revolve around his evidence, its proceedings marked throughout with the imprint of his personality. Assured at all times, even under the closest of questioning, unlike Crofton Vandeleur or Marcus Keane he did not seek to impose himself on the Committee, and his answers were unhesitating except where he paused to consult or present a document, whether report, letter, schedule or map.

In his testimony Kennedy did not condemn the general philosophy behind clearances nor landlord action in carrying them out, and he made no general indictment of the Poor Law system. These omissions, suggestive of a still conflicted attitude towards such things, did not at all redound to his credit, but they did have the effect of simplifying his testimony to the level of factual statement and the supply of information, delivered without heat or vituperation. Because he did not cede to the emotion of the moment or to the passion of personal opinion as other witnesses did, his testimony and rebuttal of his opponents' justifications were powerfully authoritative.

As the Committee sittings went on Kennedy's testimony accumulated into a body of knowledge about the Kilrush Union under his stewardship that was so detailed and complex that those of his questioners who knew little of Ireland frequently lost its thread and lapsed into a bewildered silence. In the Committee's published *Report* and minutes as they have come down to us, this evidence comprises a huge database that remains an enduring monument to Kennedy's energies and engagement with every aspect of his inspectorial duties. As we survey its awesome totality we realize why Kennedy's mind should have been so troubled, since it bespeaks an exhaustive understanding of affairs in the Kilrush Union on his part, a dangerous level of knowledge to which, try as he might, he failed so shut his mind and conscience as so many of his colleagues had succeeded in doing in analogous situations elsewhere.

Captain Kennedy, early in his colonial service. Photo courtesy State Library of Western Australia.

If Kennedy's testimony enraged the Kilrush landlords, it was deeply embarrassing to the Irish Poor Law Commissioners and beyond them to the Whig-Liberal Government in London. In the aftermath of its delivery and publication, it was obvious that Kennedy could not be allowed to remain at Kilrush or indeed in the service of the Poor Law for any length of time: Colonel Vandeleur's machinations, such as they were, now became redundant. On Kennedy's arrival home at Cappagh from London in July, celebratory bonfires were lit on the lands around, and much delight expressed at his return.[63] Within weeks, however, came the devastating news that he was to be promoted to Assistant Commissioner and transferred to the management of two Unions in Kilkenny. Within months of his transfer, Captain Kennedy was quietly eased out of service with the Poor Law.[64]

In the Kilrush district, the belief persisted for many years that his departure had been engineered by Crofton Vandeleur with the complicity of government.[65] However, it may well be that Kennedy was not at all reluctant to leave, given all he had experienced and witnessed, and the strains on his family life that his work could not but have produced. The Kilrush poor, for their part, could have been under no illusions as to what Kennedy's departure portended, and as he and his wife and children had taken their leave in early September, tattered crowds followed their party to the quay where the Shannon steamship awaited their arrival on board. 'I cannot conceal the gloomy conviction,' wrote a reporter who watched the Kennedys leave and the crowd shuffle sadly home, 'that the departure of this officer seals the fate of a multitude'.[66]

It was a prescient comment. No reform at all emerged from the Scrope Committee investigation, whose report was soon buried along with other unread parliamentary papers, where it lay for over a century before it was unearthed for scholarly analysis by Monsignor Murphy. No check at all was placed on exterminating landlords, who continued to evict until their campaigns exhausted themselves. Colonel Vandeleur was allowed reign supreme in the boardroom at Broom Hill, and with the compliance of a new and timid Inspector to oversee an even tighter restriction of the parameters of relief.[67] As mismanagement and abuse of the workhouse inmates became ever more wanton, the death toll from fever and starvation began to rise catastrophically again.

10

The Famine Landscape

A minor paradox of the Great Famine is that its impact is easier evaluated with regard to the legions of its victims, whom we cannot document, than to non-victim contemporaries, whether relief officials, outside observers or those responsible for acts of barbarity, no matter what level of documentation survives for them. The paradox, of course, loses meaning on even slight reflection: in regard to victims, even if we cannot trace individual cases, the effects of starvation or fever, flight migration, workhouse pauperdom or eviction, allow of little ambiguity. For survivors too, there is much that can be reliably inferred in terms of lasting psychological and even physiological damage. For documented witnesses on the other hand, the evidence affords little insight into mental processes, nor enables valid assessment of later behaviour patterns in terms of Famine experience.

But even if we could measure such things, the psychological fallout on non-victims might well prove to have been much less and more short term than initially supposed, and lessened even further perhaps by suppression or denial, and lives continued thereafter without appreciable disturbance. At the same time, it is reasonable to postulate a certain later-life impact, in terms of memory–trauma, for example, on the part of those disturbed by what they witnessed, or a lifelong emotional brutalization in the case of those complicit in clearance atrocity or bureaucratic harshness routinely resulting in death. As regards the figures in our Famine landscape, the most we can do is lay out the subsequent patterns of each life insofar as we can, looking for tendencies or episodes that might be of relevance to our inquiry. Given that we should not hope for much from the exercise, its greatest benefits are more likely to lie in the context thus given to each individual Famine-era experience and the satisfaction of a natural curiosity as to what happened them subsequently. For this latter reason, some extra data has been added that might not be strictly relevant otherwise.

John B. Knox's post-Famine existence can be traced in a number of sources, not least his newspaper file, across whose great expanse we note the rarity of retrospective references to the horrors of the late 1840s and early 1850s. In these years, as his young family grew up around him – four of the six children he had with Frances were born in the 1850s – he balanced domestic responsibility with his other activities and production of the *Journal*. At the beginning of 1851, he relinquished control of the newspaper to an editor, although for some years his influence on editorial policy was still apparent.[1] Uncomfortable perhaps under the new dispensation, James Knox Walker left the *Journal* shortly afterwards, and within two years started the *Clare Freeman*, a reactionary newspaper with a strident evangelical stance. Almost immediately hostilities erupted between the two Tory prints, of a viciousness that compares with that of the *Clare Journal–Limerick and Clare Examiner* wars some years before.

When Knox died in 1864, of a 'softening of the brain', he had not been associated with the *Journal* for some time.[2] At his death he had attained sufficient eminence to merit an obituary in the *Irish Times*, which described him as one of the oldest journalists in Ireland and praised his 'tolerant and conciliatory spirit' and 'promotion of the best interests of the working classes'.[3] The enemy *Clare Freeman* conceded that Knox's 'benevolent disposition and many charitable acts' had rendered him 'exceedingly popular among the lower classes of his townsfolk'.[4] With dignity, Knox's *Journal* declined to eulogize 'this good man', contenting itself with the certainty that his memory would 'live in the hearts of the people'.[5]

After Knox's death, the *Clare Journal* continued under his widow's proprietorship and a series of editors who produced it over the next four decades and into the twentieth century.[6] After her death in 1898, two of Knox's daughters in succession took over, the *Journal* continuing in family hands until it ceased printing in 1917. Its companion title, the *Saturday Record*, survived under different ownership until 1937, two years after the death at an advanced age of John Busteed Knox's last surviving daughter, Kathleen Frances.[7] Some time later, the office file of the *Clare Journal* came into the possession of its latter-day rival and successor, the *Clare Champion*, and today its bound volumes stand, row by row and year by year, much as John B. Knox last saw them, if somewhat the worse for a century and a half of wear, on the deep shelves of the *Champion*'s File Room.

It is unlikely that Captain Wynne, who had been a subscriber to the *Clare Journal* while in Ennis, ever perused the paper afterwards, or given his own woes indeed that he ever thought of it again.[8] Some months after his departure from Clare he transferred to the Poor Law as Temporary Inspector and was dispatched to the Union of Boyle and Carrick, situated in Counties Leitrim and Roscommon.[9] Establishing himself in Carrick with his wife and young children, Wynne became absorbed in new duties, and according to one authority displayed a level of humanity towards the suffering poor that had been conspicuously lacking during his time in Clare.[10] In fact the evidence for this new-found kindness is equivocal, but it is true that he showed little sign of the emotional instability that had marked his conduct earlier, the anchoring proximity of his wife and young children perhaps being a significant factor in this regard.

But Wynne had lost none of his foolhardy aggression and in his new appointment alienated even the Tory gentry, and much more dangerously attracted the enmity of the Marquis of Westmeath, a major landowner in the Union and a figure of political influence. The vindictive Westmeath was not satisfied with engineering the departure of Wynne from Carrick (September 1849), but went to enormous trouble to instigate a parliamentary Select Committee investigation into his conduct as Inspector. Almost unbelievably then, Wynne had succeeded in drawing upon himself two major parliamentary inquiries in as many years.

In the course of the Committee's hearings, very damaging allegations were made by a number of witnesses that Wynne had received sexual favours from certain female paupers in exchange for distress relief to which they were not entitled.[11] With difficulty he extricated himself from these allegations whose apparently solid basis was undermined by the intemperate anger of his accusers. The accusations, however, left his reputation 'hopelessly smeared', in David Fitzpatrick's phrase, and Wynne without any further possibility of public employment.[12]

After this he vanishes into the obscurity from which his appointment to the Board of Works had summoned him. One source ascribes him a hero's death during the Crimean War – a letter from a private soldier writing home from the front, in which he declares excitedly that he was beside 'Captain Wynn [sic] that was in Ennis in the Board of Works', when the latter's head 'was blown off by a cannon ball'.[13] Alas, we have to disregard this persuasive suggestion of a glorious battlefield death for Wynne, since David Fitzpatrick has tracked the ex-Inspector through a number of later addresses; from the Georgian splendour of Esker House, Lucan, in 1848, to a more modest terraced house in Fairview, Dublin, in 1857 and finally to his brother's house in North George's Street in the capital, where he died in 1872 at the age of sixty-eight.[14]

The closing of John Singleton's diaries in February 1851 frustrates us with the loss of such a rich source, and there is so much more that we would wish to view from its perspective; how his estate management progressed in post-Famine times, for example, or anything regarding the county election of 1852, where he acted as nominator of Crofton Vandeleur, and was present at the scenes in Sixmilebridge when police opened fire on an agitated crowd, killing five bystanders.[15] But at worst we work in penumbral light in regard to Singleton and never in total darkness, and a trickle of other evidence keep us apprised of his doings. For many years he continued to participate in gentry gatherings, functioning as before as Justice of the Peace and maintaining his attendance on various public bodies. After the death of his beloved Isabella, Singleton remarried in 1867 and died ten years later, at the age of eighty-five.[16]

Of his children, we know that Johnny, the scapegrace subaltern of the diaries, served with gallantry during the Crimean War, for which he received the thanks of Lord Raglan. His service during the Indian Mutiny earned him further honours, and following a distinguished career he retired with the rank of Major-General. For a very brief period, he succeeded his father at Quinville, but died childless and prematurely in 1880 at the age of fifty-four, just three years after his father's passing. General Singleton was succeeded by his brother, Edward, whom we last met as a holidaying schoolboy, helping out with the reordering of boundaries following a clearance at Baltard in 1849. Edward lived until 1896.[17] Of John Singleton's beloved girls, we know that Susan and Sarah married acceptably into landed gentry families elsewhere in Ireland. We have no information on Mary. Marcella never left Quin and died unmarried in 1857. Isabella, also unmarried, died in 1890.[18]

Of Singleton's friend, Father Corbett, we only know that he broke with Singleton over the 1852 election and lived until 1893.[19] Of the hundreds expelled by Singleton from Baltard, we learn nothing more at any point: in the consolidations that followed their eviction or coerced 'voluntary surrender', their cabins were razed, no trace of them remaining in the large fields created afterwards. John Singleton's gracious home, Quinville Abbey, on the other hand, remained the architectural ornament it had been in his time; in 1872, it was described as nestling 'in the bosom of cherishing foliage'.[20]

The Cullinan-Healy feud sputtered on for a few years more following the confrontations recounted in Chapter 4, but lost its *raison d'etre* when for reasons that remain uncertain, Dr Healy resigned his institutional employments in 1855.[21] But resignation made little difference to Healy's testy nature, and in that same year, he quarrelled with his neighbours in Bindon Street; with the Town Commissioners, with the ever-volatile John B. Knox, and again and for other reasons with Dr Cullinan.[22] His death, of a 'tiresome' illness in August 1862, elicited just two newspaper obituaries, brief notices which referred to Healy's position as surgeon to the Clare Militia, the only post he obtained after the confrontations with Cullinan were over.[23] Dr Healy appears to have left little after him, and the life progress of his six children cannot be followed far in the sources. It is uncertain where his remains lie.[24]

Although Healy had seen off Cullinan in the last active stage of their feud, in post-Famine times it was Cullinan whose career flourished. Driven as ever by a thirst for the accumulation of income-generating employments, in 1862, the year of Healy's death, and unusually for a professional man, he became a Justice of the Peace, and shortly afterwards first visiting physician to the Clare County Lunatic Asylum.[25] At this point in his life, between institutional positions old and new and his private practice, Dr Cullinan's earnings comprised a veritable lake into which copiously flowed individual streams comprising salaries, emoluments, stipends and fees, as well as the more informal income enhancements now within his reach.

And even when in gathering old age he began to withdraw from his longest-held appointments, Cullinan fought spirited rearguard actions in order to retain portions of the income from them. When he retired as workhouse physician in 1871, for example, 'in consequence of multiplied avocations and advancing years', he battled for months with the Board of Guardians for what he referred to as 'the usual superannuation allowance', or in lieu thereof the right to select an assistant 'to whom a portion of his salary might be given'. Conscious of Cullinan's connections, the Board was careful in its deliberations on these proposals before refusing them on the grounds that there was no provision for either in the Poor Law.[26] As late as 1878, when he was seventy-one, he mounted a vigorous campaign for an increase in his remuneration as physician to the Lunatic Asylum.[27] It is hardly to be wondered then, that when he died in 1895, he was a wealthy man who included among his assets over 900 acres of land.[28]

Dr Cullinan lies in Dromcliffe Cemetery, in a large vault that dwarfs the modest granite cross marking the resting place just below of John B. Knox who had died more than thirty years earlier. The Cullinan vault is topped by a memorial identifying deceased familial occupants, including Cullinan's wife and the three children who predeceased him; sixteen-year-old Rachel, and William and Max, who died in their forties, the former a civil servant, the latter a Cambridge don.[29] Another son, Fitzjames, also a senior functionary, survived him, but had no children and is buried elsewhere.[30]

We do not know if Reverend Henry Murphy followed any of the episodes of the Cullinan–Healy feud; given his incurious nature and his own concerns, it doesn't seem probable that he would have been interested enough. After spending just two years as headmaster of the Clergy Sons' School at Lucan, he chose to follow a career path in the northern counties of Antrim and Down, where he would have felt less isolated in confessional terms and where perhaps advancement might be more likely. What followed in the event was a succession of parish appointments combined with chaplaincies and the odd sinecure, all of it badly needed to support a family which had grown fearfully large – in total he and his wife Frances had eight sons and five daughters.[31] From 1849 to 1853 Reverend Murphy was Vicar of Dunluce; from 1853 to 1863 while Rector of Magheralin he was also Rural Dean of Moira and Precentor of Dromore, and from 1864 to the time of his death, Prebendary of Dromaragh; all positions held concurrently with other employments that brought him to locations such as Cultra, Holywood, Downpatrick and Coleraine. At different times he was also Secretary to the Bishop of Connor, the first Dean of Residence for Church of Ireland students at the new Queen's College in Belfast and, of course, Inspector of Colonel Wyndham's Schools.[32]

Murphy's connection to Clare in these years was limited to ongoing correspondence with Colonel Wyndham and Samuel Ball regarding the Miltown schools, lasting well into the early 1860s; twice each year he appeared in west Clare in order to carry out his schools' inspections. In 1861, he became involved in a rather recondite theological disputation in the *Clare Freeman*, which reveals him to have been a more radical exponent of evangelical ideology even than editor-owner James Knox Walker. More importantly, this amiably pursued controversy reveals that all along Murphy had been a pre-Millenialist, an adherent of a hardline evangelical tendency which favoured conversion methods of the type he denied had been practiced at Miltown.[33]

Some of Reverend Murphy's children died in infancy; three of the girls married into clerical families in the north, while two of his younger sons became clergymen. Henry, the eldest, whom we saw earlier as a child locking himself into the dressing room at Green Park, became a naval officer, and another, George Wyndham, named for his father's patron, a medical practitioner who died in South Africa in 1902.[34] Reverend Murphy himself died at Kingsfield, Downpatrick, in 1878, at the age of seventy-three.[35]

By the time of Reverend Murphy's death, his association with Marcus Keane was long past, the latter's time now taken up with estate affairs and the still flourishing agency. During these years Marcus lived quietly at Beech Park and summered at Doondahlin, surrounded by family and the many nephews and nieces to whom he was devoted. A slightly later diary kept by a grand-niece, Amy Griffin, reveals evidence of an idyllic life at Doondahlin, along with her cousins amid scenes of carefree familial amusements similar to those we find in the Singleton ménage more than twenty years earlier.[36]

During the 1860s, Marcus had taken to antiquarian pursuits, over time developing a hypothesis that the round towers of tenth-century Ireland had been built, not by Irish ecclesiastics, but by a pagan race he called the Cuthites, an absurd theory he was to enshrine in print in a privately published volume.[37] But behind tranquil country life and harmless antiquarian dottiness, the Exterminator General still lurked, and in 1863 Marcus carried out a series of evictions in Kilkee, whose chilling precision replicated the *modus operandi* of his Famine-era clearances; in the first phase alone seventy-four dwellings were emptied and levelled, their occupants dumped on the street beside their broken belongings.[38]

When Marcus died in October 1883, in his sixty-ninth year, the *Clare Journal* eulogized the 'sound sense, sagacity and earnestness' of this 'kind and generous landlord and agent', and of his funeral reflected how appropriate it was 'that the last earthly tribute paid to so popular a man should bear some proportion to the usefulness of his life'.[39] Descendants of his victims, however, marked his passing in a very different manner.[40] Because the family tomb at Kilmaley was full, his body and that of a family nurse who had died months earlier had been placed temporarily in an empty vault adjoining pending completion of a burial plot on the estate. The following September, however, workmen sent to remove the coffins to Beech Park found the vault empty, the entry stone in place and no clue as to what had happened. The vacuum in information concerning the bodies was filled in with wild speculation, which soared to even greater heights eight years later when to their astonishment, gravediggers reopening a plot adjacent to the empty vault came on the coffins, stacked neatly just underneath the soil.[41]

More than a century was to elapse before this apparently unsolvable mystery was explained, or at least became known outside the Beech Park area. This was when, in conversation with the present author, the late Colm Casey, owner of part of the old demesne, revealed that his grandfather had been one of the group responsible for the escapade, comprising seven young men, all from families affected by Marcus's clearances. Their intention of desecrating Marcus's body by throwing it in the river was thwarted when they failed to distinguish the heavy coffins from each other in the dark, or indeed to open either of them. Rather than abandon them where they were, they reburied the coffins in a nearby grave, hiding their deed in the soil disturbance of a recent burial.[42]

After the building of the Moneen chapel, Michael Meehan had little to do with Marcus Keane and was already six years in his grave when the latter's remains disappeared from the Kilmaley vault.[43] In post-Famine times, Father Meehan's concerns were those of any rural parish priest in Ireland, although in the mid-1860s he did spend three years in the United States raising funds for his educational programmes and for a flock that was once again teetering on the verge of food shortage. He returned home to a pastoral ministry that remained uneventful in the years leading up to his death in Limerick in 1878, at the age of sixty-eight.[44] His body was brought back to west Clare via the Shannon steamer, and during the funeral ceremonies the Little Ark was placed outside the chapel door at Moneen as it had been during the dedication ceremony years before.[45] In this manner, myth-making in relation to the Ark began at Michael Meehan's death.

Ark mythology is of two broad types: the first relating to the assertion of personal roles within the narrative by certain individuals or families; the second the elaboration of a genre of folktale relating to Father Meehan. Notable in the first category is the account, much repeated over a long life, by Thomas Casey, who had served Meehan's Mass as a teenager. Although Casey's version of events is consistent, it features his own presence at too many significant junctures of the story to be entirely credible and has to be treated with caution.[46] Benign scepticism has to be exercised also in regard to the claims of the Harris family of Limerick, Michael Meehan's in-laws, to have prefabricated the Ark at Mount Kennett Steam Mills and shipped it by steamer in secrecy to west Clare. Certainly the version offered by Richard Harris, the screen actor, a direct Harris descendant, is highly inaccurate, although it is not impossible that the family had some minor connection to the Ark episode.[47]

By the time of its centenary in 1952, the Ark story had developed into a kind of cult, one carefully managed by Church authority. The centenary was an officially organized event, and it was marked by ceremonies in which the Ark was placed on the spot where Meehan had deployed it during the souper wars.[48] Mass was again said by a priest inside to a devout congregation gathered around it, and photographs of the day show the re-enactment to have been strikingly faithful to the story. Speeches were notable for an angry rehearsal of Famine horror and evangelical wickedness, indications not alone of the strength of inherited memory but also of the confessional nature of Irish society during the 1950s.

By contrast, strong emotion was absent from the 150-year anniversary commemoration in 2002, which was as much community festival as religious occasion. The Little Ark being too fragile for removal from the chapel, a replica was constructed and brought to the foreshore for the re-enactment. Unlike his predecessor of a half-century earlier, Bishop Walshe's address framed the Ark story as a metaphor for the difficulties of the modern Church and the necessity for internal unity in combating them.[49] But even in the light of its changing inspirational function, as it sits innocuously in its annexe the Ark remains too uncomfortable a reminder of denominational antagonisms to represent just a great human story and nothing more.

Crofton Vandeleur would have been little aware of the Little Ark drama: Kilbaha was twenty miles away after all, and when home from his travels, his attention was still fixed on the reordering of his estate, and also on the Kilrush town project in which he became interested again in the early 1850s. Both of these endeavours soon foundered, as a direct and rather ironic outcome of his very success in removing surplus tenants. The social desolation and population loss that resulted from clearances he had carried out and those he had encouraged triggered a massive human flight from Kilrush Union, an outflow of all classes, from comfortable tenants to near-paupers; the anticipated influx of industrious, well-capitalized tenants to the consolidated farms never took place.

As the Union's population sagged and went into reverse, the hinterland was no longer able to sustain existing levels of business activity in Kilrush town, let alone that projected in Crofton's civic vision. The hoped-for Atlantic Packet station went elsewhere, the port traffic declined from year to year and soon Kilrush acquired the semi-abandoned look it would carry into modern times, its stagnation graphically encapsulated in the manner in which Frances Street ever afterwards was to bear magnificently down on nothing more grand than a muddy tidal creek.[50] For generations in Kilrush suppressed memories of mass horror lay beneath the surface of everyday life, a corner of the collective unconscious focused immovably on the bleak grave pits of Shanakyle just outside the town where unknown thousands of the Famine dead lay, a great portion of them from Vandeleur's evicted tenant families. Along the Creek, the name Paupers' Quay attached itself indelibly to that section of pier from which thousands of desponding workhouse inmates were shipped out to uncertain futures in the decades after the Famine.

In the next generation, Crofton's heir, Captain Hector Vandeleur, would also achieve notoriety as an evictor, with a short series of some twenty or so ejectments whose scale was miniscule by comparison with those perpetrated by his father. But because they were carried out in the glare of the international media and in the presence of photographers, they attracted intense criticism of a kind his father had not had to contend with.[51] Hector's evictions, in fact, represented a last manifestation of his family's dynastic capriciousness, and when Kilrush House was gutted in an accidental fire in 1897, its destruction heralded the demise of Vandeleur suzerainty in Kilrush in the land purchase schemes of the early twentieth century.[52]

Crofton lies in the family mausoleum in the old churchyard of Kilrush where he was placed after his death in 1881. 'His existence was spent in endeavouring to do good amongst all those around him', his chosen epitaph reads, and into it we might read evidence of repression on Crofton's part of the horrendous crimes he had committed during the Famine. More likely, however, the inscription reflects no more than contemporary platitude: perpetrators of mass atrocity do not generally repent their deeds, and it is improbable that Crofton's conscience ever bothered him, at conscious or subconscious levels.

As with the Murphy and Singleton narratives, certain literary resonances and possibilities adhere to Vandeleur's story, and there are specific reasons why it might indeed have attracted the creative energies of one particular giant of modern letters. Unfortunately, we have no way of knowing how deeply – we know he understood a good deal – did George Bernard Shaw care to delve into the life and career of Crofton Moore Vandeleur, whose biological grandson he believed himself to be and almost certainly was.[53]

Any literary associations in Captain Kennedy's later career will have to remain unexplored, although its dimensions were certainly epic, involving travel to the farthest corners of the British Empire and a wide variety of career situations and experiences. In 1852, shortly after joining the Colonial Service, Kennedy was appointed governor of the Gambia Settlements, and some time later to Sierra Leone where he battled against slave traders and revenue fraudsters.[54] A major promotion to Western Australia followed in 1856, and six years later to Vancouver. This was followed by a return to the West African Settlements and Sierra Leone and then to Hong Kong. Kennedy's last appointment was to Queensland in 1877.[55] By the time he arrived in Brisbane a lifetime's service and achievement had transformed the young Captain Kennedy of Kilrush into Sir Arthur Kennedy, GCMG, CB, a vastly experienced administrator and one of the great public men of his time.

Throughout his colonial service Kennedy was noted for traits which we recognize from his Kilrush days: an autocratic disposition and concern with economy and corruption, balanced by a sympathy with the oppressed and downtrodden.[56] Whether these characteristics were innate to him or seared into his psyche by events in west Clare cannot be known; but Kennedy certainly never forgot the Kilrush Union and on several occasions during later crises sent money there, most notably during the disastrous seasons of the late 1870s when it seemed for a time that another horrific famine crisis was about to descend on the impoverished people of Ireland.[57]

In 1872, while in England between appointments and staying at Lord Carnarvon's bristling neo-Elizabethan Hampshire pile, Highclere (the fictional Downton Abbey), Kennedy was questioned by his host regarding his Famine experiences. 'I can tell you, my lord', another guest recorded him as replying, 'that there were days in that western county when I came back from some scene of eviction so maddened by the sights of hunger and misery I had seen in the day's work that I felt disposed to take the gun from behind my door and shoot the first landlord I met'.[58] The reality, however, was that at no time did Kennedy confront any of the landlords with their criminal inhumanity, and until the Scrope Committee hearings remained on good terms with all of them. From what we have come to know of him, however, we can be confident that the vehemence of his Highclere remarks are reflective of a long-held guilt on Kennedy's part that he had not behaved otherwise and that as Union Inspector he had been complicit in the murderous workings of the Poor Law machine.

After retiring from the Queensland governorship in 1883, Kennedy was on his way to England when he died suddenly at Aden. His daughter, Elizabeth, seven years old when we last met her, in adult life married a naval officer, Captain Richard James, who eventually became fourth Earl of Clanwilliam.[59] Vanishing into the ranks of the aristocracy, Elizabeth is not heard from again in the sources. And by a strange quirk of popular memory, neither she nor her extraordinary father, who had been such a champion of the poor, feature at all in the oral tradition of the west.

From what has just been said, therefore, and as we suspected at the outset of this chapter, examining what happened to them subsequently tells us very little regarding any possible lasting impact, psychological or otherwise, of the Great Famine on the lives of our protagonists. What the exercise has established, however, is that for each of them the Famine was a brief interlude, occurring for the most part in relative youth, and that as resumed afterwards the lives of some of our figures went on as before, others were nudged in a new direction and in one or two cases radically altered, although not necessarily as a direct outcome of interface with Famine horror.

Another incidental result of our investigation is that it necessarily extends the paradigm of the Famine landscape forward in time. Authoring the book in fact has entailed a recalibration of the entire concept, since parallel with the writing came a growing realization that the Famine landscape still exists, concealed though so much of it is under the contour-disguising accretions of modern roads, phone masts, urban sprawl and the ubiquitous one-off new homes that now litter the countryside. Often indeed it is not concealed at all, as in the case of the abandoned Board of Works roads still to be found in the rock-strewn uplands of the Burren, or the consolidated field systems still discernible across the countryside, most dramatically in the massive grids around Kilbaha. Its most eerie manifestation lies in the unexpected materialization in empty fields from time to time of 'lazy beds', abandoned Famine-era cultivation ridges, highlighted with ephemeral clarity in the long shadows cast by evening or morning sunshine.

For me as author, the sense of connection with the Famine landscape became ever stronger as the writing proceeded and the chapters unfolded, bringing a closeness with the people and the era I had been writing about; as the writing drew to a close it culminated, as we shall see in a moment, in a series of what appeared to be jaw-dropping coincidental links to those people and that era. It took some time and some thinking to realize that these startling associations were not really coincidental at all, nor even surprising given where I had chosen to dig in the historical landscape.

Even the digging itself emerged as less a matter of choice than I had believed. With an ancestry that on both sides was replete with smallholding tenants, among whom 'tracing' those who had gone before was the fascination of winter evenings, my father, the late Seán Ó Murchadha, a well-known old-style antiquarian for whom Clare's past was a lifelong passion and from whom I had learned much, it was probably inevitable that at some stage I would do so. Among my earliest childhood recollections, in addition, was of being brought to see the Little Ark at Kilbaha and being enthralled by it. At a very young age also I first heard the name of Marcus Keane, from my maternal grandmother who dropped it incidentally during reminiscences of her War of Independence activities as a young Cumann na mBan activist; ever afterwards its three solid Roman-sounding syllables lodged in my mind, along with the equally sonorous two of his Beech Park demesne.

Few beech trees remain in this once-lovely place, now a rambling expanse of stone ruins, so overgrown with scrub trees, briars and other vegetation that it is difficult to determine where offices once were and house once stood. Only the roadside wreck of the little gate lodge, still inhabited when I was a child, remains recognizable. For most residents, in fact, Beech Park signifies no more than the name for the north-western fringe of Ennis town, and the traffic roundabout at that location around whose concrete perimeter, unknowing, they motor each day.

As my awareness sharpened, the sense of continuity with the Famine landscape and of habitation within it was to be, I discovered, substantially a thing of ruins like Beech Park, as well as of standing buildings and of townscapes. Kilrush's street pattern remains much as Crofton Vandeleur left it; Kilbaha remains astonishingly unchanged from its appearance in 1852, and Ennis's present-day town centre would be immediately recognizable to a revivified John B. Knox. The premises where Drs Healy and Cullinan lived and consulted have hardly changed since both men were locked in their feud, and part of the old County Fever Hospital which they attended is still there. John Singleton's Quinville Abbey remains as gracious as ever, although long separated from its demesne and tenanted lands.[60] The little stone courthouse in Ennistymon, scene of the confrontations between Captain Wynne and the North Clare relief committees, is still in use; the Glandine 'soup school', a tractor garage for much of my life, stands unoccupied on the Ennis road at Miltown Malbay, still identifiable by its 1851 date marker.

Looking at these familiar features with new eyes as the book took form and as Famine-era associations multiplied into patterns hitherto unseen, there were strange dissonances also. Two are noteworthy: in a bizarre development some time during 2010 the Ennis Town Council erected a heritage wall plaque to Marcus Keane, the same year as the Office of Public Works, direct descendant of the Famine-era Board of Works, placed a crude modern roof on Reverend Henry Murphy's parish church, erasing all sense of its venerable history and making it impossible to imagine how he would have seen it. In other places, unsightly commemorative monuments appeared on Famine mass graves, crass intrusions on the reflective space of this hallowed ground.

But even vexations such as these were charged with resonance; the Marcus Keane plaque was promptly defaced by an unknown hand and the word 'evictor' scraped across it; subsequently it was taken down – one hopes in embarrassment. The wrecking of Reverend Murphy's old church and the cemetery intrusions are of themselves reminders that little that has survived from human history is proof against the uncomprehending or the uncaring of later generations. And among the places in which I pondered these things in the company of friends, in states of mind that varied between agitation, wonder and fatalism, was a pleasant restaurant that had once been the dining room of the old County Club, the landed and professional gentleman's refuge where Crofton Vandeleur, Marcus Keane, Edmond Wynne, John Singleton and P.M. Cullinan had all dined in their time.

Many of the later instances of connection with the Famine landscape and the figures in it came by way of sudden, startling epiphany rather than gradual apprehension. One of these occurred during events leading up to the National Famine Commemoration at Kilrush in May 2013, where I was to speak about Captain Kennedy at a venue identified to me only as the town's Teach Ceoil. I was astonished to find myself in the defunct Protestant parish church, addressing a crowd seated where nineteenth-century worshippers would have sat, and where Kennedy certainly attended Sunday service with his family each week. Crofton Vandeleur, who now lay across the churchyard in his marble mausoleum, had worshipped here also each Sunday he was in Kilrush, sitting with his family in their front pew, occasionally perhaps contemplating the sculpted memorials to deceased Vandeleurs that are still attached to its walls.

In February 2014, I was brought up short again, this time with the discovery that the building in Ennis whose first floor housed the dentist's practice I had attended for most of my adult life had in fact been the *Clare Journal* offices and home of John B. Knox. This was one of the most unsettling connections to date: how many times had I lain back on the dentist's recliner awaiting his approach with sharp steel instruments, nervously seeking visual distraction in the ceiling's decorative cornices and wondering who could have lived in such a space. And all that time in that nicely proportioned room, without knowing it I had been in what must have been Knox's drawing room, situated directly over the *Journal* offices on the ground floor.[61]

Other memorable moments came in November the same year, on a lowering, atmospheric Sunday afternoon at graveyards in Tulla and Newmarket-on-Fergus. In the Tulla cemetery, now disused, as I looked down at an array of mildewed, dirt- and leaf-covered commemorative tablets salvaged from several long-demolished Protestant churches, some of them broken or with pieces missing, I spotted two relating to the Quinville Singletons. These clearly had once lined the walls of the old church in Quin, along with others destroyed at the same time as the building.[62] Marcella and Johnny, as we know of them from the diaries, were the subjects of these two tablets, the new data they added to what I knew already making sad reading. Marcella's early death in 1857 had been due to 'a fearful accident from fire', and she had lingered, probably in agony, for a fortnight. The early death of Johnny – Major-General John Singleton – at the age of fifty-four had occurred 'after a long illness and much suffering'.

Marcella's memorial tablet referred to her burial at Kilnsoolagh, Newmarket-on-Fergus, in the family vault, which after a lengthy search in fading drizzle-filtered light I found later that afternoon. A low-lying structure in a corner behind the church, more than half buried under accumulated debris, it was here also that John Singleton's remains were carried after his funeral in 1877. Of the family inscriptions only the word 'Edward' could be made out above the impacted detritus concealing the entrance.

But notwithstanding the sad *memento mori* of the wall-tablets and the buried tomb with its Emily Dickinson 'cornice in the ground' echoes, the Singletons in their time at least had had the comfort of an ancestral burial place, in contrast to the Famine dead and many of those who survived the calamity. It is salutary to reflect that we have no idea where Bridget O'Donnell of Garraunnatooha lies, nor indeed Nancy Hoare, John Singleton's evicted Baltard tenant, nor Patrick Mullins, Marcus Keane's vanished Gotbofarna smallholding occupier. As for the vast majority of the Famine dead, they lie in anonymity, many of them yet undiscovered where they perished in roadside ditches, in turf-bogs or in weed-grown crags or scrub hollows in fields. Those of them who received formal coffined burial – hurriedly and without dignity, ceremony or familial presence – rest for the most part in inexpressibly moving bare corners of graveyards all across the landscape of John Singleton's county, in places with names such as Dromcliffe, Kilmaley, Killerenan, Shanakyle, Farahy, Kilfearagh, Moyarta, Kilkeedy, Poll na Dóib and many, many more.

NOTES

Introduction
1. More often known as Carrigaholt and Cross. The parish was divided on Fr Meehan's death in 1878; Ciarán Ó Murchadha, *The Diocese of Killaloe: An Illustrated History* (New Edition, Belfast, 2011), p. 117.
2. An inscribed dedication to Bishop Vaughan of Killaloe identifies the drawing as contemporary. The painting may be slightly later.
3. Michael Hewson, 'The Diaries of John Singleton of Quinville, Co. Clare', in *North Munster Antiquarian Journal*, vol. xvii (1975), p. 103.
4. H. Montgomery-Massingbred (ed.), *Burke's Irish Family Records* (London, 1976), under Keane.
5. Thomas Leigh Goldie to Randolph Routh, National Archives of Ireland, Relief Commission Papers 3/1/1670, 25 May 1846.
6. *Clare Journal*, 24 April 1851.

Chapter 1
1. For more on Knox, see Chapter Two of my earlier study, *Sable Wings over the Land: Ennis, County Clare and Its Wider Community during the Great Famine* (Ennis, 1998).
2. W.G. Wheeler, 'The Spread of Provincial Printing in Ireland up to 1850', in *Irish Booklore*, vol. iv, no. 1 (1978), p. 12.
3. *A Catalogue of the Bradshaw Collection of Irish Books in the University Library Cambridge* (Cambridge, 1916), vol. II, pp. 863–864, 1338. *Clare Journal*, 1 October 1846; *Limerick and Clare Examiner*, 3 October 1846.
4. Estimate based on regression from the 1861 Census, when Clare's Church of Ireland population stood at 2 per cent; before the Famine, the proportion has been considerably less. See W.E. Vaughan and A.J. Fitzpatrick (eds.), *Irish Historical Statistics: Population 1821–1971* (Dublin, 1979), p. 52.
5. *C.J.*, 2 June 1842.
6. James McGuire and James Quinn (eds.), *Dictionary of Irish Biography from the Earliest Times to the Year 2002* (Cambridge, 2009), vol. vi, under Meany.
7. *D.I.B.*
8. Lucille Ellis, *Ennis at Work in the Nineteenth Century* (Ennis, 2014), p. 63.
9. Ibid., p. 63.

10 See *C.J.*, 10 April, 4 September 1837, 20 April 1846, 17 January 1848.
11 Ó Murchadha, *Sable Wings*, p. 28.
12 *C.J.*, 1 September 1845; Ó Murchadha, *Sable Wings*, p. 29.
13 *C.J.*, 16 October 1845.
14 *C.J.*, 3, 6 November 1845.
15 Ó Murchadha, *Sable Wings*, pp. 32–33.
16 Ibid., p. 33.
17 *C.J.*, 27 November 1845, Ó Murchadha, *Sable Wings*, p. 35.
18 *C.J.*, 17 November 1845.
19 *C.J.*, 20 November 1845.
20 *C.J.*, 29 December 1845.
21 Ó Murchadha, *Sable Wings*, p. 40.
22 Act I Victoria Cap 21 (1837).
23 Ó Murchadha, *Sable Wings*, pp. 41–42.
24 Ó Murchadha, 'The Onset of Famine', in *The Other Clare*, vol. xx (1996), p. 49.
25 *C.J.*, 12, 16, 30 March, 2 April 1846; Ó Murchadha, *Sable Wings*, p. 49.
26 See *C.J.*, 20, 23, 27 April 1846.
27 *C.J.*, 2 July 1846.
28 *C.J.*, 29 June 1846; Peter Gray, *Famine, Land and Politics: British Government and Irish Society 1843–50* (Dublin, 1999), p. 93.
29 *C.J.*, 16 July 1846.
30 *C.J.*, 10 August 1846.
31 *C.J.*, 10, 17, 20 August 1846.
32 *C.J.*, 3 September 1846.
33 *C.J.*, 24 September 1846.
34 *C.J.*, 5 October 1846.
35 *C.J.*, 8 October 1846.
36 *C.J.*, 1 October 1846.
37 *C.J.*, 15 October 1846.
38 *C.J.*, 2 November 1846.
39 *The Times*, 16 November 1846.
40 See *Limerick and Clare Examiner*, 25 March, 28 October 1846.
41 *C.J.*, 2 November 1846.
42 *Limerick Reporter*, 30 October 1846.
43 *L.R.*, 30 October 1846.
44 *C.J.*, 15, 29 October 1846.
45 See *C.J.*, 31 August 1846.
46 *C.J.*, 26, 29 October, 2 November, 3 December 1846; *L.R.*, 30 October 1846.

47 *C.J.*, 7 January 1847.
48 *C.J.*, 22 February 1847.
49 *C.J.*, 25 February 1847.
50 *C.J.*, 7, 22 February, 11, 19 April, 24 May 1847.
51 *C.J.*, 8 June 1847.
52 *C.J.*, 8 April 1847.
53 *C.J.*, 7 June 1847.
54 See *L.&C.E.*, 4 November 1846.
55 For Knox comment on Wynne controversy, see *C.J.*, 3 December 1846.
56 *C.J.*, 1 February 1847.
57 *C.J.*, 5 April 1847; Ó Murchadha, *Sable Wings*, p. 108.
58 Ó Murchadha, *Sable Wings*, p. 107; *C.J.*, 19 April 1847.
59 Ó Murchadha, *Sable Wings*, p. 108.
60 *C.J.*, 5 April, 1847. For later Macbeth dispute see *C.J.*, 10, 13 April, *L.R.*, 11 April 1848.
61 Ó Murchadha, *Sable Wings*, pp. 141, 252.
62 *C.J.*, 23 September 1847.
63 *C.J.*, 1 October 1846.
64 *C.J.*, 17 January 1848.
65 See for example, *C.J.*, 20 March 1848.
66 *C.J.*, 24, 27 July, 3, 14 August 1848; Ó Murchadha, *Sable Wings*, pp. 180–182.
67 *C.J.*, 12, 19 October 1848; *C.J.*, 17 June 1850 (Smith O'Brien).
68 See *C.J.*, 5 May 1836, 2, 9 January 1843.
69 *C.J.*, 19, 22 January 1846.
70 *C.J.*, 13 March 1848.
71 *C.J.*, 15 March 1849.
72 *C.J.*, 4 October 1849.
73 *C.J.*, 16 August 1849.
74 *C.J.*, 18 March 1850.
75 See *C.J.*, 14 August 1848 and *L.&C.E.*, 9, 12, 19 August 1848 (holy well); *C.J.*, 20 August, 3, 10 September 1849 and *L.&C.E.*, 29 August, 5, 12, 19, 29 September 1849 (Society of Saint Vincent de Paul).
76 *C.J.*, 8 February 1847.
77 Rev. Wallace Clare (ed.), *A Young Irishman's Diary: Being Extracts from the Early Journal of John Keegan of Moate* (Dublin, 1928), p. 82.
78 For a representative comment, see that made at a public meeting, *L.&C.E.*, 26 November 1851: 'When they had master Henry Keane reading the Bible and Johnny Knox in Ennis moralising for them surely they had some reason to hope for the future improvement of the country.'

Chapter 2

1. David Fitzpatrick, 'Famine, Entitlements and Seduction: Captain Edmond Wynne in Ireland 1846–1851', in *English Historical Review*, vol. cx (June 1995), pp. 596–619; Cormac Ó Gráda, *Black '47 and Beyond: the Great Irish Famine in History, Economy and Memory* (Princeton, 1999), pp. 59–69.
2. Fitzpatrick, 'Entitlements', p. 599.
3. Ibid., pp. 599–600.
4. Thomas P. O'Neill, 'The Organisation and Administration of Relief', in R. Dudley Edwards and T. Desmond Williams (eds.), *The Great Famine: Studies in Irish History 1845–1852* (Dublin, 1956), p. 228.
5. Lieutenant-Col. Jones to Charles Trevelyan, 24 October 1846, *Correspondence from July 1846 to January 1847, relating to the Measures adopted for the Relief of the Distress in Ireland, Board of Works Series* (London, 1847), p. 152.
6. Cecil Woodham Smith, *The Great Hunger* (London, 1962), p. 31; Austin Bourke, '*The Visitation of God*'? *The Potato and the Great Irish Famine* (Dublin, 1993), pp. 112–113.
7. *C.J.*, 1 October 1846. John B. Knox helpfully published the official instructions in relation to relief committees in the same issue.
8. Wynne to Jones, 5 November 1846, *Correspondence from July 1846 ... Board of Works*, p. 170.
9. *C.J.*, 9 November 1846.
10. 'Extract from Report of Captain Wynne', 8 November 1846, *Correspondence from July 1846 ... Board of Works*, p. 181.
11. Wynne to Jones, 19 November 1846, *Correspondence from July 1846 ... Board of Works*, p. 270; Ó Murchadha, *Sable Wings*, p. 84.
12. Wynne to Jones, 19 November 1846, *Correspondence from July 1846... Board of Works*, p. 271.
13. *C.J.*, 26 November 1846; *L.C.*, 28 November 1846.
14. *C.J.*, 30 November 1846.
15. See for example *C.J.*, 30 November, 3, 17 December 1846.
16. *C.J.*, 3 December 1846.
17. *C.J.*, 17 December 1846.
18. *C.J.*, 3 December 1846.
19. For O'Brien and duelling see *D.I.B.*
20. *C.J.*, 3 December 1846.
21. *C.J.*, 10, 17 December 1846; Wynne to Secretary of the Board of Works, 5 December 1846, *Correspondence from July 1846 ... Board of Works*, p. 300.
22. *C.J.*, 7, 10 December 1846.
23. *C.J.*, 10 December 1846.
24. *C.J.*, 14 December 1846.

25 *C.J.*, 17 December 1846.
26 *C.J.*, 7, 14 November 1846.
27 *C.J.*, 14 December 1846.
28 See also letter by Cornelius O'Brien, *C.J.*, 21 December 1846.
29 *C.J.*, 14 December 1846.
30 'From Captain Wynne', n.d., *Correspondence from July 1846 ... Board of Works*, p. 333.
31 For Russell, see *D.I.B.*
32 From Captain Wynne', p. 333.
33 *Report from the Select Committee on Captain Wynne's Letters, together with the Minutes of Evidence, Appendix and Index* (London, 1847), henceforward *Aglionby Committee*, pp. 325–326.
34 *C.J.*, 21, 31 December 1846.
35 Ó Murchadha, *Sable Wings*, pp. 92–93.
36 Cited in Ó Murchadha, *Sable Wings*, p. 93.
37 Woodham Smith, *Great Hunger*, p. 153; Wynne to Jones, 24 December, 1846. *Correspondence from July 1846 ... Board of Works*, pp. 434–435.
38 Ó Murchadha, *Sable Wings*, pp. 93–94.
39 *C.J.*, 17, 24, 31 December, 1846; Ó Murchadha, *Sable Wings*, p. 93.
40 Wynne to Mr Walker, 17 January 1847, *Correspondence from January to March 1847 relating to the Measures adopted for the Relief of the Distress in Ireland, Board of Works Series*, Second Part, p. 16.
41 *C.J.*, 14 January 1847; *Aglionby Committee*, pp. 106–108.
42 *C.J.*, 14 January 1847; *Correspondence from January to March 1847, Board of Works*, Second Part, p. 7; *Aglionby Committee*, p. 107.
43 *C.J.*, 14 January 1847.
44 'Extract from a Letter of Captain Wynne', 1 January 1847. *Correspondence from July 1846, Board of Works*, p. 472.
45 Public Record Office of Northern Ireland, Ms. D1337, 8 December 1847; Wynne to Secretary of Board of Works, 5 December 1846, *Correspondence from July 1846 ... Board of Works*, p. 300.
46 Wynne to Captain Wynne, R.E., 9 January 1847, *Correspondence from January to March 1847 relating to the Measures Adopted for the Relief of the Distress in Ireland, Board of Works Series*, Second Part, pp. 8–9.
47 Wynne to Mr Walker, 17 January 1847, *Correspondence from January to March 1847, Board of Works*, Second Part, p. 15.
48 Ibid., pp. 15–16.
49 *C.J.*, 25 January 1847.
50 See Woodham Smith, *Great Hunger*, p. 152.
51 *C.J.*, 25 January 1847.
52 *Aglionby Committee*, pp. 37, 161, 169.
53 Ibid., p. 162, 170, 174, 190–191.

54 *C.J.*, 28 January 1847; *Aglionby Committee*, Appendix B, p. 841.
55 *Aglionby Committee*, pp. 9, 794–796 (Appendix B); Ó Gráda, *Black '47 and Beyond*, p. 63.
56 *Report from the Select Committee on Captain Wynne's Letters* (London, 1847); Fitzpatrick, 'Entitlements', p. 607.
57 For one very atypical letter, see Wynne to Jones, 29 December 1846, *Correspondence from July 1846 to January 1847 relating to the Measures adopted for the relief of Distress in Ireland, Commissariat Series*, First Part (London, 1847), p. 438.
58 See, for example, Woodham Smith, *Great Hunger*, pp. 152–155.
59 Jones to Trevelyan, 7 December 1846, *Correspondence from July 1846 ... Board of Works*, p. 301.
60 Trevelyan to Routh, 10 December 1846, *Correspondence from July 1846 ... Commissariat*, p. 335.
61 Ó Gráda, *Black '47 and Beyond*, pp. 63–69.
62 Leon Ó Broin, *Charles Gavan Duffy: Patriot and Statesman* (Dublin, 1967), pp. 94–95.
63 Ó Murchadha, *Sable Wings*, p. 95.
64 *C.J.*, 1 March, 1847.
65 Ó Murchadha, *Sable Wings*, pp. 95–96.
66 *C.J.*, 8 March, 1847.
67 *C.J.*, 15, February, 8 March 1847.

Chapter 3
1 *C.J.*, 18 June 1840.
2 Arthur Woolaston Button (ed.), *Arthur Young's Tour in Ireland 1776–1779* (London, 1892), vol. i, pp. 285, 287, 291.
3 As recorded in the later *Return of Landowners of One Acre and Upwards, in the Several Counties, Counties of Cities, and Counties of Towns in Ireland* (Dublin, 1876), Clare County, p. 114.
4 *Return of Landowners*, Clare, p. 114.
5 *General Valuation of Rateable Property in Ireland* (Dublin, 1855), Union of Ennis, pp. 22, 27. The farms feature often in the diaries.
6 The official valuations do not necessarily reflect ownership. Griffith's *General Valuation*, Union of Kilrush, pp. 31–32, records Singleton as one of many 'immediate lessors' at Baltard; but we know he owned the townland; see *C.J.*, 17 January 1850.
7 In September 1846, 100 destitute families (621 persons) lived at Baltard, *C.J.*, 21 September 1846.
8 National Library of Ireland Ms. 16,885, Diary of John Singleton 1845–1851 (hereinafter Singleton Diary), 26 June 1845, 1 September 1847, 26 July 1848.
9 The Kiltannon Molonys (senior branch) owned over 10,000 acres in 1876, *Return of Landowners*, Clare, p. 112.

10 For his Grand Tour, see Richard Cargill Cole, *John Singleton's Grand Tour 1815–1817* (New York, 1988).
11 Hewson, 'Diaries of John Singleton', p. 103; Clare County Archives, Singleton Papers, IE CLCCA, PP/29.
12 Hugh Weir, *Historical, Genealogical, Architectural Notes on Some Houses of Clare* (Whitegate, 1986), p. 221.
13 Weir, *Houses of Clare*, pp. 110, 220–221.
14 See for example Singleton Diary, 21, 29 August 1845.
15 See exchanges in *C.J.*, 2 June 1842.
16 See *C.J.*, 4 August 1842, 23, 30 November 1843.
17 Singleton Diary, 7 October 1845.
18 Singleton Diary, 16 February 1845.
19 The eldest son was in fact Michael Creagh Singleton, a lieutenant in the tenth foot regiment, who fought in India, mentioned just once in the diaries, Singleton Diary, 6 April 1846; Bernard Burke, *A Genealogical and Heraldic History of the Landed Gentry of Ireland* (London, 1912), under Singleton.
20 Singleton Diary, 29 October 1845.
21 *C.J.*, 6 November, 24 November 1845.
22 *C.J.*, 27 November 1845.
23 Singleton Diary, 31 December 1845.
24 Singleton Diary, 25 January–6 February 1846.
25 Singleton Diary, 24 March 1846.
26 *L.&C.E.*, 4 July 1846.
27 Singleton Diary, 2–6 May 1846.
28 Singleton Diary, 8, 9, 11, 12 May 1845.
29 See Singleton Diary, 9, 10 April, 10 June 1846.
30 *C.J.*, 12 May 1845.
31 *C.J.*, 12 February 1846.
32 Singleton Diary, 9 February 1846.
33 Singleton Diary, 28 May 1846.
34 Singleton Diary, 25 July 1846.
35 Ó Murchadha, *Sable Wings*, pp. 65, 85, 87.
36 Singleton Diary, 22–28 April 1846.
37 Singleton Diary, 27 April, 12, 14–16 May 1846.
38 Singleton Diary, 11–12 June 1846.
39 Singleton Diary, 17–21, 25 June, 3 July 1846.
40 Singleton Diary, 11 July 1846.
41 Singleton Diary, 11 August 1846; *C.J.*, 27 August 1846.
42 Singleton Diary, 11, 16, 17 August 1846; *C.J.*, 27 August, 27 September 1846; *Limerick Chronicle*, 29 August 1846; Clare County Archives, Singleton Papers, PP/3/7.

43 Singleton Diary, 12–15 August 1846.
44 Singleton Diary, 2 September 1846.
45 Singleton Diary, 23 October 1846.
46 *L.&C.E.*, 23 September 1846.
47 *L.C.*, 7 October 1846.
48 Singleton Diary, 5 October 1846.
49 Singleton Diary, 24, 26 November 1846.
50 Singleton Diary, 1 December 1846.
51 Singleton Diary, 13–15 December 1846.
52 Singleton Diary, 17 June 1847.
53 Singleton Diary, 6 July 1847; Ó Murchadha, *Sable Wings*, p. 115.
54 Singleton Diary, 9 November 1846.
55 Singleton Diary, 15, 17 February 1847.
56 Singleton Diary, 28 April–12 May, 22 May–9 June 1847.
57 Singleton Diary, 31 May 1847.
58 *L.&.C.E.*, 4 March 1846.
59 Ó Murchadha, *Sable Wings*, pp. 50–52; *L.C.*, 11 July 1846.
60 *L.C.*, 8 August 1846.
61 *C.J.*, 7 September 1846.
62 *L.C.*, 7 October 1846.
63 Singleton Diary, 18, 22 October 1846; *L.C.*, 17 October; *C.J.*, 19 October 1846.
64 *L.C.*, 11 November 1846.
65 *L.C.*, 16 September 1846.
66 *L.C.*, 24 April, 1 May 1847.
67 *L.C.*, 29 September, 2 October 1847.
68 See Singleton Diary, 23 August, 8 October 1847.
69 In contrast to Hugh who 'snapped off' shots at his attackers, *L.C.*, 24 April, 1 May 1847.
70 Singleton Diary, 27, 28 November 1846; *Dublin Evening Mail*, 2 December 1846; *C.J.*, 17 October 1846.
71 For Hugh's lunacy, see *C.J.*, 1 May 1851.
72 Ó Murchadha, *Sable Wings*, p. 169; *L.C.*, 26 January 1848.
73 *Limerick Chronicle*, 29 March 1848.
74 *L.&C.E.*, 28 October, 1848; *L.C.* 1 November 1848; *C.J.*, 16 November 1848, *L.C.*, 18 November 1848.
75 See *C.J.*, 20 January, 2 June 1842.
76 *C.J.*, 5 August 1847.
77 *C.J.*, 3 February 1848.
78 Ó Murchadha, *Sable Wings*, pp. 188–189.
79 Ibid., pp. 191, 300.

80 *C.J.*, 18 January, 15 February 1849.
81 *C.J.*, 2 March 1848.
82 Ó Murchadha, *Sable Wings*, p. 158.
83 *Reports and Returns relating to the Kilrush Union* (London, 1849), p. 16. The Baltard evictions are discussed in Matthew Lynch, *The Mass Evictions in Kilrush Poor Law Union during the Great Famine* (Miltown Malbay, 2013), pp. 94–95.
84 *C.J.*, 18 May 1848; *L.C.*, 20 May 1848.
85 Kennedy, *Reports and Returns*, p. 49.
86 *C.J.*, 20 August, 6 September 1849.
87 Singleton Diary, 12 January 1849.
88 Singleton Diary, 9 January 1849.
89 Singleton Diary, 13 January 1849.
90 *C.J.*, 17 January 1850.
91 *C.J.*, 17 January 1850. See also *L.&C.E.*, 31 October 1849.
92 Lynch, *Mass Evictions in Kilrush Poor Law Union*, p. 94; see also *Report from the Select Committee on Kilrush Union, together with the Proceedings of the Committee, Minutes of Evidence, Appendix, and Index* (London, 1850), pp. 229–230.
93 Lynch, *Mass Evictions in Kilrush Poor Law Union*, pp. 94–95.
94 *L.&C.E.*, 31 October 1849.
95 Singleton Diary, 14 November 1849.
96 Hewson, 'Diaries of John Singleton', p. 103.
97 *L.&C.E.*, 24 November 1849.
98 Singleton Diary, 25 December 1849.
99 Singleton Diary, 23 January, 23 February, 11 March 1850.
100 Singleton Diary, 19 March 1850.
101 Singleton Diary, 21 May 1850.
102 Singleton Diary, 21 June, 20 July 1850.
103 Singleton Diary, 29 July 1850.
104 Singleton Diary, 2, 3 August 1850.
105 Singleton Diary, 21 September 1850.

Chapter 4
1 W.J. Fitzpatrick, *The Life of Charles Lever* (London, 1896), pp. 53–58; See also T.G. Wilson, *Victorian Doctor, being the Life of Sir William Wilde* (London, 1974), pp. 32–34; *C.J.*, 7 November 1895.
2 *C.J.*, 28 February 1850. For Healy's mother, see Flannan Enright, 'Terry Alt; the Rise and Fall of an Agrarian Secret Society', in Mathew Lynch and Patrick Nugent (eds.), *Clare: History and Society* (Dublin, 2008), p. 231.
3 Ellis, *Ennis at Work*, pp. 50, 93.

NOTES

4   For middlemen at this level, see David Dickson, 'Middlemen', in Thomas Bartlett and D.W. Hayton (eds.), *Penal Era and Golden Age: Essays in Irish History 1690 and 1800* (Dublin, 1979), pp. 170–173; L.M. Cullen, 'Catholic Social Classes under the Penal Laws', in T.P. Power and Kevin Whelan (eds.), *Endurance and Emergence: Catholics in Ireland in the Eighteenth Century* (Dublin, 1990), pp. 57–86.

5   For these houses, see Weir, *Houses of Clare*, pp. 51, 163, 185–186, 245–246; Ellis, *Ennis at Work*, p. 93; *C.J.*, 20 July 1840.

6   Ellis, *Ennis at Work*, p. 49.

7   *Dublin Medical Press* cited in *C.J.*, 20 July 1840.

8   Wilson, *Victorian Doctor*, pp. 32–33.

9   *C.J.*, 3 May 1832.

10   *C.J.*, 10, 14 June 1832; Ignatius Murphy, 'Cholera Epidemic in County Clare', in *The Other Clare*, vol. v (1981), p. 26.

11   *C.J.*, 14 June 1832.

12   *L.C.*, 13 June 1832; *C.J.*, 18 June 1832; Joe Power, 'The Cholera in Clare Castle', in *Other Clare*, vol. ix (1985), p. 65.

13   *Lancet*, 1 September 1832, pp. 681–685; *C.J.*, 15 October 1832; Power, 'Cholera in Clare Castle', pp. 64–68.

14   *C.J.*, 30 August, 17 September, 15 October, 24 December 1832, 4 November 1833, 16 January 1834.

15   *C.J.*, 20, 24, 27 August 1832.

16   For early examples of this scrambling see *C.J.*, 5, 12 January 1835 and 1, 5 December 1836.

17   *Thom's Irish Almanac and Official Directory with the Post Office Dublin City and County Directory for the Year 1847*, p. 458.

18   For medical squabbling see *C.J.*, 4 November 1833, 20 July 1840, 31 October 1842.

19   Samuel Lewis, *A Topographical Dictionary of Ireland* (London, 1837), vol. 1, p. 602.

20   *C.J.*, 17 March 1836; *Thom's Directory 1847*, p. 456.

21   *C.J.*, 9, 16 January 1834.

22   *C.J.*, 31 December 1840, 4 January 1841.

23   *C.J.*, 4 March 1841.

24   *C.J.*, 7, 10, 14 June 1841.

25   *C.J.*, 13 October, 3, 10 November 1842.

26   *C.J.*, 25 March 1841, 26 February, 6 July 1846.

27   See *C.J.*, 31 March 1845, 26 February 1846.

28   *C.J.*, 17, 27 November 1845, 26 February 1846; *L.&C.E.*, 4 March, 8 July 1846.

29   *C.J.*, 22 June 1846; *L.&C.E.*, 4 July 1846; *L.C.*, 8 July 1846.

30 *C.J.*, 9 February 1846.
31 *C.J.*, 9 February, 2 March 1846.
32 Ó Murchadha, *Sable Wings*, pp. 122–123.
33 Ibid., pp. 123–124.
34 Ibid., p. 121.
35 For confident pre-Famine remarks see *C.J.*, 29 June 1843.
36 *C.J.*, 7, 14 January 1847.
37 *Dublin Quarterly Journal of Medical Science*, vol. vii, p. 93.
38 *L.&C.E.*, 20 March 1847.
39 *C.J.*, 2 December 1847.
40 *L.C.*, 14, 17 July 1847. For County Jail salary, see *L.&C.E.*, 4 July 1846.
41 *L.C.*, 17 July 1847; *L.&C.E.*, 20 March 1847.
42 *C.J.*, 19 August 1847.
43 *C.J.*, 23, 26 August 1847.
44 For medical profession discontent, see Peter Froggatt, 'The Response of the Medical Profession to the Great Famine', in E. Margaret Crawford (ed.), *Famine: The Irish Experience 900–1900* (Edinburgh, 1989), pp. 144,146.
45 The dispute can be followed in *C.J.*, 23, 26, 30 August, 2, 6, 20 September 1847, 24 February 1848, 2 March 1848; *L.&C.E.*, 15 September 1847, 4, 11 March 1848.
46 *C.J.*, 26 August, 6, 20 September 1847, 2 March 1848; *L.&C.E.*, 15 September 1847.
47 *C.J.*, 2 March 1848.
48 *L.&C.E.*, 4 March 1848.
49 *L.&C.E.*, 1 March 1848.
50 Cullinan's salary had been raised to £65 in February 1847, *C.J.*, 6 April 1848.
51 *C.J.*, 6, 20 April 1848.
52 *C.J.*, 20 April 1848.
53 *C.J.*, 4, 11, 25 May, 8, 22 June 1848.
54 *C.J.*, 14 September 1848.
55 *C.J.*, 21, 28 September 1848; *L.C.*, 4 October 1848. For Hehir, see *C.J.*, 31 March 1845.
56 For this gratuity, see *C.J.*, 11 September 1848.
57 *C.J.*, 7 December 1848.
58 Froggatt, 'Medical Profession', p. 147; *C.J.*, 14, 28 December 1848.
59 *C.J.*, 28 December 1848, 1 January 1849.
60 *C.J.*, 8 January, 15 March 1849.
61 *C.J.*, 19 March 1849.
62 *C.J.*, 14, 18 June, 26 July 1849.
63 *C.J.*, 4, 7 June 1849.

64 *C.J.*, 18 June 1849.
65 *Dublin Medical Press*, 20 June 1849.
66 *D.M.P.*, 27 June 1849.
67 Reproduced in *C.J.*, 5 July 1849.
68 *C.J.*, 29 July, 13 August, 6, 10 September, 4, 8 October 1849.
69 *C.J.*, 1 November 1849.
70 Froggatt, 'Medical Profession', p. 147.
71 Ó Murchadha, *Sable Wings*, p. 232.
72 *C.J.*, 16, 25 September 1850.
73 *C.J.*, 24 January 1850.
74 *C.J.*, 10, 17 June, 16 September 1850.
75 *C.J.*, 30 September, 3 October 1850.
76 *C.J.*, 26, 30 September, 3 October 1850.
77 *C.J.*, 20, 27 May, 3, 17 June 1852.
78 *C.J.*, 13 December 1852.

Chapter 5

1 Reverend Murphy's diaries are preserved in the Public Record Office of Northern Ireland, Belfast, Ms. D1337 (henceforth referred to as Murphy Diary).
2 Lewis, *Topographical Dictionary*, under Dromcliffe; Ciarán Ó Murchadha, 'The Diary of a Country Curate: Revered Henry Murphy in Ennis 1844–1846', in *Other Clare*, vol. xiv (1990), p. 37; H.B. Swanzy, *Succession Lists of the Diocese of Dromore* (Belfast, 1933), p. 64.
3 Lewis, *Topographical Dictionary*, under Dromcliffe.
4 Ennis graveyard remained thus throughout the nineteenth century. See *C.J.*, 10 August 1846; *Clare Freeman*, 25 February 1871.
5 *Slater's National Commercial Directory of Ireland* (Manchester, 1846); Ó Murchadha, 'Country Curate', p. 38.
6 H.B. Swanzy, *Dromore Succession Lists*, p. 65.
7 Ó Murchadha, 'Country Curate', p. 38.
8 Murphy Diary, 14, 30 September, 2 October 1845.
9 Ó Murchadha, 'Country Curate', pp. 38–39.
10 Murphy Diary, 6, 23, 24, 25 October 1844; *Dublin Evening Mail*, 28 October, 28 November 1844.
11 Wyndham's behaviour before and during the Great Famine is comprehensively dealt with in Matthew Lynch, 'Colonel George Wyndham, First Baron Leconfield (1787–1869) and his Estate in Clare', in Matthew Lynch and Patrick Nugent (eds.), *Clare: History and Society* (Dublin, 2008), pp. 289–341.
12 Flannan Enright, 'Pre-Famine Reform and Emigration on the Wyndham Estate in Clare', in *Other Clare*, vol. viii (1984), p. 33; Lynch, 'Colonel George Wyndham', pp. 300–303.

13 Lynch, *Mass Evictions in Kilrush Poor Law Union*, p. 68.
14 Max Egremont, *Wyndham and Children First* (London, 1968), p. 52.
15 Ibid., p. 45.
16 Murphy Diary, 24 October, 27 December 1844; Egremont, *Wyndham and Children First*, p. 45.
17 Murphy Diary, 21 October 1846.
18 See for example *C.J.*, 31 August 1841, 22 August, 12 September 1842, 21 March 1844.
19 Ó Murchadha, 'Country Curate', p. 38.
20 Ibid., p. 38; Murphy Diary, 18 June 1845.
21 Murphy Diary, 23 September 1845; Ó Murchadha, 'Country Curate', p. 38.
22 Murphy Diary, 15 April, 21 October 1845.
23 Ó Murchadha, 'Country Curate', p. 39.
24 Asenath Nicholson, *Ireland's Welcome to the Stranger*, ed. Maureen Murphy (Dublin, 2002), p. 282. See also Murphy Diary, 20 April 1845.
25 Murphy Diary, 27 October, 20, 25 November 1845.
26 *C.J.*, 30 May 1842.
27 Ó Murchadha, *Sable Wings*, p. 17; *C.J.*, 2 June 1842.
28 Ó Murchadha, 'Country Curate', p. 41.
29 Murphy Diary, 14, 18 October 1845.
30 Murphy Diary, 20–28 October 1845.
31 Murphy Diary, 22 November 1845; *C.J.*, 24, 27 November 1845.
32 Murphy Diary, 23–29 November 1845.
33 Murphy Diary, 23–31 December 1845.
34 Murphy Diary, 8–26 January 1846.
35 Murphy Diary, 9 February 1846.
36 Murphy Diary, 9–21 February 1846.
37 Murphy Diary, 16 March 1846; Ó Murchadha, *Sable Wings*, pp. 50–53.
38 Murphy Diary, 17–18 March 1846; *C.J.*, 19 March 1846.
39 Murphy Diary, 20 March 1846.
40 *C.J.*, 24, 30 March 1846.
41 *C.J.*, 30 March 1846; Murphy Diary, 26–27 March 1846.
42 Murphy Diary, 28 March 1846.
43 *C.J.*, 2 April 1836.
44 Murphy Diary, 29 March–2 April 1846.
45 Murphy Diary, 31 March–18 April 1846.
46 Murphy Diary, 12–14 May 1846.
47 See for example the diary of the Wicklow landlord's wife, Elizabeth Smith, for 10–20 May 1846, Patricia Pelly and Andrew Tod (eds.), *Elizabeth Grant of Rothiemurchus, the Highland Lady In Ireland: Journals 1840–50* (Edinburgh 1990), pp. 226–227.

48 Murphy Diary, 5–13 June 1846.
49 Murphy Diary, 15 June 1846.
50 Murphy Diary, 9 July 1846.
51 Murphy Diary, 20, 21, 27 July 1846
52 Murphy Diary, 27 July 1846.
53 Murphy Diary, 2–18 August 1846.
54 Murphy Diary, 12, 14, 19, 20, 23 July, 6 August 1846.
55 Murphy Diary, 20 August 1846.
56 Murphy Diary, 24 July 1846.
57 Murphy Diary, 19 September 1846; Ó Murchadha, *Sable Wings*, pp. 65–66.
58 Murphy Diary, 25 August 1846.
59 Murphy Diary, 13–16 October 1846.
60 Murphy Diary, 5, 8, 9 October 1846.
61 *C.J.*, 12 October 1846.
62 Murphy Diary, 18–24 October 1846.
63 *C.J.*, 26 October 1846; *L.&C.E.* 28 October 1846.
64 Murphy Diary, 27 October, 29 October to 4 November, 16–17 November 1846. For the Volatti affair, see also *C.J.*, 5 November 1846.
65 Murphy Diary, 1 December 1846.
66 Murphy Diary, 12–18 December 1846.
67 Murphy Diary, 19–31 December 1846.
68 *C.J.*, 15 March 1847.
69 *C.J.* 22 October 1849.
70 See *C.J.*, 3 July 1851 for another account of prize giving ceremony at Glandine.
71 Harry Hughes, 'The Glandine School Controversy', in *Clare Association Yearbook, 1995–1997*, p. 71; Harry Hughes, 'Civilizing and Enlightening the Population of Miltown; the Souper School at Glandine', in *Cumann na Meanmhúinteoirí Éire, Comhdháil Bhliantúil Inis 1995* (Ennis, 1995), p. 21; Lynch, 'Colonel George Wyndham', pp. 319–332.
72 For Reverend Murphy's evangelical credentials see *C.F.*, 16, 23, 30 March 1861.
73 Hughes, 'Civilizing and Enlightening', p. 20.
74 Hughes, 'Glandine School Controversy', p. 71; Lynch, 'Colonel George Wyndham', p. 323.
75 Murphy Diary, 30 June 1855 (PRONI D1337/2).

Chapter 6
1 *Burke's Irish Family Records*, under Keane; *Proceedings Royal Irish Academy*, Vol. IX (1864–1866), Series I, p. 41. Luke McInerney, *Clerical and Learned Lineages of Medieval County Clare* (Dublin, 2014), p. 33.
2 See Anon, 'Remarks on Some Statements of Marcus Keane in His Work, "Temples and Towers of Ancient Ireland"', in *Irish Ecclesiastical Record*, vol. V (1869), pp. 376–377.

3   For nickname, see *Burke's Irish Family Records*; for popularity of Long Bob, *C.J.*, 12 December 1842; *L.&C.E.*, 12 April 1848.
4   Kieran Sheedy, *The Clare Elections* (Dun Laoghaire, 1993), pp. 461–463.
5   *C.J.*, 11, 29 March 1841.
6   *Digest of Evidence Taken before Her Majesty's Commissioners of Inquiry into the State of the Law and Practice in Respect to the Occupation of Land in Ireland*, vol. ii (London, 1848), p. 461.
7   *Correspondence Relating to the Measures Adopted for the Relief of Distress in Ireland (Board of Works Series)* First Part, p. 308; *Correspondence Relating to the Measures Adopted for the Relief of Distress in Ireland (Commissariat Series)*, Second Part, p. 203; *L.C.*, 28 March, 29 April 1846; *L.&C.E.*, 15, 29 April 1846; *C.J.*, 27 April 1846.
8   *C.J.*, 20 July 1846.
9   *C.J.*, 18 January, 1 February 1847.
10 *C.J.*, 18 February 1847.
11 *Burke's Irish Family Records*, under Keane.
12 *C.J.*, 20 December 1847.
13 See Ó Murchadha, *Sable Wings*, pp. 87–89, 91–97, 111–113; Ó Gráda, *Black '47*, pp. 59–69.
14 Keane, for example, persuaded Fishbourne that tenants were hiding their seed in order to obtain free government supplies, *Correspondence … Commissariat Series, Second Part*, p. 203.
15 See *General Valuation of Rateable Property*, Union of Ennistimon, pp. 33, 44, 47.
16 *Return of Owners of Land*, Clare, pp. 108, 110, 115.
17 *Minutes of Evidence Taken before the Select Committee on the Clare Election Petition; Together with Proceedings of the Committee* (1853), p. 20; *Report of Her Majesty's Commissioners of Inquiry into the Working of the Landlord and Tenant (Ireland) Act, 1870* (London, 1881), p. cxxvii.
18 *Return of Owners of Land*, Clare, p. 110.
19 James S. Donnelly, *The Land and People of Nineteenth Century Cork* (Dublin, 1975), p. 173; *Report from the Select Committee on Kilrush Union, Together with the Proceedings of the Committee, Minutes of Evidence, Appendix, and Index* (London, 1850), p. 196 [*Scrope Committee*]; P.P. Patrick White, 'Proselytism in West Clare: A Retrospect', in *Irish Ecclesiastical Record*, third series, vol. viii, no. 5 (May 1887), p. 415.
20 Ignatius Murphy, *A People Starved, Life and Death in West Clare, 1845–1851* (Dublin, 1996), p. 53.
21 Famine evictions are profiled in Chapter 2 of Perry Curtis's recent work, *The Depiction of Evictions in Ireland 1845–1910* (Dublin, 2011); for west Clare see pp. 38–39 and 43–44.
22 James S. Donnelly Jr, *The Great Irish Potato Famine* (Stroud, England, 2001), pp. 147, 156.

23 Ciarán Ó Murchadha, 'One Vast Abattoir: County Clare, 1848–1849', in *Other Clare*, vol. xxi (1997), pp. 65–66.
24 Ciarán Ó Murchadha, *The Great Famine: Ireland's Agony 1845–1852* (London, 2011), pp. 116–117.
25 *L.&C.E.*, 22 September, 3 November 1847.
26 Ignatius Murphy, 'Captain A.E. Kennedy, Poor Law Inspector and the Great Famine in the Kilrush Union 1847–1850', in *Other Clare*, vol. 3 (1979), pp. 16–25.
27 *L.&C.E.*, 2 May 1849. See also *L.&C.E.*, 18, 25 April 1849.
28 *L.&C.E.*, 11 March 1848.
29 Scariff Vice-Guardians to Irish Poor Law Commissioners, 19 February 1848, in *Papers Relating to Proceedings for the Relief of Distress and State of the Unions and Workhouses in Ireland*, Sixth Series, vol. lvi (1848), pp. 508, 509.
30 *C.J.*, 13 March 1848.
31 *L.&C.E.*, 11 March 1848.
32 Ibid.
33 *Reports and Returns*, pp. 21–23.
34 *L.&C.E*, 2 September 1818.
35 *L.&C.E.*, 20 September 1848.
36 *L.&C.E.*, 23, 30 September 1848.
37 *L.&C.E.*, 25 October 1848.
38 *L.&C.E.*, 18, 24, 29 November 1848.
39 *Reports and Returns*, pp. 37, 38, 40.
40 *C.J.*, 10 May 1849.
41 *L.&C.E.*, 31 March 1847.
42 Marcus Keane to T.N. Redington, 25 April 1848; Report of Sub-Inspector Donovan. National Archives of Ireland, Outrage Reports, Clare, 1848, 5/380, 5/319.
43 Keane to Redington, 25 April 1848; Donovan Report, O.R., Clare 1848, 5/319.
44 *L.&C.E.*, 22, 25 March 1848.
45 *L.&C.E.*, 25 March 1848.
46 *Pilot*, 29 March 1848; Donovan Report, O.R. Clare 1848, 5/319; *L.&C.E.*, 8 April 1848.
47 *C.J.*, 3 April 1848; Redington to Keane, 16 April 1848; Keane to Redington, 25 April 1848, O.R. Clare, 1848, 5/380, 5/319.
48 Donovan Report, O.R. Clare 1848, 5/319.
49 *C.J.*, 3 April 1848.
50 Keane to Redington, 25 April 1848, O.R. Clare, 1848, 5/380.
51 Ibid.
52 Ibid.

53 White, 'Proselytism in West Clare', p. 415.
54 *L.&C.E.*, 13 September 1848.
55 *L.&C.E.*, 2 December 1848.
56 *L.&C.E.*, 16 December 1848.
57 For Dan Sheedy, see *L.&C.E.*, 8 April 1848; 25, 29 August, 29 September 1849.
58 For Davoren, see *C.J.*, 29 January 1846; *L.&C.E.*, 14 February 1849.
59 *L.&C.E.*, 2 December 1848. The *Examiner* would use the term 'slaughterers of houses' as a term of derision later; see *L.&C.E.*, 1 September 1849.
60 *Clare Election Petition*, pp. 19–20.
61 *L.&C.E.*, 14 February 1849.
62 *L.&C.E.*, 24 February 1849.
63 Ibid.
64 See *Clare Election Petition*, pp. 7–33.
65 For examples of Henry's drunkenness, see *L.&C.E.*, 27 August 1852, 23 March 1853.
66 *L.&C.E.*, 28 February 1849.
67 *L.&C.E.*, 28 February 1849. The Keanes returned to Meelick in May and October, and again in August 1852, for further clearances; *L.&C.E.*, 16 May, 13, 17 October 1849, 21 August 1852.
68 *Scrope Committee*, p. 86.
69 *Scrope Committee*, p. 218.
70 *L.&C.E.*, 11 August 1849.
71 For Keane's petition and ancillary material see *C.J.*, 20 August 1849; *L.&C.E.*, 11, 15, 18, 22 August 1849. The manuscript petition is in the papers of Sir Lucius O'Brien, who presented it to the House of Commons on his behalf, National Library of Ireland, Inchiquin Ms. 4632.
72 *L.&C.E.*, 18 August 1849; Donnelly, *Great Irish Potato Famine*, p. 145.
73 *Scrope Committee*, pp. 86–104, 189–196.
74 *Scrope Committee*, pp. 87, 88, 98, 102.
75 *Scrope Committee*, pp. 95, 96, 193, 195.
76 *Scrope Committee*, pp. 89, 90.
77 *Scrope Committee*, p. 89.
78 *Scrope Committee*, p. 90.
79 *Scrope Committee*, p. 97.
80 *Scrope Committee*, p. 196.
81 Donnelly, *Great Irish Potato Famine*, p. 155; *Scrope Committee*, p. 98.
82 *Scrope Committee*, p. 89.
83 *Scrope Committee*, p. 95.
84 *Scrope Committee*, p. 196.
85 See Donnelly, *Great Irish Potato Famine*, p. 146; *Scrope Committee*, p. 217.

86 *Scrope Committee*, p. 220.
87 *L.&C.E.*, 29 March 1848.

Chapter 7

1   Ignatius Murphy, *Michael Meehan and the Ark of Kilbaha* (private publ., 1980), pp. 1, 17.
2   For pre-Famine in one west Clare parish (Kilfearagh), see Ignatius Murphy, *Before the Famine Struck: Life in West Clare 1844–1845* (Dublin, 1995), especially pp. 44–72; for Ó Míocháin, see Brian Ó Dálaigh, 'Tomás Ó Míocháin and the Ennis School of Poetry c. 1730–1804', in *Dál gCais*, vol. xi (1993), pp. 55–72.
3   Murphy, *Ark*, p. 2.
4   Ignatius Murphy, *The Diocese of Killaloe 1800–1950* (Dublin, 1992), p. 362.
5   Murphy, *Ark*, p. 3; *C.J.*, 22, 26 October 1840.
6   *C.J.*, 26 October, 9 November 1840.
7   *C.J.*, 26 October 1840.
8   *C.J.*, 9 November 1840; Murphy, *Ark*, p. 4.
9   In January 1843 Meehan was lampooned in the *Clare Journal* for a Repeal speech made in Kilrush, *C.J.*, 23 January 1843. See also Murphy, *Ark*, p. 4.
10 Kerr, '*A Nation of Beggars*'?: *Priests, People and Politics in Famine Ireland 1846–1852* (Cambridge, 1994), p. 128, citing the *Nation*, 22 July 1846.
11 Evidence of Meehan's radicalization can be seen in *L.C.*, 18 July 1846; *L.&C.E.*, 11, 15 July 1846; see also Murphy, *Killaloe 1800–1850*, pp. 205–207; Paddy Nolan, 'My Dear Doherty', in *Other Clare*, vol. xxvii (2003), pp. 48–50.
12 O'Neill, 'Administration of Relief', pp. 226–227.
13 Murphy, *Killaloe 1800–1850*, pp. 210–211.
14 *L.C.*, 7 July 1847; *L.&C.E.*, 7 July 1847.
15 *Tablet*, 14 August 1847.
16 *C.J.*, 19 January, 2 February 1846.
17 See for example, *C.J.*, 2, 19 February 1846.
18 *L.&C.E.*, 11 March 1848.
19 *L.&C.E.*, 11, 29 March 1848, 8 April 1848; *C.J.*, 27 March 1848.
20 *L.&C.E.*, 13 May 1848; Kennedy, *Reports and Returns*, pp. 8–10. Another 'Hieros' swipe at Keane a few days later drew no response from Beech Park: *L.&C.E.*, 17 May 1848.
21 *L.&C.E.*, 30 September 1848.
22 Two accounts of the O'Donnell eviction exist: one in *L.&C.E.*, 25 August 1849; the second in the *Illustrated London News*, 22 December 1849. Both accounts, which would appear to be connected, render the name as Gurranatuaha.
23 *Scrope Committee*, pp. 143–144.
24 *Scrope Committee*, p. 143.

25 *L.&C.E.*, 25 August 1849; *I.L.N.*, 22 December 1849.
26 Curtis, *Depiction of Eviction*, p. 48.
27 *Scrope Committee*, p. 144.
28 *Scrope Committee*, p. 107.
29 *Scrope Committee*, p. 107.
30 White, 'Proselytism in West Clare', p. 413; White, *History of Clare and the Dalcassian Clans* (Dublin, 1893), pp. 358–359.
31 Murphy, *Ark*, p. 6.
32 *L.&C.E.*, 6 June 1849.
33 Ó Murchadha, *Diocese of Killaloe: An Illustrated History*, pp. 97–98.
34 *Scrope Committee*, pp. 104–105.
35 George Clune, *The Little Ark* (Dublin, 1936), p. 6.
36 Weir, *Houses of Clare*, pp. 52, 106.
37 *L.&C.E.*, 7 April 1852 (reprint of article from *The Lamp*, 27 March 1852).
38 Murphy, *Ark*, p. 7.
39 *L.&C.E.*, 7 April 182; Murphy, *Ark*, p. 7.
40 Murphy, *Ark*, p. 7.
41 Ibid., p. 7; *L.&C.E.*, 7 April 1852.
42 White, 'Proselytism', p. 416.
43 Ibid., p. 416.
44 *C.J.*, 11 September 1851; Murphy, *Ark*, p. 8.
45 *C.J.*, 11 September 1851.
46 *L.&C.E.*, 27 September 1851. See also *C.J.*, 18 September 1851.
47 *L.&C.E.*, 7 April 1852 (reprinted from *The Lamp*, 27 March 1852). The proverb is directly translated from the Irish: *Nuair a bhíonn do lámh i mbéal an mhadra, tarraing go réig [sic] í*: see Thomas F. O'Rahilly, *A Miscellany of Irish Proverbs* (Dublin, 1922), p. 36.
48 White, 'Proselytism', p. 419.
49 *C.J.*, 6 October 1851.
50 Murphy, *The Diocese of Killaloe 1850–1904* (Dublin, 1995), p. 39; Murphy, *Ark*, p. 8.
51 *C.J.*, 20 October 1851.
52 For references to curse *Report of the Society for Irish Church Missions*, Clare Mission, June 1852, p. 169; *C.J.*, 16 October 1851; *L.&C.E.*, 7 April, 11, 25 August 1852 (coverage in *London Standard; Leicester Mercury, Aris's Birmingham Gazette*).
53 Desmond Bowen, *The Protestant Crusade in Ireland* (Dublin, 1978), p. 238.
54 *C.J.*, 6 November 1852; *L.&C.E.*, 7 April 1852.

55 *Limerick Reporter and Tipperary Vindicator*, 12 June 1852. Nine children were in Killtrellig, nine in Kilballyowen and three in the third school (Moyarta) at Doonaha.
56 Murphy, *Killaloe 1850–1904*, p. 43. *Census of Ireland 1851*, County Clare, General Table.
57 *L.R.&T.V.*, 11 June 1852.
58 *L.&C.E.*, 7 April 1852.
59 *L.&C.E.*, 24 July 1854.
60 *C.F.*, 14 April 1855.
61 Bowen, *Protestant Crusade*, p. 243; Irene Whelan, 'The Stigma of Souperism', in Cathal Póirtéir (ed.), *The Great Irish Famine* (Dublin, 1995), pp. 149–153.
62 White, 'Proselytism', p. 418.
63 Patrick J. Hamell, 'The Ark of Kilbaha', in *I.E.R.* (August 1952), pp. 132–133.
64 See, for example, *C.F.*, 22 October 1853.
65 White, 'Proseltysism', p. 419; Murphy, *Ark*, p. 11.
66 Murphy, *Ark*, p. 11; Clune, *Little Ark*, p. 15.
67 Murphy, *Ark*, p. 13.
68 Murphy, *Ark*, p. 14.

Chapter 8
1 *Aglionby Committee*, pp. 142, 794.
2 Lewis, *Topographical Dictionary*, vol. ii, pp. 204–205; Matthew Lynch, *The Mass Evictions in Kilrush Union during the Great Famine* (Miltown Malbay, 2013), p. 32.
3 Murphy, *Diocese of Killaloe 1800–1850*, pp. 288–289, 300; *L.R.*, 8 November 1839.
4 *L.&C.E.*, 28 February 1849.
5 *Burke's Irish Family Records*, under Vandeleur.
6 Thomas Johnson Westropp, 'Notes on the Sheriffs of County Clare 1570–1700', in *Journal of the Royal Society of Antiquaries in Ireland*, vol. i, part i (1890), p. 73; Weir, *Houses of Clare*, p. 164.
7 William Shaw Mason, *Statistical Survey of Ireland*, vol. ii (Dublin, 1816), p. 496; John Clancy, 'Gleaning in Seventeenth Century Kilrush', in *North Munster Antiquarian Journal*, Autumn (1943), pp. 211–212.
8 For nickname, see *C.J.*, 1 July 1841; *L.&C.E.*, 21 July 1852.
9 James Frost, *The History and Topography of the County of Clare* (Dublin, 1893), p. 620; *Burke's Irish Family Records*.
10 Sheedy, *Clare Elections*, p. 467; Murphy, *Before the Famine Struck: Life in West Clare 1834–1845* (Dublin, 1996), p. 44; *C.J.*, 1 June 1843.
11 Sheedy, *Clare Elections*, pp. 184–186.
12 Lynch, *Mass Evictions*, pp. 30–31.

13 *CJ*, 18, 21, 25 April, 5, 9 May 1836.
14 For J.O. Vandeleur's Kilrush projects see Shaw Mason, *Parochial Survey of Ireland*, vol. ii (Dublin, 1814, 1816, 1819), pp. 421–426.
15 *C.J.*, 2 January 1836.
16 *C.J.*, 11 February 1841.
17 Lewis, *Topographical Dictionary*, vol. ii, p. 205.
18 Ibid.; *C.J.*, 9 December 1841.
19 *C.J.*, 9 December 1841.
20 *C.J.*, 1, 12 July 1841.
21 *First Report from His Majesty's Commissioners for Inquiring into the Condition of the Poorer Classes in Ireland* (London, 1835), citations are to republished Clare extracts in *Poverty before the Famine: County Clare 1835* (Ennis, 1996).
22 *Poverty before the Famine*, p. 77.
23 Ibid., p. 86.
24 See Michael Meehan comment regarding Fitzgerald and Vandeleur, *L.&C.E.*, 30 January 1850.
25 Ó Murchadha, *Sable Wings*, p. 34.
26 *C.J.*, 9 April 1846; *L.C.*, 11 April 1846; *C.J.*, 18 May 1846.
27 *C.J.*, 21 January 1847.
28 See for example *L.&C.E.*, 28 February 1849.
29 *L.&C.E.*, 16 January 1847.
30 See *L.&C.E.*, 13 February 1849.
31 National Archives, Relief Commission Papers, Incoming letters sub-series, RLFC3/1 750; RLFC3/1/2122 (9 May 1846), RLFC3/1/2363 (15 May 1846), RLFC3/1/2536 (23 May 1846).
32 RLFC3/2/5, 10, 20, 37.
33 RLFC3/2/5, 37.
34 *C.J.*, 18 February 1847.
35 *L.&C.E.*, 12 May 1847.
36 *C.J.*, 17 June 1847; *L.&C.E.*, 16, 19 June 1847.
37 *C.J.*, 29 September 1847.
38 Ó Murchadha, *Sable Wings*, pp. 131–138; Sheedy, *Clare Elections*, pp. 197–200.
39 Murphy, *A People Starved*, p. 62; Captain Kennedy to the Irish Poor Law Commissioners, 2 December 1847, *Papers Relating to the Relief of the Distress and State of Unions and Workhouses in Ireland*, Fifth Series, pp. 386–387.
40 *C.J.*, 18 February 1847.
41 The Kilrush Guardians petitioned government on emigration, *L.C.*, 28 November 1846; *Times*, 28 November 1846.
42 Cited in *C.J.*, 19 January 1846.

43 The Moyasta and Tullycrine evictions can be followed in *Limerick Reporter*, 14 April 1846; *C.J.*, 19, 22 January, 2 February 1846.
44 *L.C.*, 29 September 1847; *Scrope Committee*, pp. 117–118.
45 *L.&.C.E.*, 25 September 1847; *C.J.*, 27 September, 4 October 1847.
46 *L.&C.E.*, 3 November 1847.
47 *L.&C.E.*, 30 September 1848.
48 *L.&C.E.*, 18 October 1848.
49 *Reports and Returns*, pp. 26–28.
50 Ibid., p. 31.
51 Ibid., pp. 34, 37.
52 Ibid., p. 42.
53 *L.&C.E.*, 14 February 1849.
54 *Reports and Returns*, p. 53.
55 Ibid., p. 57.
56 *L.&C.E.*, 15, 22 August 1849.
57 *L.&C.E.*, 19 September 1849.
58 *L.&C.E.* 19 September 1849; *L.C.*, 22 September 1849.
59 *L.&C.E.*, 14 February 1849.
60 *L.&C.E.*, 12 August 1848; *C.J.*, 17 August 1848; Nolan, 'My Dear Doherty', pp. 48–49; White, *History of Clare*, p. 364.
61 Sidney Godolphin Osborne, *Gleanings in the West of Ireland* (London, 1850), pp. 153–155; *L.&C.E.*, 1, 11, 15, 18 May 1850.
62 For notice see Osborne, *Gleanings*, p. 153.
63 *C.J.*, 16 May 1850.
64 *C.J.*, 16 May 1850.
65 *L.&C.E.*, 11, 15, 18 May 1850.
66 Osborne, *Gleanings*, p. 153.
67 Cited in *L.&C.E.*, 15 May 1850.
68 *L.&C.E.*, 8 May 1850. Reverend Osborne describes another scene from late the previous year that is very similar, Osborne, *Gleanings*, pp. 14–15.
69 *L.&.C.E.*, 15 June 1850.
70 *L.&C.E.*, 15 June 1850.
71 For Shannon, see *Scrope Committee*, pp. 125–128.
72 *Scrope Committee*, p. 212.
73 *Scrope Committee*, p. 137.
74 *Scrope Committee*, p. 236; Donnelly, *Great Irish Potato Famine*, pp. 26, 144, 149; Ó Murchadha, *Ireland's Agony*, p. 122.
75 *Scrope Committee*, p. 151.
76 *Scrope Committee*, p. 151.

77 *Scrope Committee*, p. 152.
78 Ó Murchadha, *Ireland's Agony*, p. 122.
79 *Scrope Committee*, p.154.
80 *Scope Committee*, p. 155.
81 *L.&C.E.*, 19 September 1849.
82 Coffee was paid £29 and eight shillings in expenses by the Committee; *Scrope Committee*, p. xix.
83 Donnelly, *Great Irish Potato Famine*, p. 146.
84 *Scrope Committee*, p. 220.
85 *C.J.*, 4 August 1851.
86 *Times*, 31 March 1851.
87 *L.&C.E.*, 12, 19 April, 24 May, 25 June, 9 August 1851; *C.J.*, 13 March, 7, 14, 25, 5 April, 5 May, 4 August, 9, 14, 18 August 1851.
88 Cited in *L.&C.E.*, 20 August 1851.
89 *L.&C.E.*, 23 March 1853.

Chapter 9
1 Burke, *Landed Gentry of Ireland*, under 'Kennedy of Cultra'.
2 Jennifer Harrison, 'Old World Famine, New World Plenty: The Career of Sir Arthur Edward Kennedy', in *Journal of the Royal Historical Society of Queensland*, vol. xvii, no. 4 (November 1999), pp. 155–171; Peter Connell, *The Land and People of County Meath, 1750–1850* (Dublin, 2004), pp. 206–208.
3 For Kennedy's salary see *Return of All Persons … Receiving Salaries, Pensions, Pay, Profit, Fees, Emolument, Allowances or Grants of Public Money in the Year 1848* (London, 1849), p. 264.
4 The illustration used by Weir, *Houses of Clare*, p. 57, for Cappagh Lodge, is actually Cappagh House, Kennedy's residence, which he doesn't discuss.
5 Auction notice, *L.&C.E.*, 28 August 1850.
6 Harrison, 'Career of Sir Arthur Edward Kennedy', p. 159.
7 Kennedy's ancestral property, at 4,000 acres, was smaller than the Vandeleur estate, Fionuala Carragher, 'The Kennedy Family of Cultra', in *Ulster Folklife*, vol. xxxvii (2001), p. 54.
8 Kennedy to Irish Poor Law Commissioners, 11 and 18 November 1848, *Papers Relating to Proceedings for the Relief of the Distress and State of the Unions and Workhouses in Ireland*, Fourth Series (London, 1847), pp. 155–158.
9 Kennedy to Commissioners, 11 November 1847, *Papers Relating … Fourth Series*, p. 155.
10 Kennedy to Commissioners, 24 February 1848, *Papers Relating to Proceedings for the Relief of Distress and State of the Unions and Workhouses in Ireland*, Sixth Series (London, 1848), p. 796.

11 Kennedy to Commissioners, 18 November 1847, *Papers Relating* ... Fourth Series, p. 157.
12 *Papers Relating* ... Fourth Series, pp. 155, 157.
13 Kennedy to Commissioners, 18 November 1847, *Papers Relating* ... Fourth Series, p. 156.
14 *Papers Relating* ... Fourth Series, p. 156.
15 Kennedy to Commissioners, 25 November 1847, *Papers Relating to Proceedings for the Relief of the Distress and State of the Unions in Ireland*, Fifth Series (London, 1848), p. 381.
16 Kennedy to Commissioners, 25 November 1847, *Papers Relating* ... Fifth Series, p. 381.
17 Kennedy to Commissioners, 24 December 1847, *Papers Relating* ... Fifth Series, p. 392.
18 Copy of letter from Captain Kennedy, dated 18 January 1848, National Archives of Ireland, Outrage Reports, Clare, No. 3183/48.
19 Kennedy to Commissioners, 11 February 1848, *Papers Relating* ... Sixth Series, p. 789.
20 Kennedy to Commissioners, 26 March 1848, *Papers Relating* ... Sixth Series, p. 807.
21 Kennedy to Commissioners, 29 January 1848, *Papers Relating* ... Fifth Series, p. 402.
22 Kennedy to Commissioners, 16 March 1848, *Papers Relating* ... Sixth Series, pp. 803–804.
23 Kennedy to Commissioners, 9 April 1848, *Papers Relating* ... Sixth Series, p. 818.
24 Kennedy to Commissioners, 1 December 1848, *Papers Relating* ... Fifth Series, p. 383; Commissioners to Kennedy, 3 December 1848, *Papers Relating* ... Fifth Series, pp. 383–384.
25 Kennedy to Commissioners, 2 December 1847, *Papers Relating* ... Fifth Series, pp. 386–387; Commissioners to Kennedy, 21 December 1847, *Papers Relating* ... Fifth Series, pp. 388–389. See also pp. 397–398.
26 Kennedy to Commissioners, 1, 4 January 1848, *Papers Relating* ... Fifth Series, pp. 394–395; O.R. Clare, 5 January 1848, 6673/48.
27 Commissioners to Captain Kennedy, 4 April 1848, *Papers Relating* ... Sixth Series, p. 813.
28 Kennedy to Commissioners, 11 February 1848, *Papers Relating* ... Sixth Series, p. 790.
29 *Papers Relating* ... Sixth Series, p. 796. See also p. 808.
30 Kennedy to Commissioners, 24 February, 26 March 1848, *Papers Relating* ... Sixth Series, pp. 797, 807.
31 Kennedy to Commissioners, 22 January 1849, *Papers Relating to Relief of the Distress and State of Unions and Workhouses in Ireland*, Eighth Series (London, 1849), p. 82.
32 L.C., 2 February, 7 June 1848.

33 Kennedy to Commissioners, 5 January 1848, *Papers Relating* ... Sixth Series, p. 396. Vandeleur was less than truthful on this issue to the Scrope Committee, p. 117.
34 Ciarán Ó Murchadha, 'The Years of the Great Famine', in Lynch and Nugent (eds.), *County Clare: History and Society*, pp. 256–257; Christine Kinealy, *This Great Calamity: the Irish Famine 1845–1852* (Dublin, 1994), pp. 210–216.
35 *Reports and Returns*, pp. 4–6; Kennedy to Commissioners, 13, 15 April 1848, *Papers Relating* ... Sixth Series, pp. 820–821.
36 *C.J.*, 30 March 1848; *L.C.*, 5 April 1848.
37 *L.&C.E.*, 1 November 1848.
38 *L.&C.E.*, 9 December 1848.
39 *L.&C.E.*, 15 May 1849.
40 See for example *C.J.*, 2 February 1849; *L.&C.E.*, 28 February, 15, 19 December 1850.
41 *L.C.*, 22 April 1848.
42 Ó Murchadha, *Sable Wings*, pp. 187, 195.
43 *C.J.*, 18 May 1848; *L.C.*, 20 May 1848.
44 *C.J.*, 9 April 1849. See also *L.&C.E.*, 19 May 1849.
45 *L.&C.E.*, 18 August 1849.
46 *L.&C.E.*, 18 April 1849.
47 *Reports and Returns*, p. 47; *L.&C.E.*, 9 June 1849.
48 *L.&C.E.*, 15 August 1849.
49 *L.&C.E.*, 16 June 1849.
50 Some sources refer to her as being eight years of age.
51 *L.&C.E.*, 31 October 1849.
52 *L.&C.E.*, 24 November 1849.
53 *Illustrated London News*, 22 December 1849.
54 *L.&C.E.*, 28 November 1849.
55 *I.L.N.*, 22 December 1849.
56 See, for example, *LCE*, 13 October 1849.
57 Kennedy to Commissioners, 18 February 1848, *Papers Relating* ... Sixth Series (London, 1848), p. 793.
58 *L.&C.E.*, 10 November 1849; *Kilrush Union Minute Book*, p. 316.
59 *L.&C.E.*, 20 December 1849; *C.J.*, 24 December 1849.
60 *C.J.*, 11 November 1850.
61 *L.&C.E.*, 5, 12 January 1850
62 *L.&C.E.*, 26 January 1850.
63 *L.&C.E.*, 31 July 1850.
64 Murphy, 'Captain Kennedy', p. 23.
65 *L.&C.E.*, 21 July 1852.

66 *L.&C.E.*, 4 September 1850.
67 See S.G.O. letter in *L.&C.E.*, 20 August 1851.

Chapter 10

1   Ellis, *Ennis at Work*, pp. 63, 65, 75; *C.J.*, 11, 21 November 1850.
2   Ibid., p. 65; *C.J.*, 20 June 1864.
3   *Irish Times*, 22 June 1864.
4   *Clare Freeman*, 26 June 1864.
5   *C.J.*, 20 June 1864.
6   Ellis, *Ennis at Work*, pp. 65–66.
7   *Catalogue of the Bradshaw Collection*, p. 1338; Ellis, *Ennis at Work*, pp. 65–66, 86.
8   *Aglionby Committee*, p. 414.
9   Fitzpatrick, 'Entitlements', p. 607.
10 Ibid., pp. 608–609.
11 Ibid., pp. 609–617; David Thomson, *Woodbrook* (London, 1974), pp. 157–172.
12 Fitzpatrick, 'Entitlements', p. 618.
13 *C.F.*, 18 November 1854.
14 Fitzpatrick, 'Entitlements', pp. 618–619.
15 See Sheedy, *Clare Elections*, pp. 208–214.
16 Burke, *Landed Gentry of Ireland*, under Singleton; Hewson, 'Diaries of John Singleton', p. 103.
17 *C.J.*, 30 April 1896.
18 Burke, *Landed Gentry of Ireland*, under Singleton.
19 Sheedy, *Clare Elections*, p. 208; Murphy, *Diocese of Killaloe 1850–1904*, p. 465.
20 See description in Weir, *Houses of Clare*, pp. 220–221; Hewson, 'Diaries of John Singleton', p. 103.
21 *C.J.*, 26 June 1855.
22 For quarrels in 1855 alone, see *C.J.*, 14 May, 29 June, 13 August, 15 September 1855.
23 *C.J.*, 4 August 1862; *C.F.*, 9 August 1862.
24 Lucille Ellis, *Bindon Street and Bank Place* (Ennis, 2015), p. 40.
25 His Newmarket-on-Fergus colleague, Dr S. Patterson Evans, had made the county magistracy a year earlier; Frost, *History and Topography*, p. 621. See also Eddie Lough, 'The Establishment and Development of Ennis District Lunatic Asylum in the Nineteenth Century', Unpublished Dissertation, University College Cork, 1998, Appendix G.
26 *C.J.*, 8 June 1871.
27 Cullinan to Governors, Ennis District Asylum, 4 February 1878 (manuscript letter attached to Dunboyne News cuttings).

28 *Return of Owners of Landowners*, Clare, p. 108.
29 Inscription on Cullinan vault.
30 Bernard Burke and Ashworth P. Burke, *Genealogical and Heraldic History of the Peerage and Baronetage, The Privy Council, Knightage and Companionage* (London, 1912), under Cullinan.
31 Swanzy, *Dromore Succession Lists*, p. 65.
32 Ibid., pp. 64–65; notes to Murphy Diaries, P.R.O.N.I., D.1337.
33 For the disputation, see, for example. *C.F.*, 16, 23, 30 March, 23 April 1861.
34 Swanzy, *Dromore Succession Lists*, p. 65.
35 Ibid., p. 64.
36 Excerpts from the Griffin Diary, which is in private hands, have been published in Laura Hogan (ed.), *The Loop Head Gathering* (Kilbaha, c. 2006), pp. 46–47.
37 *Towers and Temples of Ancient Ireland, Their Origin and History Discussed from a New Point of View* (Dublin, 1867).
38 Ignatius Murphy, 'A Town for Sale: Landlord Tenant Relations in Kilkee in the 1860s', in *Dál gCais*, vol. x (1991), pp. 21–35.
39 *C.J.*, 1, 5 November 1883. For a very different obituary, see *Clare Independent*, 3 November 1883.
40 *C.J.*, 18 September 1884.
41 *L.C.*, 16 September 1884; *C.J.*, 18 September 1884, 5 October 1891; *C.I.*, 20 September 1884.
42 More than a half-century on from these events, a full decade after the Keanes had departed from Beech Park, during the 1940s another attempt was made to desecrate Marcus's remains; in 2006 the gouges left by the would-be desecrators were indicated to me by Colm Casey.
43 Apart from one brief newspaper spat in 1860, see *C.F.*, 31 March 1860.
44 Murphy, *Ark*, p. 16.
45 *C.I.*, 2 February 1878.
46 See, for example, Clune, *Little Ark*, p. 11; Murphy, *Ark*, p. 13.
47 I am grateful to Fr Pat O'Neill, formerly Parish Priest of Carrigaholt and Cross, for showing me a letter from Richard Harris, dated 2002, in which these things are contained.
48 Anon, 'Clare's Glorious Lead: Commemoration of Historic Struggle', in *Molua*, 1952, pp. 9–19.
49 For the 2002 commemoration, see *Clare Champion*, 9, 14, 28 June 2002.
50 Until the building of the modern marina, that is.
51 For these evictions, see Noel J. Mulqueen, *The Vandeleur Evictions and the Plan of Campaign in Kilrush* (Cappa, Kilrush, 1988).
52 Weir, *Houses of Clare*, p. 164.
53 Michael Holroyd, *George Bernard Shaw, A Biography* (London, 1998), pp. 12–14.

54 Harrison, 'Career of Sir Arthur Edward Kennedy', pp. 162–163.
55 J. S. Battye, *The Cyclopedia of Western Australia* (Adelaide, 1912), Vol. 1, pp. 293–294.
56 Ibid., p. 293; Harrison, '*Career of Sir Arthur Edward Kennedy*', p. 162.
57 Harrison, 'Career of Sir Arthur Edward Kennedy', pp. 164–167.
58 Sir W.F. Butler, *An Autobiography* (London, 1911), p. 12.
59 Burke, *Landed Gentry of Ireland*, under Kennedy; Harrison, 'Career of Sir Arthur Edward Kennedy', p. 162.
60 At the time of writing, the property had been for sale for over a year; *Irish Independent*, 10 October 2014.
61 I am grateful to Lucille Ellis, for elucidating the Knox connection with the O'Connell Street building.
62 I am indebted to Anne McNamara for bringing the wall-tablets to my attention, and to Jane Halloran Ryan for showing them to me, and for joining in the Kilnasoolagh search.

BIBLIOGRAPHY

Manuscript and Single-copy Printed Sources, and Photographic Collections
National Archives of Ireland, Dublin
Outrage Reports
Relief Commission Papers

National Library of Ireland
Conyngham Papers
Diary of John Singleton
Dunboyne Newscuttings
Dunboyne Photographic Album
Inchiquin Manuscripts

Clare County Archives, Ennis
Minute Books of the Ennis Board of Guardians
Minute Books of the Kilrush Board of Guardians
Singleton Papers
Vandeleur Collection

Public Records of Northern Ireland, Belfast
Diaries of Reverend Henry Murphy

Clare County Library, Local Studies Centre Ennis
Grand Jury Presentment Books

Killaloe Diocesan Archives, Westbourne, Ennis
Papers of Ignatius Murphy

Representative Church Body Library, Dublin
Leslie's Biographical Succession List, Killaloe Diocese

Printed Primary Sources: Parliamentary and Other Official Papers
Abstract Return of Number of Temporary Fever Hospitals in Unions in Ireland and Expenditure; Number of Fever Hospitals Supported by Poor Rate; Number of Dispensaries, Fever Hospitals and Infirmaries (London, 1849).
Census of Ireland for the Year 1841 (Dublin, 1843).
Census of Ireland for the Year 1851 (Dublin, 1856).
Correspondence from July 1846 to January 1847, Relating to the Measures Adopted for the Relief of the Distress in Ireland, Board of Works Series (London, 1847).

Correspondence from July 1846 to January 1847, Relating to the Measures Adopted for the Relief of the Distress in Ireland, Commissariat Series (London, 1847).
Correspondence from January to March 1847, Relating to the Measures Adopted for the Relief of the Distress in Ireland, Board of Works Series, Second Part (London, 1847).
Correspondence from January to March 1847, Relating to the Measures Adopted for the Relief of the Distress in Ireland, Commissariat Series, Second Part (London, 1847).
Digest of Evidence Taken before Her Majesty's Commissioners of Inquiry into the State of the Law and Practice in Respect to the Occupation of Land in Ireland, two vols. (London, 1847 and 1848).
First Report from His Majesty's Commissioners for Inquiring into the Condition of the Poorer Classes in Ireland (London, 1835).
Minutes of Evidence taken before the Select Committee on the Clare Election Petition, Together with Proceedings of the Committee (London, 1853).
Papers Relating to Proceedings for the Relief of the Distress and State of the Unions in Ireland, Fourth Series (London, 1847).
Papers Relating to Proceedings for the Relief of the Distress and State of the Unions in Ireland, Fifth Series (London, 1848).
Papers Relating to Proceedings for the Relief of the Distress and State of the Unions in Ireland, Sixth Series (London, 1848).
Reports and Returns Relating to the Kilrush Union (London, 1849).
Report from the Select Committee on Captain Wynne's Letters (London, 1847).
Report from the Select Committee on Kilrush Union, Together with the Proceedings of the Committee, Minutes of Evidence, Appendix, and Index (London, 1850).
Report of Her Majesty's Commissioners of Inquiry into the Working of the Landlord and Tenant (Ireland) Act, 1870, and the Acts Amending the Same (London, 1881).
Return to an address of the Honourable the House of Commons, dated 7 March 1849, for a list, alphabetically arranged, of all persons in England receiving salaries, pensions, pay, profit, fees, emoluments, allowances or grants of public money, in the year 1848, the amount of which exceeds £150; and also a similar list and return for Scotland, and a similar list and return for Ireland (London, 1849).
Return of Landowners of One Acre and Upwards, in the Several Counties, Counties of Cities, and Counties of Towns in Ireland (Dublin, 1876).

Catalogues, Directories and Family Records

A Catalogue of the Bradshaw Collection of Irish Books in the University Library Cambridge, three vols. (Cambridge, 1916).
Burke, Sir Bernard and Burke, Ashworth P., *Genealogical and Heraldic History of the Peerage and Baronetage, the Privy Council, Knightage and Companionage* (London, 1912).
Burtchaell, George and Sadleir, Thomas, *Alumni Dublinensis: A Register of the Students, Graduates, Professors and Provosts of Trinity College in the University of Dublin 1593–1860*, three vols. (Dublin, 1924).
General Valuation of Rateable Property in Ireland (Dublin, 1852, 1855).
Montgomery-Massingbred, Hugh (ed.), *Burke's Irish Family Records* (London, 1976).
Slater's National Commercial Directory of Ireland (Manchester, 1846).
Swanzy, H.B., *Succession Lists of the Diocese of Dromore* (Belfast, 1933).

Thom's Irish Almanac and Official Directory with the Post Office Dublin City and County Directory for the Year 1847 (Dublin, 1847).
Vaughan, W.E. and Fitzpatrick, A.J. (eds.), *Irish Historical Statistics: Population 1821–1971* (Dublin, 1979).

Other Printed Primary Sources

Anon, 'Remarks on Some Statements of Marcus Keane in His Work, "Temples and Towers of Ancient Ireland"', in *Irish Ecclesiastical Record*, vol. v (1869).
Butler, Sir W.F. Butler, *An Autobiography* (London, 1911).
Button, Arthur Woolaston (ed.), *Arthur Young's Tour in Ireland 1776–1779*, three vols. (London, 1892).
Clare, Rev. Wallace (ed.), *A Young Irishman's Diary: Being Extracts from the Early Journal of John Keegan of Moate* (Dublin, 1928).
Keane, Marcus, *Towers and Temples of Ancient Ireland, Their Origin and History Discussed from A New Point of View* (Dublin, 1867).
Lewis, Samuel *Lewis's Atlas comprising the Counties of Ireland, and a General Map of the Kingdom* (London, 1837).
Murphy, Maureen (ed.), Asenath Nicholson, *Ireland's Welcome to the Stranger* (Dublin, 2002).
Osborne, Sidney Godolphin, *Gleanings in the West of Ireland* (London, 1850).
Pelly, Patricia and Tod, Andrew (eds.), *Elizabeth Grant of Rothiemurchus: The Highland Lady in Ireland, Journals 1840–50* (Edinburgh, 1990).
Report of the Society for Irish Church Missions, June 1852.
Shaw Mason, William, *Parochial Survey of Ireland*, three vols. ii (Dublin, 1814, 1816, 1819).

Newspapers and Periodicals

Clare Champion
Clare Freeman
Clare Independent
Clare Journal
Dublin Evening Mail
Dublin Medical Press
Dublin Quarterly Journal of Medical Science
Evening Press
Freeman's Journal
Illustrated London News
Irish Builder
Irish Independent
Irish Times
Lancet
Limerick and Clare Examiner
Limerick Reporter
Limerick Reporter and Tipperary Vindicator
Molua
Pilot
Times

Secondary Sources

Anon, 'Clare's Glorious Lead: Commemoration of Historic Struggle', in *Molua* (1952).
Battye, J.S., *The Cyclopedia of Western Australia* (Adelaide, 1912).
Berry, Róisín, 'The Vandeleur Family: A Photographic Archive', in *Other Clare*, vol. 31 (2007).
Bourke, Austin, *'The Visitation of God'?: The Potato and the Great Irish Famine* (Dublin, 1993).
Bowen, Desmond, *The Protestant Crusade in Ireland* (Dublin, 1978).
Cameron, Charles A., *History of the Royal College of Surgeons in Ireland* (Dublin, 1916).
Carragher, Fionnnuala, 'The Kennedy Family of Cultra', in *Ulster Folklife*, vol. xxxvii (2001).
Clune, George, *The Little Ark* (Dublin, 1936).
Cole, Richard Cargill, *John Singleton's Grand Tour 1815–1817* (New York, 1988).
Connell, Peter, *The Land and People of County Meath, 1750–1850* (Dublin, 2004).
Cullen, L.M., 'Catholic Social Classes under the Penal Laws', in T.P. Power and Kevin Whelan (eds.), *Endurance and Emergence: Catholics in Ireland in the Eighteenth Century* (Dublin, 1990).
Curtis, L. Perry, Jr., *The Depiction of Evictions in Ireland 1845–1910* (Dublin, 2011).
Dease, Charlotte, 'The Little Ark', in *The Irish Educational Review*, vol. vi (1912).
Dickson, David, 'Middlemen', in Thomas Bartlett and D.W. Hayton (ed.), *Penal Era and Golden Age: Essays in Irish History 1690 and 1800* (Dublin, 1979).
Donnelly, James S., Jr., *The Great Irish Potato Famine* (Stroud, England, 2001).
Donnelly, James S., Jr., *The Land and People of Nineteenth Century Cork* (Dublin, 1975).
Edwards, R. Dudley and Williams, T. Desmond, *The Great Famine: Studies in Irish History 1845–1852* (Dublin, 1956).
Egremont, Max, *Wyndham and Children First* (London, 1968).
Ellis, Lucille, *Bindon Street and Bank Place* (Ennis, 2015).
Ellis, Lucille, *Ennis at Work in the Nineteenth Century* (Ennis, 2014).
Enright, Flannan, 'Pre-Famine Reform and Emigration on the Wyndham Estate in Clare', in *Other Clare*, vol. viii (1984).
Enright, Flannan, 'Terry Alt; the Rise and Fall of an Agrarian Secret Society', in Mathew Lynch and Patrick Nugent (eds.), *Clare: History and Society* (Dublin, 2008).
Fitzpatrick, David, 'Famine, Entitlements and Seduction: Captain Edmond Wynne in Ireland 1846–1851', in *English Historical Review*, vol. cx (June 1995).
Fitzpatrick, W.J., *The Life of Charles Lever* (London, 1896).
Frogatt, Peter, 'The Response of the Medical Profession to the Great Famine', in E. Margaret Crawford (ed.), *Famine: The Irish Experience, Subsistence Crises and Famine in Ireland, 900–1900* (Edinburgh, 1989).
Frost, James, *The History and Topography of the County of Clare* (Dublin, 1893).
Gernsheim, Helmut, *Lewis Carroll; Photographer* (London, 1949).
Gray, Peter, *Famine, Land and Politics: British Government and Irish Society 1843–50* (Dublin, 1999).
Hamell, Patrick J., 'The Ark of Kilbaha', in *I.E.R.* August 1952.

Harrison, Jennifer, 'Old World Famine, New World Plenty: The Career of Sir Arthur Edward Kennedy', in *Journal of the Royal Historical Society of Queensland*, vol. xvii, no.4 (November 1999).

Hewson, Michael, 'The Diaries of John Singleton of Quinville, Co. Clare', in *North Munster Antiquarian Journal*, vol. xvii (1975).

Hogan, Laura (ed.), *The Loop Head Gathering* (Kilbaha, c. 2006).

Holroyd, Michael, *George Bernard Shaw: A Biography* (London, 1998).

Hughes, Harry, 'Civilizing and Enlightening the Population of Miltown; the Souper School at Glandine', in *Cumann na Meanmhúinteoirí Éire, Comhdháil Bhliantúil Inis 1995* (Ennis, 1995).

Kinealy, Christine, *This Great Calamity: the Irish Famine 1845–1852* (Dublin, 1994).

Lough, Eddie, 'The Establishment and Development of Ennis District Lunatic Asylum in the Nineteenth Century', Unpublished Dissertation, University College Cork, 1998.

Lynch, Matthew, 'Colonel George Wyndham, First Baron Leconfield (1787–1869) and his Estate in Clare', in Matthew Lynch and Patrick Nugent (eds.), *Clare: History and Society* (Dublin, 2008).

Lynch, Matthew, *The Mass Evictions in Kilrush Poor Law Union during the Great Famine* (Miltown Malbay, 2013).

McGuire, James and Quinn, James (eds.) *Dictionary of Irish Biography from the Earliest Times to the Year 2002*, six vols. (Cambridge, 2009).

McInerney, Luke, *Clerical and Learned Lineages of Medieval County Clare* (Dublin, 2014).

Mulqueen, Noel, *The Vandeleur Evictions and the Plan of Campaign in Kilrush* (Kilrush, 1988).

Murphy, Ignatius, *Before the Famine Struck: Life in West Clare 1834–1845* (Dublin, 1996)

Murphy, Ignatius, 'Captain A.E. Kennedy, Poor Law Inspector and the Great Famine in the Kilrush Union 1847–1850', in *Other Clare*, vol. 3 (1979).

Murphy, Ignatius, 'Cholera Epidemic in County Clare', in *Other Clare*, vol. v (1981).

Murphy, Ignatius, *The Diocese of Killaloe 1800–1850* (Dublin, 1992).

Murphy, Ignatius, *The Diocese of Killaloe 1850–1904* (Dublin, 1995).

Murphy, Ignatius, *Michael Meehan and the Ark of Kilbaha* (private publ., 1980).

Murphy, Ignatius, *A People Starved: Life and Death in West Clare, 1845–1851* (Dublin, 1996).

Murphy, Ignatius, 'A Town for Sale: Landlord Tenant Relations in Kilkee in the 1860s', in *Dál gCais*, vol. x (1991).

Murphy, Ignatius, 'William Smith O'Brien and the Teaching of Irish in West Clare', in *North Munster Antiquarian Journal*, vol. xvi (1973–1974).

Nolan, Paddy, 'My Dear Doherty', in *Other Clare*, vol. xxvii (2003).

O'Brien, Pius, *Sisters of Mercy of Kilrush and Kilkee* (Ennis, 1997).

Ó Broin, Leon, *Charles Gavan Duffy: Patriot and Statesman* (Dublin, 1967).

Ó Dalaigh, Brian, *Irish Historic Towns Atlas No. 25: Ennis* (Dublin, 2012).

Ó Dálaigh, Brian, 'Tomás Ó Míocháin and the Ennis School of Poetry c. 1730–1804', in *Dál gCais*, vol. xi (1993).

Ó Gráda, Cormac, *Black '47 and Beyond, the Great Irish Famine* (Princeton, 1999).

Ó Murchadha, Ciarán, 'One Vast Abattoir: County Clare, 1848–1849', in *Other Clare*, vol. xxi (1997).
Ó Murchadha, Ciarán, *Sable Wings over the Land: Ennis, County Clare and its Wider Community during the Great Famine* (Ennis, 1998).
Ó Murchadha, Ciarán, *The Diocese of Killaloe: an Illustrated History* (Belfast, 2007, new edn 2011).
Ó Murchadha, Ciarán, 'The Years of the Great Famine', in Matthew Lynch and Patrick Nugent (eds.), *County Clare: History and Society* (Dublin, 2008).
O'Neill, Thomas P., 'The Organisation and Administration of Relief', in R. Dudley Edwards and T. Desmond Williams (eds.), *The Great Famine: Studies in Irish History 1845–1852* (Dublin, 1956).
O'Rahilly, Thomas F., *A Miscellany of Irish Proverbs* (Dublin, 1922).
Póirtéir, Cathal (ed.), *The Great Irish Famine* (Dublin, 1995).
Sheedy, Kieran, *The Clare Elections* (Dun Laoghaire, 1993).
Thomson, David, *Woodbrook* (London, 1974).
Weir, Hugh, *Historical, Genealogical, Architectural Notes on Some Houses of Clare* (Whitegate, 1986).
Westropp, Thomas J., 'Notes on the Sheriffs of County Clare 1570–1700', in *Journal of the Royal Society of Antiquaries in Ireland*, vol. i, part i (1890).
Wheeler, W.G., 'The Spread of Provincial Printing in Ireland up to 1850', in *Irish Booklore*, vol. 4, no. I (1978).
Whelan, Irene, 'The Stigma of Souperism', in Cathal Póirtéir (ed.), *The Great Irish Famine* (Dublin, 1995).
White, Patrick, *History of Clare and the Dalcassian Clans* (Dublin, 1893).
White, Patrick, 'Proselytism in West Clare: A Retrospect', in *Irish Ecclesiastical Record*, third series, vol. viii, no. 5 (May 1887).
Wilson, T.G., *Victorian Doctor, being the Life of Sir William Wilde* (London, 1974).
Woodham Smith, Cecil, *The Great Hunger* (London, 1962).

INDEX

Note: individual 'Figures' are not indexed for chapters specifically devoted to them, the exception being with regard to illustrations, which are designated in the usual manner by italicized numbers.

Act of Union 10, 119
Aglionby Committee 44
Aglionby, Henry, MP 44
America 120, 133
Annaghneal 106
Antrim, County 177
Arthur, Miss 93
Arthur's Row 57
Atlantic Packet Station 140, 180

Ballinahinch 55
Ball, Major William 41, 42, 44
Ball, Mrs Samuel 96
Ball, Samuel 96–8, 177
Ballyea 11
Ballyerra 146
Ballyvaughan 43
Baltard 48, 51, 52, 53, 55, 58, 165, 176, 185
Baltard evictions 60–2, 63
Banemore 146, 149
Barons Lyndhurst 49
Bedford, Mr 93
Beech Park 6, 41, 66, 87, 99, 100, 101, 102, 103, 106, 134, 178, 179, 183
Beech Park estate 103, 110
Bell, Mr 90
Bessborough Commission 103
Bindon Street, Ennis 70, 176
Birr Castle telescope 93
Bishop of Connor (Anglican) 177
Bishop of Killaloe (Anglican) 84, 89, 94
Bishop of Killaloe (Catholic) 131
Black Forty Seven 57
Blake Butler, James 60
Bloxham, Mr 93

Board of Works 30, 32, 36, 39, 42, 44, 146, 175, 182
Borrisokane 93
Boulogne, France 53
Boyle and Carrick Poor Law Union 174
Brady Brownes (landlord family) 49
Bresla 160
Britain 57, 126, 147, 156
Broom Hill 139, 163, 169, 172
Bunahow 49
Bunratty Lodge 64
Bunratty Lower (barony) 52
Burren 6, 182
Butler, James 51
Butler, Miss 57
Butler, Mrs 51, 57
Butlers (landlord family) 49
Butt, Isaac 64

Cabin, The 127
Cahercon 93
Caherfeenick 146, 147, 149
Caherush school 89, 92, 94, 95–8
Cahircalla 87, 92
Cambridge, England 139, 177
Canada 156
Cappagh (Kilrush) 156, 161, 172
'caretakers' 111
Carey, Francis 108, 109
Carhue 146
Carmody, Widow 61
Carnacalla 146, 149, 158
Carnane 146
Carnarvon, Lord 181–2
Caroline (yacht) 145, 148

Carrick, Pierce 40, 57, 58, 90
Carrick-on-Shannon 174
Carrigaholt 117, 118, 125, 127, 165
Carr, Miss 92
Carrowdotia 139, 144, 179
Casey, Thomas 179
Castlecrine 57
Catholic Emancipation 10
Central Board of Health 77, 78, 79
Central Relief Committee (Islands and Inchiquin Baronies) 90
Cherry, Widow 108, 109
cholera 67, 125
Clare Abbey 39, 44
Clare Abbey Relief Committee 34, 38, 45
Clare Castle barracks 67, 86
Clare Champion 174
Clare, County 1, 3, 4, 6, 15, 30, 32, 43, 49
Clare County Lunatic Asylum 176
Clare Freeman 174, 177
Clare glebe 91
Clare Journal 9–10, 12, 16, 18, 21, 24, 26, 27, 31, 37, 61, 62, 71, 78, 86, 95, 96, 109, 128, 130, 131, 153, 164, 173, 178, 184–5
Clare Medical Association 80
Clare Medical Society 70, 101
Clarendon, Lord (Lord Lieutenant) 78
Clare (village) 39, 85, 91, 94
Clarke, Reverend J.A. 62
Clashmore 14
clearances. *See* evictions
Clergy Sons' School, Lucan 83, 92, 93, 95, 177
Cliffs of Moher 6
Clogán Óir 100
Clohessy, Denis 160
Cloncullen 146
Clondagad 31
Clonderlaw (barony) 153
Clonmel 9
Coffee, Francis 115, 151–2
Coffey, J. 91
Coleraine, County Derry 177
'collectors' 110
Collins's Hotel, Ennis 91
conacre men 31

Conyngham estate 103, 104, 106, 110
Conyngham, Marquis 102, 107, 109, 164
Copley, John Singleton 49
Corbett, Father Daniel 47, 59, 118, 176
Corcomroe Barony 32, 36
Cork 53, 119
Corn Laws 15
Corofin 34, 36
Corofin Relief Committee 34
Coroners Act 72
County Assizes 15, 55, 64, 72, 74, 76, 88, 142
County Club, Ennis 57, 184
County Fever Hospital 15, 68, 69, 70–2, 74, 76, 79, 84, 89, 183
County Infirmary 68, 69, 79, 80, 84
County Jail 60, 68, 69, 72, 84, 87
County Lying-in Hospital 68, 69
County Meetings 14, 51, 88, 101, 141
County Militia 137, 138, 176
Creek, the (Kilrush) 140, 141, 145, 180
Crimea 6, 78
Crimean War 175
Cross 132
Cross Chapel 130
Crowe, Captain 90
Crowes (landlord family) 67
Crowe, Tom 97, 98
Crowe, Wainwright 92
Cruise's Hotel, Limerick 94
Crystal Palace 152
Cullinan, Dr P.M. 5, 7, 176, 177, 183
Cullinan, Fitzjames 177
Cullinan, Max 177
Cullinan, William 177
Cultra, County Down 156, 177
Cumann na mBan 183
Cuthites 178

Dangan 58
Davenport, Captain 90
Davoren, Basil Lukey 112
Devon Commission 100
Dickinson, Emily 185
Doherty, Cornelius 150
Doherty, Garrett 146
Donovan, Sub-inspector 109–10
Doodys (tenant family) 60

Doolin 36
Doon 53
Doonbeg 62, 63, 146
Doondahlin 99, 117, 127, 178
Doonmore 62, 63
Doora 53, 118
Down, County 98, 177
Downpatrick, County Down 177, 178
Downton Abbey 182
Doyle, Daniel 120
'drivers' 110
Drogheda 138
Dromaragh, County Down 177
Dromcliffe 66, 83
Dromcliffe Cemetery 177
Dromoland 24, 47, 49, 68, 87
Dromore, County Clare 66
Dromore, County Down 177
Dublin 11, 36, 43, 49, 51, 88, 95, 175
Dublin Castle 63
Dublin Evening Mail 170
Dublin Medical Press 77
Duffy, Charles Gavan 45
Duggan, Father Malachy 125
Dunluce, County Antrim 177
Dysart 146

Edenvale 87, 92
Edinburgh 49, 57, 66
Egremont, Max 85
Egremont, third earl of 85
Eighth Hussars 57
Elliott, Henry 96
Emlagh 121
Encumbered Estates Court 64
England 182
Ennis 7, 9, 10, 11, 17, 30, 39, 48, 118, 142
Ennis District Dispensary 82
Ennis Old Friary (Church of Ireland parish church) 83–4
Ennis Poor Law Guardians 13, 15, 51, 59–60, 71, 74–6, 78, 80, 81, 100, 176
Ennis Poor Law Union 103, 165
Ennis Relief Committee 15, 20, 22, 90
Ennis Town Commissioners 13, 14, 15, 176
Ennis Town Council 184

Ennistymon 7, 32, 41, 68, 183
Ennistymon courthouse 36, 36–7, 39, 40, 183
Ennistymon Union 104
Ennis Union Fever Hospital 76, 77, 78
Ennis Union workhouse 77, 84
Enright, Dr John 68
Erasmus Smith School 90
Esker House, Lucan 175
Evans, Dr S. Patterson 13
evictions 24–5, 60–1, 85, 96, 103–16, 121–4, 130, 145–9, 151–3, 158, 160–2, 163
executions 23
Exeter Hall, London 26
exterminators 24, 25

Fahy, Father John 97
Fairview, Dublin 175
Farahy, Kilkee 185
Faussett, Reverend J.S. 127, 132
Fenloe 58
Fergus River 53
Fever Act (1847) 76, 78
fever epidemics 72, 165
Finnoe glebe 93
Fishbourne, S. Gardiner 102
Fitzgerald, Francis (land agent) 141, 147
Fitzgerald, Jonas 92
Fitzpatrick, David 175
Flannery's omnibus 88, 94
Foley, Dr 165–6
Fortfergus 41, 44
Frances Street, Kilrush 139, 180
Freeman's Journal 10, 150
Freemasons 73

Gallagher (tenant) 108, 109
Galvin, James 61
Galway 7, 50
Galway Bay 6
Galway Vindicator 147, 149
Gambia Settlements 181
Gamble, Samuel 34–5, 36, 38, 41, 42, 46
Garraunatooha 24–5, 122, 123, 185
Gibson, Peter 135
Gibsons (large farmer family) 118
Glandine school 97–8, 183

Glenwilliam 60
Goldie, Colonel T.L. 6–7, 51
Gordon, Captain 43
Gore's Quay 53
Gormans (tenant family) 60
Gort 24, 92, 119
Gortbofarna, Inagh 101, 102, 185
Grand Jury 15, 50, 68, 69, 74, 88, 138, 142
Great Exhibition 152
Green Lawn 87
Green Park 84, 86–7, 88, 89, 91, 93, 94
Gregg, Reverend 94
Griffin, Amy 178
Griffin, J. Nash 126, 127, 128

Hanrahan, Father (Catholic curate) 38
Harmony House 70
Harris, Richard 179
Harrow, England 139
Hastings, Stephen 61
Haughs (tenant family) 60
Healy, Dr Michael 5, 73, 183
Hehir, Dr Andrew 76–8, 80
Henn estate 103
Heytesbury, Lord (Lord Lieutenant) 14
Hibernian Bible Society 86
Hickey, Cornelius 15
Hickey, Patrick 108, 109–10
Hickman, Hugh 58
Hieros 121
Highclere Castle 181–2
Hill, Captain 143
History of Clare and the Dalcassian Clans 125
Hoare, Nancy 61, 64, 165, 185
Hobbawns 52
Holy Well incident 26
Hong Kong 181
horse-shootings 23, 30
Horsman, Edward, MP 63
House of Commons (British) 114
Hurley, John 66

Ibrickane (barony) 153
Illustrated London News 123, 155, 168
imposition, imposture 31, 33, 161
Inagh 101, 102, 106
Inch 100

Inchiquin Barony 36
Indian meal 120
Irish Confederation, Confederates 24, 106, 119–20
Irish Poor Law Commissioners 75, 79, 157, 160–3, 170, 171–2
Iron Bridge Road 52–3
Islandmacnavin 48

Jail Street 9, 11, 19, 20, 86
James, Captain Richard, Earl of Clanwilliam 182
Jewish Missionary Society 86
Johnson, Mr and Mrs 90
Jones, Colonel Harry 30, 32, 38, 44

Keane, Dr Charles 67, 100
Keane, Henry 95, 100, 103, 112–13, 126, 127, 128, 131, 133
Keane, Marcus 1, 5, 24, 25, 41, 45, 64, 67, 93, 95, *105*, 117, 121, 126, 127, 128, 133, 134, 142, 149, 152, 170, 178–9, 183, 184
Keane, Maria 87
Keane, Misses 86, 95
Keane, Robert Fada 100
Keane's Store 80
Keane, Thomas (Tom) 90
'keepers' 110
Kells, County Meath 168
Kells Union 156
Kelly, Father Timothy 125, 141
Kellys (tenant family) 60
Kennedy, Captain Arthur E. 6, 26, 59, 60, 104, 106, 115, 121, 143, 146, 147, 150, 151, *167*, 181–2, 184
Kennedy, Hugh 156
Kennedy, Miss Elizabeth 156, *167*, 167–9, 182
Kennedy, Mrs Georgina 156
Kilbaha 1, 99, 117, 118, 126, 132, 135, 180, 182, 183
Kilballyowen 125, 127
Kildare 95
Kildysert 42, 43, 106, 157
Kilfearagh 125
Kilkee 7, 60, 63, 92, 115, 120, 132, 134, 140, 146, 165, 178
Kilkeedy 185

Kilkee Petty Sessions 132
Kilkenny 172
Killaloe 7, 66, 94
Killard 42, 47, 55
Killard Relief Committee 42
Killerenan 185
Killofin 164
Kilmacduane 106, 159, 160
Kilmaley 39, 66, 84, 106, 178, 185
Kilmaley Relief Committee 45–6
Kilmurry 160
Kilnacrandy 57
Kilnasoolagh 185
Kilraghtis 83
Kilrush 5, 6, 7, 26, 68, 92, 119, 120, 121, 122, 138, 139–40, 143, 144, 145, 147, 148, 149, 151, 152, 153, 155, 156, 165, 166, 171, 180, 181, 183, 184
Kilrush Board of Guardians 137, 138, 143, 145, 148, 150, 151, 152, 153, 157–8, 163, 169, 170
Kilrush clearances 26
Kilrush House 49, 62, 87, 157, 181
Kilrush Poor Law Union 25, 59, 63, 103, 104, 106, 113–16, 121, 139, 147, 149, 151, 152, 157–8, 159, 162, 164, 169, 170, 180, 181
Kilrush Relief Committee 141, 142
Kilrush Vice-Guardians 163
Kilrush workhouse 157
Kiltrellig 127, 128, 130
Kinnavanes (tenant family) 112–13
Knock 147
Knox, Eliza 11
Knox, John Busteed 4, 33, 35, 51, 53, 60, 67, 72, 76, 78, 86, 87, 91, 92, 95, 142, 173, 174, 177, 183, 184–5
Knox, Kathleen Frances 174
Knox, Mary 11
Knox, Mrs Frances 10, 172
Knox, T.S. 10
Krause, Reverend 94

labourers 31
Labour Rate Act 55
Lady Grace (ship) 140
Lancashire 87
Lancet 67

'lazy beds' 182
Leadmore 146, 158
Le Fanu, Sheridan 64
Leitrim, County 174
'levellers' 107, 108, 111
Lever, Charles 65
Limerick 7, 9, 17, 59, 88, 108, 119
Limerick Chronicle 164, 165
Limerick and Clare Examiner 18, 22, 26, 63, 74, 104, 106, 107, 111, 113–14, 121, 122, 142, 146, 147, 149, 174
Limerick Fever Hospital 109
Limerick Reporter 18–19
Limerick workhouse 108
Lindsay, Captain 57
Lissycasey 52, 96, 97, 106
Little Ark 1, 2, 3, 117–18, 133–5, 179–80, 183
London, England 49, 57, 172
Loop Head 1, 117, 125, 157
Lough Cutra 92
Luby, Reverend Dr 94
Lucan, County Dublin 83, 92, 93, 177
Lynch, Daniel 59
Lynch, Denis 52, 59
Lynch, Ellen 165
Lynch, James 59

MacBeth, John 22
MacCatháin (old Gaelic sept) 100
Mac Cuilleanáin, Cormac 66
Macnamara, Captain Francis 39
Macnamara, Major W.N. 36–7, 39, 44, 45, 138–9, 142
Magheralin, County Down 177
Mahon, Thomas 20, 22, 92
Mahony, James 123
Mansion House Committee 14, 52
Manus House 66
Mathew, Father Theobald 119
Maynooth 118
Mayo Telegraph 16
McDonnells (tenant family) 60–1
McMahon, Denis 61
McMahon, Father Michael 128
McMahon, Simon 61
McMahons (tenant family) 60
McNamara, Michael 61

Meany, Stephen Joseph 11, 24
Meath 12
Meehan, Father Michael 1, 5, 24, *129*, 130, 145, 146, 147, 152, 155, 179
Meelick 106, 107–13
Menzies, Mr 94
Millett (engineer) 37
Miltown Malbay 7, 55–6, 97, 126, 183
Moira, County Down 177
Molony, Croasdale 57
Molonys (landlord family) 49
Moneen 1, 2, 117, 118, 179
Monmore 146
Morning Chronicle 38
Morris, Frederick 92
Mount Callan 6
Mount Kennett Steam Mills 179
Moyarta 125, 132, 146, 185
Moyarta (barony) 153
Moyarta and Kilballyowen 1, 117, 118, 122, 125, 126
Moyasta 120, 145, 146
Mullins, Patrick 101, 102, 185
Murphy, Emma 84
Murphy, George Wyndham 178
Murphy, Henrietta 84
Murphy, Henry, Jr. 84, 89, 95, 178
Murphy, Jane 84
Murphy, Monsignor Ignatius 155, 172
Murphy, Mrs Frances (Fanny) 84, 89, 90, 91, 92, 93
Murphy, Reverend Henry 5, 128, 177–8, 184

National Famine Commemoration 184
New Hall 87
Newmarket-on-Fergus 6, 13, 25, 48, 52, 55–6, 57, 58, 67, 109, 185
Newmarket-on-Fergus Relief Committee 52
Nicholson, Asenath 3, 86
Norbury, Lord 138
North George's Street, Dublin 175

O'Brien, Captain H.H. 45
O'Brien, Cornelius 36–7, 38, 39, 44, 45, 138, 142
O'Brien, Dr George 53, 68, 76, 79
O'Brien, Mary 160

O'Brien, Sir Lucius 24, 48, 49, 68, 139, 143
O'Brien, William Smith 24
O'Connor, James 81
O'Dea, Fanny 52
O'Donnell, Bridget 24–5, 122–3, *124*, 185
O'Donnell, John 120
O'Donoghue, Michael 57
Office of Public Works 184
Ogashin 84
O'Gorman, Richard 120, 145
Ó Gráda, Cormac 45
O'Keeffe, Hugh 10
O'Keeffe, Timothy 160
'Old Doctors' 68
O'Loghlens (Catholic landlord family) 49
O'Loghlen, Sir Michael 64
Ó Míocháin, Tomás 118
Ó Murchadha, Seán 183
O'Neill, Dennis 58
Osborne, Reverend Sidney Godolphin 148, 152–3
O'Shaughnessy, Dean Terence 66, 72, 87
O'Sullivan, Catherine 81
outrage 23, 30

Palmer, Mr 94
Paradise, Ballinacally 93
Parkinson, Miss 92
Parliament, British 15
Paupers' Quay, Kilrush 180
'pauper warrens' 62
Peel, Robert 14, 15, 55
Penal Laws 66
Petworth, Sussex 85
Pilkingtons (lesser gentry family) 87
Pilot 109
Poll na Dóib, Ennistymon 185
Poor Law 6, 50, 62, 70, 103–4, 143, 153, 156, 159, 160, 165, 169, 170, 172
Poor Law Amendment Act 161
Poor Law Commissioners 71. *See also* Irish Poor Law Commissioners
Poor Law Inspectors 33
potato blight 12, 88, 93
Poulnasherry Bay 168
pre-Millennialism 86, 178

'priest's curse' 130
proselytism 97–8
Protestant Orphan Society 86, 87
Public Works Act (1837) 15, 53

Queen's Colleges 84, 177
Queensland 181, 182
Quin Abbey 64
Quinn, Father Thomas (P.P. Inagh and Kilnamona) 38
Quinn, John 61
Quinns (tenant family) 60
Quin Relief Committee 52, 55, 57, 59
Quin village/parish 47, 48, 53, 56, 57, 118, 176
Quinville Abbey 4, 11, 47, 48, 49, 51, 53, 57, 87, 176, 183, 185

Raglan, Lord 175
Redington, T.M. (Under Secretary) 109, 110
Reidy, John 159–60
Relief Commissioners 142
relief committees 32, 33, 35, 41, 102
Repeal Association 120
Repeal, Repealers 14, 15, 18, 21, 119
Rhadamanthus 92
Rineanna 57
Rineen 64
Rising (1798) 10, 24
Rising (1848) 24
Roscommon, County 174
Rosslewin, Reverend 43
Routh, Randolph 18, 45
Rowe House 34
Ruan 39, 40, 43
Russell, Lord John 17, 20, 45
Russell, William Howard 38

Sable Wings over the Land ix
Saddler's Cross 58
Saint Senan 100
Saturday Record 174
Scariff 68
Scientific Commission 13
Scrope Committee 114–16, 122, 123, 149–52, 163, 170–2, 182
Scrope, George Poulett 25, 114
seaweed gatherers 31

Second Reformation 26, 126
Shanakyle 180, 185
Shannon Estuary 6
Shannon, James 150, 169
Shannon, River 7
Shannon Steamer 179
Shanvoy 66
Shaw, George Bernard 181
Sheedy, Brian 112
Sheehan, Father John 19, 32, 35, 38
Shepperton 58
Sierra Leone 181
Silver, Dr 67
Singleton, Edward 48
Singleton, Edward, Jr. 51, 57, 176
Singleton, Hugh 48, 58
Singleton, Isabella 53, 60, 175
Singleton, John 4, 5, 54, 75, 91, 102, 142, 165, 175, 185
Singleton, John (*grand-père*) 48
Singleton, John, Jr. 51, 53, 57, 175–6, 185
Singleton, Marcella 53, 176, 185
Singleton, Mary 53, 59, 176
Singleton, Miss 59
Singleton, Sara 51, 176
Singleton, Susan 51, 176
Sirius (ship) 53
Sixmilebridge 175
Sligo 29
smallpox 81
Smith, Elizabeth 3
Smith, Major 23
Smith, W.J. 66
Smyth, John Blood 91
Society of Friends 59
Society of St Vincent de Paul 26, 141, 165
Soup Kitchen Act 156
South Africa 178
Southampton, England 49
Spancil Hill 52, 88, 90
Special Judicial Commission 23
Square Road, Kilrush 166
Stackallan 51, 91
Stacpoole, Miss 92
Stacpoole, William 92
Stanley, Lord 18
Starlight, Captain 40–1

Stoker, Bram 64
Studdert, Fitzgerald 92
Studdert, Frank 93
Studdert, Jonas 92
Studdert, Mary 93
Studdert, Tom 93
Suffolk (England) 12
Susex (England) 84
Synge, Colonel 34
Synod of Thurles 26

Tablet 120
Teach Ceoil, Kilrush 184
Temperance 11, 119
Templemaley 83
Termon 100
Terry Alts 23, 30, 56, 58
Thomond estate 138
Tiernaclohane 146
Times 18, 20, 152
Tipperary, County 4, 30, 32, 93
tithes 83
Tomkinson, Mr 57
Toomevara 89
Tory, Tories 10, 14, 17, 18, 45
Tralee 9
Treasury, British 44, 141
Trenahow 48, 52, 57
Trevelyan, Charles 44, 45
Trinity College, Dublin 66, 83
Trollope, Anthony 5
Tulla 118, 185
Tullabrack 121
Tullagower 121
Tullig 122, 152
Tullycrine 120, 145, 149
Turnpike Auxiliary 80

under-agents 112

Vagrant Act 148
Vandeleur Arms (Kilrush hotel) 140
Vandeleur, Crofton Moore 5–6, 14, 24, 26, 45, 49, 62, 63, 76, 104, 121, *144*, 155, 157, 158, 162, 163, 164, 169–70, 172, 175, 180–1, 183, 184
Vandeleur estate 120, 139
Vandeleur, Hector 180–1
Vandeleur, John Ormsby 138, 139, 146

Vandeleur, Lady Grace 138, 152
Vandeleur, Maximilian 138
Vandeleur, Miss 57, 152
Vard, Mrs 91
Vaughan, Dr 131
Vice-Guardians 163–4
Victoria, Queen 20
Volatti, Signor 94

Walker, James Knox 11, 27, 37, 95, 96, 177
Walshe, Bishop Willie 181
Ward, Reverend Charles 87, 128
War of Independence 183
Water Park, Ennis 87, 91
West African Settlements 181
Westby estate 103, 104, 106, 127
Westby, Louisa 101
Westby, Nicholas 64, 101, 102, 121, 126
West Clare 15, 24, 48
Western Australia 181
Westmeath, Marquis of 175
Westminster 57
Whately Commission 140
Whig-Liberals 17, 18, 23, 30, 36, 53, 90, 120, 143, 171
Whiteboy notice 162
Whiteboys 23, 30, 38, 56
White, Father Patrick 123, 125, 128, 130
White King, Dr Luke 90, 94
Whitestone, Dr 79
Wilde, Oscar 66
Wilde, William 66–7
Williamson, Reverend 94
Wilson, Professor Alexander 89
worklists 31
'wreckers'. *See* 'levellers'
Wyndham, Colonel George 26, 84–6, 89, 92, 95–8, 104, 164, 176
Wyndham, Mrs 96
Wynne, Edmond 4, 22, 57, 102, 136, 138, 139, 174–5, 183, 184

xerophthalmia 81

Young, Arthur 48
Young Ireland 11, 18
Young, Reverend 92